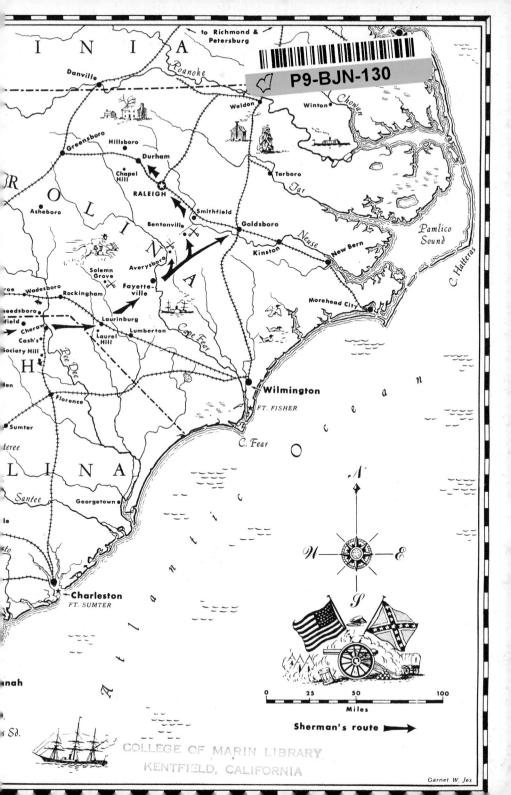

to Richmond & Petersburg

Danville

Roanoke

Weldon

Winton

Chowan

Greensboro

Hillsboro

Durham

Chapel Hill

RALEIGH

Tarboro

Tar

Asheboro

Smithfield

Bentonville

Goldsboro

Neuse

Kinston

New Bern

Pamlico Sound

C. Hatteras

Averysboro

Solemn Grove

Fayette-ville

Wadesboro

Rockingham

Morehead City

oe

eedsboro field

Laurinburg

Lumberton

Cape Fear

Cheraw

Laurel Hill

Cash's

ociety Hill

Pee Dee

H

en

Florence

Wilmington

FT. FISHER

Sumter

teree

C. Fear

O

L I N A

Santee

Georgetown

le

Charleston

FT. SUMTER

Atlantic

Ocean

nah

s Sd.

$\mathcal{N}$

$\mathcal{W}$ — $\mathcal{E}$

$\mathcal{S}$

0   25   50   100

Miles

Sherman's route ▶

Garnet W. Jex

THOSE 163 DAYS

THOSE
163
DAYS

A SOUTHERN ACCOUNT
OF SHERMAN'S MARCH FROM ATLANTA
TO RALEIGH

By JOHN M. GIBSON

Coward-McCann, Inc.

NEW YORK

© 1961 BY JOHN M. GIBSON

Library of Congress Catalog
Card Number: 61-5423

MANUFACTURED IN THE UNITED STATES OF AMERICA

VAN REES PRESS • NEW YORK

TO MY WIFE, VIRGINIA

ACKNOWLEDGMENTS

THE author gratefully acknowledges permission of the following to quote copyrighted material from their publications:

Oxford University Press, New York, N.Y., for excerpts from *When the World Ended: The Diary of Emma LeConte,* edited by Earl Schenck Miers (Copyright 1957 by Oxford University Press)

Louisiana State University Press, Baton Rouge, La., for excerpts from *With Sherman to the Sea, The Civil War Letters, Diaries & Reminiscences of Theodore F. Upson,* edited, with an Introduction, by Oscar Osburn Winther (Copyright 1943 by Louisiana State University Press)

Indiana University Press, Bloomington, Ind., for excerpts from *Three Years in the Army of the Cumberland, The Letters and Diary of Major James A. Connolly,* edited by Paul M. Angle (Copyright © 1959 by Indiana University Press)

Yale University Press, New Haven, Conn., for excerpts from *Marching with Sherman, Passages from the Letters and Campaign Diaries of Henry Hitchcock, Major and Assistant Adjutant General of Volunteers, November 1864–May 1865,* edited, with an Introduction, by M. A. DeWolfe Howe (Copyright 1927 by Yale University Press)

Appleton-Century-Crofts, Inc., New York, N.Y., for excerpts from *A Diary from Dixie,* by Mary Boykin Chesnut, edited by Isabella D. Martin and Myrta Lockett Avary (Copyright 1905 by D. Appleton & Company)

Mrs. W. H. Bason, Raleigh, N.C., for excerpts from *History of North Carolina,* by Samuel A'Court Ashe (Copyright 1925 by Samuel A. Ashe)

North Carolina Department of Archives and History, Raleigh,

7

ACKNOWLEDGMENTS

N.C., for excerpts from *The Correspondence of Jonathan Worth,* collected and edited by J. G. de Roulhac Hamilton (Copyright 1909 by North Carolina Historical Commission)

University of California Press, Berkeley, Cal., for excerpts from *'Ware Sherman, A Journal of Three Months of Personal Experience in the Last Days of the Confederacy* (Copyright 1937 by University of California Press)

CONTENTS

9

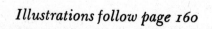

Illustrations follow page 160

AUTHOR'S NOTE

Like millions of Southerners, I grew up in an atmosphere of animosity to Sherman, with the natural result. My highly unfavorable opinion of the man has not been entirely reversed by college, living in the North, and the years of research that went into the writing of this book. I still find much to dislike. He was unnecessarily cruel, bringing hunger and misery to innocent people. He used terror as a weapon of war. Directly or indirectly, by action or inaction, he was, I am still convinced, responsible for the burning of Columbia. He was guilty of many other violations of the rules of civilized warfare. But I have found another and a better side to his nature. He hated war and contended that he waged it ruthlessly in order to end it quickly. Unlike most military heroes, he refused to capitalize on his fame. Like Grant, he showed generosity and kindness to a defeated, impoverished and helpless enemy. He had no patience with those who made Reconstruction in many respects more frightful than war.

The task of authorship has been greatly lightened by the generous and willing help of many others. Only a few can be mentioned here. The unmentioned will know I am grateful to them as well.

Miss Martha Russell, curator of manuscripts at Duke University Library, and her assistant, Miss Faye Locke, not only allowed unrestricted access to the manuscripts in their custody but made as easy as possible the inevitably onerous task of examining and copying this valuable material. Dr. James W. Patton, director of the Southern Historical Collection at the University of North Carolina Library, Robert W. Hill, keeper of manuscripts at the

New York Public Library, and William S. Powell, librarian of the U.N.C. Library's North Carolina Collection, also opened their treasures for inspection and use. Microfilmed newspaper files, especially those at the New York Public Library, revealed much unfamiliar information. Mrs. Eva R. McKenna, of the U.N.C. Library Interlibrary Center, members of the staff of the Library of Congress, Mrs. Lois Neal, Miss Annie Lee Yates and Miss Gladys Johnson of the North Carolina State Library, and Miss Clyde Smith, librarian of Raleigh's Olivia Raney Library, supplied many books, magazines and other material and helped in their use. Mrs. Pattie B. McIntyre, of the U.N.C. Library's Humanities Division, helped with some difficult problems. H. B. Harshbargers, acting director of the U. S. Department of Commerce Weather Bureau at Asheville, N.C., added to the meager information regarding South Carolina weather conditions in 1865. James A. Servies, College of William and Mary librarian, furnished copies of unpublished letters from General Joseph E. Johnston which had come into his possession.

Manly Wade Wellman read an earlier draft of the manuscript, offered some excellent suggestions for changes and, in general, acted as friendly counselor. My wife Virginia helped with the copying of manuscripts and kept the typing going while I was busy with other tasks. Dr. Frank G. Slaughter, who had reviewed two of my earlier books, spoke a good word for this one when it was submitted for publication. And finally, members of the Coward-McCann staff have been most helpful and co-operative.

JOHN M. GIBSON

RALEIGH, N.C., FEBRUARY 4, 1961

THOSE 163 DAYS

I

———————— ∿ ————————

"YOU MAY BE SURE OF ONE THING—WHAT HE SAYS HE CAN DO, HE *CAN*"

IT was a brisk day in the fall of 1864. In front of a headquarters tent in the village of Gaylesville in northern Alabama, three major generals of the United States Army huddled over a map. The man in the center spoke vigorously, with the assurance of one accustomed to giving orders to men who gave orders. The other two intently followed his finger as it moved planchette-like across the map. William Tecumseh Sherman, Oliver Otis Howard and Henry Warner Slocum, conquerors of Atlanta, were plotting their next campaign.

Sherman's finger moved slowly and deliberately from Atlanta in a southeasterly direction to Milledgeville, the state capital, and stopped. From there they might turn northeast and march on Augusta, or, if military exigencies dictated, they might swing toward Richmond or Petersburg. Pensacola was also a possibility; so were Charleston and Wilmington. But, Sherman emphasized, unless there should be some unexpected change in the plans, they would continue their southeasterly march to Savannah. That he had fixed as his first major objective.

He outlined in some detail the plans for the campaign. The elite units of the large, powerful army that had won Atlanta would form a sharply efficient, compact force of from 60,000 to

65,000 men for a kind of warfare virtually unknown on the North American continent.[1]

There would undoubtedly be fighting, but not much. The objective would be to tear up railroads supplying Lee's armies in Virginia, bleed the economy of the white South and strike a mortal blow at Southern morale, both civilian and soldier. That kind of army would have to travel rapidly. And it would have to travel light. It would carry along a minimum of food, forage and nonmilitary supplies. The rest it would get from the country.

Actually, the campaign to which Sherman was looking forward so eagerly was not altogether unique, even in North America. General Philip Henry Sheridan had carried on a similar one since mid-August in the Shenandoah Valley of Virginia. The devastation Sherman was scheming for Georgia and the Carolinas, the Army of the Shenandoah had taken with dreadful effectiveness to the peaceful towns and countrysides between Staunton and Winchester. On orders from General Grant to destroy that fruitful area as a source of food and supplies for the Confederate army, Sheridan had unleashed a force which had reduced it to a wilderness.

But Sheridan's campaign differed in some respects from what Sherman had in mind. It had been confined to a few counties. Sherman contemplated destroying the war potential of three large states. The Shenandoah Valley had been an active war theatre, with General Jubal Early's resolute army ready to contest the Yankee advance. By contrast, the route to Savannah and beyond was almost free of enemy troops, except weak garrisons here and there that would offer little threat to Sherman's seasoned veterans.

Sheridan had never been out of contact with other armies that could have come to his assistance when needed. His lines of communication had been firmly maintained. There had been no time when he could not have safely retreated. Sherman, on the other hand, was about to plunge off into the unknown. His

16

lines of communication would be snapped. He would be out of touch for weeks not only with his military superiors and with Washington but with the rest of the United States. If he should meet a newly formed, strong enemy force, he would have to fight without outside reinforcements. Defeat deep inside the enemy's country would mean the annihilation of his army.

Sherman's confidence in the success of the enterprise was largely due to his faith in his two chief lieutenants. After being accused of blundering at Chancellorsville and Gettysburg, the 34-year-old Howard had gone on to demonstrate in numerous battles that he was an able general.

Slocum, three years older than his Right Wing counterpart, had escaped the criticism which had brought so much pain to the sensitive, conscientious Howard. In lieu of blame at Gettysburg, he had won from General George Meade high praise as "an officer of honor, dignity of character, and firmness of purpose." He had more recently stirred the admiration of the independent Sherman by resigning his commission after the Battle of Chicamauga rather than serve under General Joseph Hooker, whom he had disliked intensely after a quarrel at Chancellorsville. Then, after his resignation was rejected, he had served loyally under Hooker—although avoiding so far as possible personal contact with him.

Both Howard and Slocum were as confident as their commander, first, that a successful march could be made to the sea and then through the heart of the Carolinas to the rear of Lee's embattled armies in Virginia, and second, that such a campaign was the best means of speeding the end of the war.

Major Henry Hitchcock, Assistant Adjutant General of Volunteers, to whom Sherman described his plan soon after outlining it to Slocum and Howard, agreed heartily when Sherman told him "It's a big game, but I can do it." Not only could Sherman march to the sea and on to Lee's rear, Hitchcock was confident, but he could do anything else he made up his mind to

17

do: ". . . you may be sure of one thing—what he says he can do, he *can.*"

Major Hitchcock's confidence in Sherman's capabilities was based upon a short-time acquaintance, but a comradely feeling had marked their relationship from the first. Many entries in Hitchcock's carefully kept diary already reflected highly favorable impressions he had gained of the man with whom he was now working so closely. At their very first meeting Sherman's "frank, kind, off-hand way" had captivated him. This "straightforward, simple, kind-hearted, nay, warm-hearted man" struck him as "scrupulously just and careful of the rights of others."

II

REQUIEM FOR ATLANTA

HITCHCOCK'S OPINION of his new chief was hardly shared by the people of Atlanta. The city was to be destroyed to prevent it from ever again becoming a Southern stronghold. All civilians were ordered to evacuate within ten days. Those wishing to go north were promised free transportation, with their possessions, beyond the Federal lines. The others—those scorning to leave the Confederacy—would be taken at Federal expense to Rough and Ready, a neutral point agreed upon by Sherman and General John Bell Hood, commanding Confederate troops in the Atlanta area. Hood had protested against the evacuation order, calling it "unprecedented, studied and ungenerous cruelty." But he had agreed to the armistice which stipulated it.

Mayor James M. Calhoun, who had formally surrendered the city on September 2, and Councilmen E. E. Rawson and S. C. Wells, wrote Sherman that the area south of Atlanta was already crowded with refugees retreating from the northern part of the state before the Federal advance. Where would the displaced Atlantans go?

There was a grave lack of houses to shelter the new arrivals. Many "are staying in churches and other out-buildings." How, they asked, "is it possible for the people still here (mostly

women and children) to find shelter?" How could they survive
the winter just ahead, with neither houses nor subsistence, "in
the midst of strangers who know them not, and without the
power to assist them much if they were willing to do so?"

The conditions they had described they called "a feeble picture" of the results of the Sherman civil evacuation order:

> You know, the woe, the horror and the suffering cannot be
> described by words. Imagination can only conceive of it, and
> we ask you to take these things into consideration. We know
> your mind and time are continually occupied with the duties of
> your command, which almost deters us from asking your atten-
> tion to the matter, but thought it might be that you had not
> considered the subject in all its awful consequences, and that,
> on reflection, you, we hope, would not make this people an ex-
> ception to all mankind; for we know of no such instance ever
> having occurred—surely not in the United States. And what has
> this helpless people done that they should be driven from their
> homes, to wander as strangers, outcasts and exiles, and to subsist
> on charity?

In his reply Sherman did not deny that the evacuation would
bring great hardship. But he refused to revoke or soften the
order, because it was "not designed to meet the humanities of
the case, but to prepare for the future struggles, in which
millions, yea, hundreds of millions, of good people outside of
Atlanta have a deep interest."

Atlanta, the Federal commander insisted, must never again
serve the Confederacy. Under its new regimen, there would be
"no manufactures, commerce, or agriculture here for the main-
tenance of families." Therefore, "sooner or later, want will compel the inhabitants to go." Why then, he asked, not go
immediately, "when all the arrangements are completed for the
transfer, instead of waiting until the plunging shot of contending armies will renew the scene of the past month?"

In that rambling, sixteen-page handwritten letter, Sherman
contended that the people of the South had brought on them-

selves all the hardships and suffering they had been made to endure:

> War is cruelty, and you cannot refine it; and those who brought war on our country deserve all the curses and maledictions a people can pour out. I know I had no hand in making this war, and I know I will make more sacrifices today than any of you, to secure peace. But you cannot have peace and a division of our country.... Once admit the Union, once more acknowledge the authority of the National Government, and, instead of devoting your houses and streets and roads to the dread uses of war, I and this Army become at once your protectors and supporters, shielding you from danger, let it come from what quarter it may....
>
> You might as well appeal against the thunder storm, as against these terrible hardships of war. They are inevitable; and the only way the people of Atlanta can hope once more to live in peace and quiet at home, is to stop this war, which can alone be done by admitting that it began in error and is perpetuated in pride. We don't want your negroes or your horses, or your houses or your land, or anything you have; but we do want, and will have a just obedience to the laws of the United States. That we will have, and if it involves the destruction of your improvements, we cannot help it....

The evacuees' lot was worsened by a Union officer, identified only as "Captain S——," who was designated to provide the free transportation out of Atlanta. Recognizing a golden opportunity, he connived with railroad workers to make the refugees pay extravagantly to get away. To those crowding the Atlanta depot almost to suffocation, employees would announce that each train would be the last. That would set the mob to bidding against each other for the limited space available. Consequently, many of those free passages were sold for two hundred dollars or more apiece, some of the successful bidders giving up the last money they had in the world. Railroad workers would let part of a family aboard, then inform the remaining members that they would be left behind unless they produced outrageous bribes. Since separation at a time like that might have meant the permanent breaking up of a family, those who could possibly pay did so.

A further contrivance of "Captain S——" was assuring evacuees that it would be safe to leave their furniture behind in his custody. Soon after they were gone, it was sold to his enrichment. He promised to move into one woman's house and protect it and its contents from damage or theft. Her train was barely out of Atlanta when he began arranging to have the furniture crated for shipment to his home in the North.

"I wanted myself to get a poor soldier who was going home to die, inside one of the cars," a disgusted Yankee wrote. "Though they were full of strapping, healthy Negroes, who were either servants of the extortioner, or had the almighty dollar to pay their way, I could not gain admittance for the poor fellow. A few dollars in a conductor's pocket were of more importance than his comfort or safety. I gave him my blanket and oil-cloth, but I have since learned he never reached home, for when taken off the top of the cars at Chattanooga, he was found dead."

The New York Times correspondent with the army called these depot dramas "heart-rending in the extreme." War-hardened as he was, he was touched by "old age and tottering infancy huddled together, awaiting their chance of escape." Those milling hordes of refugees, he wrote, "cast many a long lingering look at their once happy home, which they were now about to abandon, perhaps forever." Men and women too old or too sick to get away, wrung their hands as they said good-by to their children. That visitor had seldom witnessed "a more affecting scene of separation." Those who touched him especially were the men who until recently had been rich but now had only a few dollars with which to bid for tickets.

He went on to tell of a disabled soldier with no money who managed, in spite of his feeble condition, to climb atop one of the coaches. The correspondent begged the conductor to allow the shivering invalid inside the car, but the appeal was "rudely and impertinently" turned down. All the correspondent could do was to give the traveler his own rug and overcoat.

High-ranking army officers did not condone these depredations. Brigadier General L. C. Easton, Sherman's chief quartermaster, was especially vigorous in tracking down the culprits. But he and the others were severely handicapped, almost to the point of impotence. An extortionist, for instance, could be convicted only on the testimony of the victim and two witnesses, and he was usually clever enough to operate in such a way as to prevent such evidence from being used against him. Many witnesses were loath to delay their departures by remaining to testify.

At Rough and Ready trains and wagons dumped their human cargo. The new arrivals mechanically gathered up their simple belongings and began looking about forlornly for friendly faces. Many of the women were on the verge of childbirth. As they struggled from their conveyances they could see no answer to their overwhelming problem: how would they get medical care, and who would see to it that they and their babies had shelter and food?

Miss Mary A. H. Gay saw the Atlanta population that had refused to go north "dumped out upon the cold ground without shelter." An "autumnal mist or drizzle" filled the atmosphere, "saturating every article of clothing upon them." Among the milling, confused, bewildered crowd of evacuees were "aged grandmothers upon the verge of the grave, tender girls in the first bloom of young womanhood, and little babes not three days old in the arms of sick mothers." These and other refugees from war's cruelties "were driven from their homes." All were "thrown out upon the cold charity of the world."

Piled high on wagons and railway cars was a conglomeration of barking, purring and bleating animals which their owners did not have the heart to leave behind. There was furniture covering the entire range of normal household needs: ancient pianos, tables of all kinds, disassembled beds, bureaus, chairs, heirloom sofas.

The lugubrious aspect of this crude exodus was relieved somewhat by an air of friendliness. Men in blue and men in gray fraternized in the most comradely fashion. As a visitor commented: "One could scarcely realize that these laughing, chatting groups were deadly enemies, who tomorrow would strive for each other's blood."

At Sherman's camp preparations for the march steadily progressed. No man unable to make his full contribution to the common task would be taken along. The sick and wounded were transferred to other units. Orders went out that baggage and personal equipment were to be cut to the barest necessities. With few exceptions, the men were to travel for several winter weeks with only a single blanket apiece.

The artillery was reduced to one gun per thousand men. Each man was to carry forty rounds of ammunition in his cartridge box and pockets, and two hundred rounds more per man were to be carried in wagons, along with artillery ammunition and other equipment and supplies. Twenty-five hundred wagons would be pulled by fifteen thousand mules, a caravan that would stretch twenty miles or more in an unbroken line. In addition, there would be six hundred ambulances, which could serve other purposes when not needed for the sick and wounded.

Although most of the men were looking forward eagerly to the campaign as a great adventure, as marching time approached, an epidemic of resignation fever swept through the army. Officers in particular were afflicted.

"A great many officers are resigning to avoid the coming campaign," Major James Austin Connolly told his wife in his final letter from the Atlanta area, "and a great many others are trying to resign but cannot. They are being laughed at by the whole army here, and by their present conduct they are losing such soldierly reputation as they have made . . . Perhaps they have been away so long that their wives are urging them to come home, and the great boobies are consequently backing out and trouping off home as fast as they can get away. . . . They will all be sorry for going home before they have been there a single month, while we will have no regrets of that kind to disturb us."

The army rapidly being organized in the Atlanta area would number 62,204 men. General Howard's Right Wing would consist of the XV and XVII Corps, while the XIV and XX Corps would comprise General Slocum's Left Wing. The two divisions comprising the cavalry corps would be dissociated from the two wings. Their commanding officer, Brigadier General Judson Kilpatrick, would take orders directly from Sherman.

On November 8 Sherman issued an order describing the impending campaign. The new army had been organized, it said, for a specific purpose, "well known to the War Department and to General Grant." The campaign "involves a departure from our present base and a long and difficult march to a new one." Special Field Orders, No. 119, went on:

> All the chances of war have been considered and provided for, as far as human sagacity can. All he [the writer] asks of you is to maintain that discipline, patience, and courage, which have characterized you in the past; and he hopes, through you, to strike a blow at our enemy that will have a material effect in producing what we all so much desire, his complete overthrow. . .

Special Field Orders, No. 120, issued the same day, specified that wherever practicable, the four corps would march on four approximately parallel roads, converging at agreed-upon rendezvous points. Each column would start out at 7 o'clock in the morning and march about fifteen miles a day, unless contrary orders were issued. The army "will forage liberally on the country," but indiscriminate seizure or destruction of private property would not be countenanced. To that end, "each brigade commander will organize a good and sufficient foraging

party, under the command of one or more discreet officers."
Those officers would supervise the assembling at appropriate
places along the route of "corn or forage of any kind, meat of
any kind, vegetables, cornmeal, or whatever is needed by the
command." Their aim at all times would be to keep in the
wagons food enough for at least ten days and a three-day supply
of forage for the animals. The men were forbidden to enter private residences or trespass in any way. However, while in camp
or enjoying the customary halts for rest, "they may be permitted
to gather turnips, potatoes, and other vegetables, and to drive
stock in sight to their camp."

The burning of houses, mills, cotton gins and other buildings
would be done only by order of the four corps commanders.
Whether they would order such destruction would be determined by the attitude of the people: "In districts and neigh-
borhoods where the army is unmolested, no destruction of such
property should be permitted; but should guerrillas or bush-
whackers molest our march, or should its inhabitants burn
bridges, obstruct roads, or otherwise manifest local hostility,
then army commanders should order and enforce a devastation
more or less relentless, according to the measure of such
hostility."

Cavalry and artillery units might "appropriate freely and
without limit." They were expected, however, to discriminate
between "the rich, who are usually hostile," and "the poor and
industrious, usually neutral or friendly." The orders authorized
regular foraging parties to seize horses and mules needed to
replace worn-out animals or to serve as pack mules. Those seizing private property—foraging parties and individuals looking
for animals—were forbidden to use abusive or threatening language. If the officer in charge of a foraging party chose, he might
give householders or landowners "written certificates of the
facts," but no receipts. No family was to be forced to give up
enough of its foodstuffs to endanger its survival or bring on
acute need.

Able-bodied Negroes were to be allowed to join the marching columns provided the work they seemed capable of doing would compensate for the food they would eat. But each high-ranking officer was cautioned about the necessity for maintaining ample food supplies at all times. He was to turn back any outsiders who might become a drain upon them. A commander's primary duty, Special Field Orders, No. 120, emphasized, "is to see to those who bear arms."

At about 3 o'clock on the afternoon of November 12, Sherman wrote out a dispatch to General George Henry Thomas, whom he was leaving behind to keep Hood's army from attacking his rear, and stood by while the operator ticked it out. As soon as the last dot-and-dash telegraphic signal had flashed northward, the operator, at his command, broke the wires. At that moment Atlanta ceased to be in telegraphic communication with the rest of the world.

Sherman's mind was now more at ease. The lack of enthusiasm for the projected campaign shown by General Grant, Secretary of War Edwin M. Stanton and President Lincoln had caused him great concern. More than once they had gone so far as to actually oppose it. So long as there were live telegraph wires between Atlanta and Washington, there was the possibility that the plan might have to be abandoned. That silent ticker meant that he was virtually on his way, and Grant's friendly "Great good attend you" of four days before still stood as official Washington's approval.[2]

With the departure less than three days away, Sherman ordered the units of the new army to leave their north Georgia encampments and concentrate in the Atlanta area. This was accomplished in two days.

Although busy with large plans and small details, the commander found time to get off two letters. One was to Admiral David D. Porter, commanding Federal sea forces along the Atlantic coast. The admiral, he wrote, could expect him and his army somewhere between Hilton Head and Savannah about

27

Christmastime. They would need great quantities of everything except food after that long, hard march and would look to him to have it ready. And in the second missive, "my last letter from here," he told Mrs. Sherman not to worry about him or to become concerned over reports of disaster. She was to remember always that the only news she would have would come from "rebel sources."

Throughout the night of November 14-15, profane, sweating troops staggered under heavy loads as they piled mountains of supplies into the twenty-five hundred wagons. The austerity rule was strictly enforced. The men went carefully through their personal possessions to separate what they would like to carry from what they could not safely leave behind. Infantry was funneled to the middle of the streets, to protect the inflammables in the wagons from carelessly thrown matches. At dawn the vast engine of men and machines started moving. Only Slocum's XIV Corps remained, with orders to march out twenty-four hours later.

In the late afternoon of November 15, while the three corps were nearing the end of their first day's march, Sherman rode into Atlanta from his headquarters nearby. With him was his aide-de-camp, Major George W. Nichols. There was a stillness that Atlanta had never before known as their horses' hooves echoed in the streets. The order for evacuation had been all but unanimously obeyed. Those few families who had remained were now keeping themselves in the rear of their houses or peeping curiously and apprehensively out of curtained windows.

The general's sharp eyes saw piles of rubble here and there as he rode through the industrial districts. Factories that had been turning out vital war materials for Lee's and Hood's armies, warehouses and other structures considered potential aids to the Confederate war effort had already been leveled by the specialists he had assigned to the task.

Sherman had issued orders that no fires were to be set anywhere in the city until he was there to supervise. That was to be his final act before his departure. But already there were dark voids where buildings had stood for generations before the incendiaries came. Four nights earlier someone had set fire to some buildings on Decatur Street. Before it could be brought under control, eight had been destroyed. At about the same time, as if by prearranged signal, other fires shot skyward in other parts of the city. Those responsible, knowing that much of the city was to be burned, failed to see how a few days would make much difference. Then too, fires set ahead of time would not be supervised and would serve as excellent cover-ups for looting and other crimes.

Officers did what they could to restrain the fire-setters. Guards were doubled. Orders went out to shoot anybody seen firing a building, and rewards were posted for the apprehension of offenders. Both measures were ineffective.

Among the hundred or so remaining in Atlanta was the Berry family, with a young daughter given to diary-keeping. Even before the fires started, Carrie Berry confided to her little book her "dred" of the likely consequences of Atlanta's fall. After the last train had pulled out, she wrote: "We are erbliged to stay here now." The next few days' entries recount that she and her parents were "fritened almost to death last night, and could not sleep for fear they would set our house on fire." For two days, she stood guard at her window or made hasty excursions about the neighborhood to watch the creeping snake of flame advancing toward her part of the city. She experienced a measure of relief when a "gard" was assigned to her house, as he made her "feel a little more protected."

Those who stayed saw much to infuriate and embitter them. Soldiers unbridled cavalry horses and turned them loose in cemeteries to graze on the grass and shrubbery, where their heavy metal-shod hooves sank deeply into the soft ground above the caskets. Marble lambs adorning the headstones of children, religious symbols placed on graves by the bereaved and other tributes to the departed were broken and scattered about in fragments. Caskets and the bodies of the dead were not safe from vandal hands. General William P. Howard of the Georgia militia described the removal of the dead from vaults in the cemetery, stripping coffins of their silver name plates and tippings and placing the Federals' own dead in the vaults. These depredations he called "the crowning act of all their wickedness and villainy."

The *official* destruction began on November 15. Sherman's orders to Captain O.M. Poe, his chief of engineers, were to destroy everything that would be of use to the enemy.

The foundry, a half-million-dollar stucture, was the first to go. Next came the oil refinery, followed by the freight warehouse, containing several bales of cotton, the railway depot and turn-tables, the freight sheds and other nearby buildings. Breaking out of the center area, the flames crawled to the Atlanta Hotel. From there they spread to other hotels, clothing stores, places of amusement and saloons. Soon all were burning furiously as one. Soldiers used their muskets to smash the doors and windows of a partially destroyed warehouse and rushed in and out with armloads of liquor, clothing, tobacco and other articles just before the building fell in. Hair and eyebrows were singed, uniforms scorched and a few of the looters suffered painful burns, but they had little to fear from their officers, who generally took the position that it was all right for the men to get what they could, since what they didn't get would be burned.

"The streets were now in one fierce sheet of flame; houses were falling on all sides, and fiery flakes of cinders were whirled about," wrote Captain David P. Conyngham, reporting the campaign for the New York *Herald*. "Occasionally shells exploded, and excited men rushed through the choking atmosphere, and hurried away from the city of ruins."

Conyngham apparently did not linger long himself, for he gives us this picture of dying Atlanta as seen in perspective:

Requiem for Atlanta

At a distance the city seemed overshadowed by a cloud of black smoke, through which, now and then, darted a gushing flame of fire, of projectiles hurled from the burning ruin.

The sun looked, through the hazy cloud, like a blood-red ball of fire; and the air, for miles around, felt oppressive and intolerable . . . the "Gate City" was a thing of the past.

A correspondent from the New York *Evening Post* wrote:

A grand and awful spectacle. The heaven is one expanse of lurid fire; the air is filled with flying, burning cinders; buildings covering two hundred acres are in ruin or in flames; every instant there is a sharp detonation or the smothered booming sound of exploding shells and powder concealed in the buildings, and then the sparks and flame shoot away up into the blackened red roof, scattering cinders far and wide.

The vast wall of flames kept rolling forward until it made hot ashes of more than a third of the city. Roaring-drunk soldiers, singing and shouting, staggered about or rode stolen animals amid the burning ruins. While drunk and sober alike made mincemeat of "Rally Round the Flag," the Thirty-third Massachusetts band in another part of the city played "John Brown's Body" over and over, reading the notes by the light of the flaming buildings. "I have never," averred Major Nichols, "heard that noble anthem when it was so grand, so solemn, so inspiring."

Of General Sherman, Major Connolly wrote in his diary that night, "he is somewhere nearby now, looking on at all this, and saying not one word to prevent it."

III

THE ROAD TO MILLEDGEVILLE

AT 7 O'CLOCK the next morning, Sherman, accompanied by Major Hitchcock and other officers on his personal staff, rode out of Atlanta on the Decatur road. It was choked with men, wagons, ambulances and animals of the XIV Corps, and a company of infantry and one of cavalry, which had been detailed to guard the wagon train against sudden forays by Joe Wheeler's cavalrymen. Outside the city Sherman pulled his horse to a stop on the crest of a slight hill near where the Confederate breastworks had stood during the battle for Atlanta. That very ground had been fought over furiously in the grim conflict of July 22. Not far away he could see a little patch of woods where his friend, Brigadier General James Birdseye McPherson, had been killed that bitter day leading his Army of the Tennessee against his West Point classmate, General Hood. A decade later Sherman wrote in his memoirs:

> Behind us lay Atlanta, smouldering and in ruins, the black smoke rising high in the air, and hanging like a pall over the ruined city. Away off in the distance, on the McDonough road, was the rear of Howard's column, the gun-barrels glistening in the sun, the white-topped wagons stretching away to the south; and right behind us the Fourteenth Corps, marching

steadily and rapidly with a cheery look and swinging pace, that made light of the thousand miles that lay between us and Richmond.

A regimental band struck up "John Brown's Body." The marching men started singing the refrain, the only part many of them knew, and the countryside was alive with the stirring words and music. "Never before or since have I heard the chorus of 'Glory, glory, hallelujah!' done with more spirit, or in better harmony of time and place," Sherman wrote.

He urged his horse forward. In a few minutes the ruins, the fires and the low-hanging cloud of smoke of Atlanta were hidden behind a patch of forest. Straight ahead, some 270 perilous miles away, was Savannah.

He could not have asked for a better day for the start of a new campaign. That chilly November 16 was "extremely beautiful . . . clear sunlight, with bracing air." He recalled "an unusual feeling of exhilaration" in his men. "Uncle Billy," they would shout in the free informality he had encouraged, "I guess Grant is waiting for us in Richmond," unaware that they were not on their way to meet Grant or anybody else at Richmond, at least not directly. Indeed the men's buoyant feeling that they were off on an easy march, with no anticipation of the hardships and risks to be faced, depressed Sherman's spirits. He realized success would be accepted with little appreciation. But, if he should fail, the enterprise would be condemned as "the wild adventure of a crazy fool."

Sherman, so confident of success a few weeks ago, was not alone in his doubts. As soon as news of the march reached the rest of the world there were predictions of disaster. "It will be the fault of the people inhabiting those countries [the South], if his army is not utterly destroyed long before it shall have reached either Mobile, Savannah, or Charleston," the London *Post* averred.

The Road to Milledgeville

The London *Times* said:

> The movement seems, as far as we can judge, to resemble the celebrated march of Napoleon in 1814 to St. Dizer, by which he threw himself upon the communications of the allied armies, then marching on Paris. If this enterprise be brought to a successful termination, General Sherman will undoubtedly be entitled to the honor of having added a fresh chapter to the history and practice of modern warfare. The worst of such enterprises as Sherman's is, that they allow nothing for the chapter of accidents, proverbially so potent in war, and that the slightest and most unforeseen causes may lead to their defeat and ruin. We had our own experience in the tremendous disaster of Saratoga, undertaken, it might be thought, under auspices far more promising than the expedition of Sherman; in the ruin which overtook Braddock; and in the failure against Quebec, by the brave American general, Montgomery. It will be strange, indeed, if the Army of General Sherman should arrive before Savannah, after such a march, conducted under such difficulties, in condition to attack and storm a town so well fortified and so strenuously defended.

Out of Sherman's bold adventure would come either "the most tremendous disaster that ever befell an armed host" or a world-stirring triumph, "the very consummation of the success of sublime audacity," said the London *Herald*. If the former, the long-shot gambler "will become the scoff of mankind" and "the humiliation of the United States." If the latter, the Sherman name would be "written upon the tables of fame side by by side with that of Napoleon and Hannibal." The American commander certainly would not live in a dim gray twilight of half-fame. He would be "either an Xerxes or an Xenophon."

"If Sherman really has left his army in the air and started off without a base to march from Georgia to South Carolina," the *British Army and Navy Gazette* observed wonderingly, "he has done either one of the most brilliant or one of the most foolish things ever performed by a military leader ... The date on which he goes and the plan on which he acts must really place him among the great Generals or the very little ones."

In the South a Richmond minister declared, "God has put a hook in Sherman's nose and is leading him to destruction." The Richmond *Whig* pointed out that "Sherman may be a shrewd banker, a stubborn fighter, and a prospective candidate for Presidential honors," but "we venture the prediction that he has been woefully outgeneraled this time."

> If Sherman can do all this with the force at his command, which we are disposed to think does not exceed 40,000 men, [The *Whig* editor of course considerably underestimated the size of the army.] then he is a much greater Commander than we take him to be, and the Georgians are a much tamer people than they have credit for being. For our own part, we cannot see how the contemplated campaign is to advance the design of subjugation, let it terminate as it may.
>
> It may serve as an additional annoyance to the people, but it must be destitute of results as the arrow is destitute to wound the air through which it passes. It leaves absolutely open the entire country in the rear, from Chattanooga to the Gulf, wherever the Yankee army is not for the time encamped.

The Richmond *Examiner* predicted that the march would lead Sherman to the "Paradise of Fools." The Augusta *Chronicle and Sentinel* expressed confidence that, "instead of overwhelming the State at his ease, as he has proudly boasted, he will be fortunate if he succeeds in making good his escape."

A *New York Times* editorial referred with some misgivings to the spectacle of a great army, "plunging off into the darkness of an enemy's territory, burning their shelter behind them, as Cortez his ships, never to be heard of more till the enemy reports to us victory or disaster." It called such a spectacle "something dramatic and exciting." If successful, the venture would be "the most remarkable military achievement of the war." Indeed the

Times editors "do not recall a march which can be compared with it, in modern military history."

The fear of failure and its consequences stayed with Sherman, but at the same time, he took courage from the knowledge that all was going well so far: Howard's XV and XVII Corps were a full day's march ahead on the road to Jonesboro after tearing up the Atlanta end of the railroad linking it with Montgomery. The XIV Corps, of which he was a part, was moving along at a satisfactory pace toward Covington and Shady Dale. And the XX Corps had spent much of its first day out of Atlanta tearing up the railroad leading from Atlanta to Augusta and Charleston. This was at least a fine beginning.

Captain O. M. Poe was employing with great effectiveness the technique for demolishing railroads which he had already demonstrated in north Georgia and the Atlanta area. Using equipment devised especially for this purpose, his engineers would yank the iron rails from the wooden crossties. Then the crossties would fuel bonfires in which the rails were heated to the pliability of wire and then twisted. Later, as the men got more experience, the soft rails were bent into fantastic shapes around trees, posts and fence rails. The men prided themselves on the fanciful designs they concocted, but most were satisfied to make crude *U. S.*'s. Too heavy to be carried away as trophies or souvenirs of war, they could be seen for years along Sherman's pathway, and became known as "Sherman's neckties."

Sherman had chosen with deliberation the routes to be followed by the four corps, marching in the approved manner along four roughly parallel roads. Slocum's Left Wing was moving in an easterly direction, as though headed for Augusta, while Howard's Right Wing was marching toward the southeast, in the general direction of Macon. The enemy was successfully confused. Deciding that the Yankees were about to attack Augusta and Macon, the Confederates kept their forces divided between these two places, while the main Federal forces drove on toward their real objective, Milledgeville, about thirty miles northeast of Macon. Kilpatrick's cavalry added to the enemy's confusion and military weakness by making a strong feint on Macon, capturing a train of railway cars a little east of the town, and tearing up the track for a mile or so.

The XX Corps continued its destruction of the Atlanta-Augusta railroad as far as Madison, seventy-five miles from Atlanta. But instead of going on to Augusta, Slocum turned sharply south at Madison to keep the first rendezvous at Milledgeville. In the meantime the XIV Corps was heading for the rendezvous by a short, direct inside route about half-way between those taken by Slocum's XX and Howard's XV and XVII. Kilpatrick's cavalry was acting as a screen on the right, or southwest.

The men who had so jauntily left Atlanta got a realistic foretaste of what lay ahead the fourth day out. On November 18 the head of column of Howard's Right Wing reached the Ocmulgee River at Planter's Ferry after passing through Jonesboro, McDonough and Indian Springs in its swing in the general direction of Macon. Howard's engineers set up two pontoon bridges in short order. But because of heavy rains and the steep slippery bank on the far side of the river, difficult to negotiate even when dry, the men were not able to cross over until November 20. The heads of column were at Clinton, not far from Macon, by the time the last muddy wagon and the last cursing trooper were safely over and marching again.

At Social Circle, where a small advance force of Slocum's XX almost captured a wagon train and did capture a Confederate surgeon and about three thousand dollars in gold, they found what one of them called "a dirty little village," of "shanties, superannuated negroes, wooly pickaninnies rolling in the dust, and squatting like huge monkeys on the fences, and half-naked, snuff-begrimed white women." However, they also received something much more to their liking. The wide-eyed Negroes gave them a joyous welcome. One, an old woman, shouted fervently: "I'm bressed if I thought there wuz so many of God's critters in de world at all!"

At Madison the cavalry, well in advance of the main body of troops, set fire to the depot and in general did a thorough job of tearing up the town, which had a reputation for its attractive, often beautiful, houses, many of which were surrounded by skillfully planned and well cared for lawns, flower gardens and conservatories. It had a population of about two thousand, including an uncommonly large number of pretty women and girls who peeped at them fearfully but curiously through slightly open blinds. The apertures of these blinds widened as the band played "Dixie," to disappear with a bang when it swung into "Yankee Doodle."

The main body of the XX Corps entered town the next morning, and the real job of eliminating it as a possible asset to the Confederate cause got under way vigorously. The troops destroyed railroad buildings and trackage, fired two hundred bales of cotton, and reduced other public property to debris and ashes. While this *official* devastation was going on, bluecoats not on special duty swarmed through the town, battering down shop doors and taking anything that struck their fancy. Disregarding Sherman's orders, they forced themselves into fine old private dwellings over the frightened protests of the occupants, mostly women and children, and gathered armfuls of china, small pieces of furniture, silverware and prized heirlooms, which they dumped from a window into the yard in order to go back for another load. It made no difference that much of the stuff they had no use for and did not want. They jerked a beautiful gilt-framed mirror, highly prized by its owner, off the wall and smashed it to pieces. Pianos, too heavy to be moved, were smashed. Captain Conyngham was disgusted by "a lot of bearded, rough soldiers capering about the room in a rude waltz, while some fellow was thumping away unmercifully at the piano, with another cutting ludicrous capers on the top-board." After a while, though "they got tired of this Saturnalia," and "the piano was consigned to the flames, and most likely the house with it."

Business places fared no better. Hardly a store in the little county-seat town escaped. The marauders carried away armload after armload of merchandise. What was left lay broken and torn on the floors. They took particular delight in breaking into milliners' shops and decking themselves out in fancy hats and hat trimmings, and one soldier rode down the town's main street on horseback making ardent love to a dress form.

These pranks went on until Slocum's infantrymen arrived. Guards were posted where there was danger of trouble, and normal activities were resumed.

By the time the brief stay in Madison had ended, Sherman, Howard and Slocum were giving sober thought to a problem which had been growing steadily since they left Atlanta. What were they going to do with the hordes of Negroes who wanted to march with the troops to what they knew vaguely as "freedom"? In their confused minds there had generated and blossomed the firm belief that all they had to do when the Yankees came along was to fall into line, with their squalling babies, their bleating, barking animals and their variegated personal possessions and follow the liberators to Paradise. At almost every crossroads community, and indeed at almost every plantation, there would be droves of them, eager, ready and waiting to join the procession. Many read deep religious meaning into the events they were witnessing. To them these marching men in blue were agents of God sent to end their earthly troubles. Their frenzied shouts, releasing long-pent-up emotions, echoed around the countrysides: "Glory be to de Lawd!" "Bress de Lawd!" "De day of jubilee is come!" "Dis Nigger is off to glory!" It never occurred to them that they might not be wanted or that there might not be enough food for both them and the army. Nor did they give a thought to where they would go, how they would be treated after they got there or what would happen to them eventually in that strange land in the

North about which they were dreaming but about which they knew absolutely nothing. It took some strong talk to dissuade them from going along. Many who went anyhow soon wished they hadn't.

As the troops advanced, more and more Negroes tried to attach themselves to the columns. Some shouted. Some prayed. Many wore their best, cleanest and newest clothes, like children waiting for a train. There were so many at times that Sherman and the other officers on horseback had to be careful not to trample them. As soon as he was recognized or pointed out, they would swarm upon "Mr. Sherman" in a riotous frenzy. A girl literally hugged one of the regimental banners and kept jumping up to "the feet of Jesus." When Sherman dismounted and walked up to a plantation house, the Negroes swept upon him like a suddenly undammed pond. One old fellow told him he had been looking for "the angel of the Lord" since he was a child.

Sherman told him what he had already told many others: that he and the other Negroes were not to try to follow the troops but were to stay where they were, for the present at least. When he asked him to spread that message over the neighborhood, there was a sharp drop in the size of the crowds.

As the columns got farther from Atlanta they found their foraging problem simplified. Governor Joseph E. Brown, like other Southern governors, had urged farmers to reduce their cotton acreage and plant more foodstuffs to supply Lee's and Hood's armies during the coming winter. This urging had had a strong effect. Noticeable since soon after leaving Atlanta, it was especially so now. Indeed Captain Conyngham called the Madison-Covington-Milledgeville area of the fall of 1864 "a perfect garden," and the rest of central Georgia was no less bountiful. Hogs grunted contentedly in farmyards and pens. There were multitudes of chickens and turkeys in the yards and fields. Young fodder had been gathered and stacked. The barns were bursting with shucked corn for the work animals. Other grains and other kinds of farm products were piled high in the lofts. Sweet potatoes filled the potato houses, cellars and pits. And in the kitchens and pantries shelves sagged under preserved fruits and vegetables, while salted carcasses and sides of meat hung in rigid array from the rafters.

As the Yankees neared Milledgeville, Sherman, still riding with the XIV Corps, stopped at a plantation which perfectly symbolized the Yankee conception of Southern rural aristocracy. Flanking the elegant main house, the kind of mansion in which wealthy Southern planters had lived and entertained on a lavish scale before the war, were the homes of a hundred or more slaves. Six thousand fertile acres stretched to the horizon. Sherman was informed that it belonged to Howell Cobb.

That name was familiar to any informed American, Northerner or Southerner. For this large-framed, bewhiskered, 46-year-old Georgian was a national figure. He had represented his state for ten years in Congress, two of them as Speaker of the House. He had been Governor of Georgia and Secretary of the Treasury in the Buchanan administration. After playing an influential part in aligning his state with those withdrawing from the Union, he had joined the Confederate Army and was now a major general. Had Sherman searched the South over, he could not have found a more perfect example of what he most disliked about it. This fine plantation and the four or five others Cobb owned elsewhere, his five or six hundred slaves and his wearing of the Confederate uniform after holding high official positions in the Federal government—all these made this Southern planter a symbol to Sherman to despise with consummate bitterness. Here was a place where war-making in the Sherman manner would be an unquestionable pleasure.

His animosity was further strengthend by a Macon newspaper soon after he reached the plantation. In a conspicuous position on the front page he saw an appeal from General Cobb urging his fellow Georgians to rise in their wrath and destroy the invaders. They were urged to burn everything likely to fall into enemy hands and to harass them in every way possible.

Unable to wreak personal venegance on Cobb, Sherman told the slaves and soldiers to help themselves to the vast amount of food and foodstuffs that still remained on the plantation. What was left he ordered burned.

During his brief stay there, before beginning the last lap to Milledgeville, Sherman was visited by one of the oldest and feeblest of the Cobb slaves. The old colored man shuffled up to the door and pushed it open. He stood there and took a long look at this tall, erect, dark-eyed man about whom he had heard so much. Then he shuffled away, muttering: "He's got de Linkun head, de Linkun head, he's got de Linkun head."

While Sherman was nearing his rendezvous in absentia with Howell Cobb, a brigade of infantrymen and cavalry from General Charles R. Woods' division of the XV Corps was fighting the first real battle of the campaign near Griswoldville, ten miles northeast of Macon. General Charles C. Walcutt, in command of the advance unit, had been ordered to move rapidly forward toward Macon in order to strengthen the enemy's supposition that the city was about to be attacked in force. At his approach about five thousand troops consisting mainly of Georgia militia, with a few regulars transferred from the Confederate garrison at Savannah, advanced boldly against these battle-hardened troops.

The Confederates showed, and paid dearly for, the rashness characteristic of inexperienced troops. The bluecoats threw up temporary breastworks and placed their heavy guns in position, and the Southerners with great bravery but with little knowledge of protective techniques ran into a wall of grapeshot musketry, and were cut down. The rapidly thinning ranks were refilled, and the attack went on. After a long, bitter battle, lasting from about three in the afternoon until dark, the Confederates could no longer withstand this terrific pressure. Federal sources reported that they retreated "in full flight" toward

Griswoldville. The Confederate commander, Brigadier General P. J. Phillips, said they "retired in good order." In either case, the Confederate losses were extremely heavy. And they were without even partial compensation. "The battle of Griswold-ville," General G. W. Smith, in over-all command of Confederate troops in that area, wrote in his official report, "will be remembered as an unfortunate accident, whose occurrence might have been avoided by the exercise of proper caution and circumspection. It in no wise crippled the movements of the enemy and entailed upon the Confederates a loss, which under the circumstances could be illy sustained." Major Nichols estimated Confederate losses in killed, wounded and taken prisoner at more than twenty-five hundred. Federal killed and wounded did not exceed forty, he said. Neither General Smith nor General Phillips reported on Confederate losses.

In Milledgeville, where the Legislature was in session, the people became alarmed by reports of the Yankees' steady march toward the capital. But they took comfort in the brave words of Governor Brown. This long-time day laborer who had become a power in Georgia politics in spite of a very limited education, promised to stand with lawmakers and other patriots and fight off the invaders with muskets and bayonets. They could depend upon him, he told them, to defend the Governor's Mansion to his last breath. But when an excited messenger arrived with the news that the Yankees were definitely headed that way, in Governor and legislators alike, there was a sudden and complete melting of the determination to fight to the last man, or even to fight at all. Their thoughts were of getting away.

It was not a sudden resurgence of courage that detained the emotional Governor after many had left. He was determined to leave nothing that Sherman or his men could enjoy. Frightened as he was, he took time to strip the Governor's Mansion of all its furnishings. Even the vegetables were packed up and taken to the train. He did, however, leave behind the large

44

quantity of muskets and ammunition with which he and his legislators had once planned to defend the city. Neither did he bother to save the State archives.

In spite of the government's precipitous departure, Milledgeville was not given up without a fight. Convicts in the state penitentiary were turned loose with guns in their hands if they would promise to use them against the Yankees. Fighting alongside them were teen-age military school cadets transformed quickly from students to combat troops. But they could not stand up against Sherman's veterans. Under their commander, General Harry Wayne, who had seen prewar service in the United States Army, they fell back toward the city, failing en route to destroy or even damage the bridge across the Oconee river.

Slocum's XX Corps entered Milledgeville about noon November 22, a week after leaving Atlanta. Mayor R. B. DeGraffenreid, one of the few officials who had resisted the temptation to join the mad exodus, formally surrendered the city to him and made the usual request that private property and lives be protected. Bands played as the troops marched in, and the streets were alive with many-colored banners. The Stars and Stripes were soon flying atop the Capitol. General Jeff C. Davis' XIV Corps marched in the next day.

It was apparent to the people of Milledgeville, including R. M. Orme, Sr., the local correspondent of the Macon *Confederate and Telegraph,* that the bluecoats had been living well off the country. The wagons, he noted, were as full as they could be. The men looked rugged and well fed. But they had brought distress to those along their route:

> They spread desolation broadcast—taking everything in their way in the breadth of about 20 miles. Corn, fodder, meal, flour, horses, mules, hogs, cattle, sheep, poultry of every description, servants that could be enticed and forced off, and these in great numbers, [were taken] . . . We heard of a great many private dwellings, gin houses, and much cotton being burnt by the

enemy on their different routes—some within sight; also that several private citizens were shot. It is, however, due to the Federals to say that they respected families in our cities, within doors, but at the same time robbed them of all without. In the country, families were frequently ill-treated, and their houses sacked.

The fire-setters got to work on the Milledgeville railroad depot on the afternoon of November 23, and went on to magazines, factories, storehouses containing Confederate government property, and some seventeen hundred bales of cotton.

The Capitol building was spared. So were the insane asylum, the town's leading factory and the Governor's Mansion, which Sherman requistioned for his headquarters. Sherman was not disconcerted by the absence of furniture. This tough veteran of many hardships always carried a roll of blankets and a haversack full of hardtack. At night he spread his blankets on the bare floor and lay down.

To prevent a repetition of the outrages that had occurred in Madison and elsewhere, General Slocum posted guards for the protection of private homes, but the troops nevertheless enjoyed full freedom in many, and in the Capitol and places of business. In the State Library, on the first floor of the Capitol, Major Connolly looked on in strong disapproval, though without protesting, while a mob attacked the accumulation of valuable volumes and carried away what struck their fancies. He blamed his commander in chief for allowing such a thing to happen: "Sherman will, some day, regret that he permitted this library to be destroyed and plundered."

From other rooms drunken soldiers and Negroes grabbed up handfuls of valuable fossils and mineral specimens. Many left with armfuls of Georgia state bonds and paper currency, which they found in the treasurer's office. One colored man, dazzled by all this wealth, shouted his delight: "Bress de Lord, we're richer dan poor massa now!" Soon the soldiers and Negroes fell to fighting amongst themselves for the treasures.

The Road to Milledgeville

A number of the officers wondered about Sherman's failure to prevent these outrages and others which he presumably condemned. General Jeff Davis, for one, mentioned that many of the troops believed Sherman actually approved and was pleased by the burning of private dwellings, in spite of his orders against it. From time to time a fire-setter or looter, acting without orders, would be caught. His standard defense was that he had done what everybody knew Sherman wanted done. Some of Sherman's officers were asking each other whether their chief, to whom they were personally devoted, really possessed the rare qualities of military generalship they had attributed to him. "I am bound to say I think Sherman lacking in enforcing discipline," Hitchcock observed. "Brilliant and daring, fertile, rapid and terrible, he does not seem to me to carry out things in that respect. Staff organization [is] not systematic nor thorough—not as well selected as it ought to be. . . . "

Sherman certainly gave reason for these conjectures. He had a way of exploding in moments of excitement or anger and saying things that may or may not have represented his true feelings. An incident of this kind happened near Milledgeville. When his troops were temporarily halted by a burned bridge, he ordered a house in the neighborhood picked at random to be set afire in retaliation. Major Hitchcock protested that the identity of the bridge-burner could have been discovered and his own house chosen for burning. "In war," Sherman replied defensively, "everything is right which prevents anything. If bridges are burned, I have a right to burn all houses near it [sic]. . . . Let him [the owner of the house] look to his own people; if they find that their burning bridges only destroys their own citizens' houses, they'll stop it."

This struck many people as queer reasoning. Statements of that kind, as well as Sherman's acts, left them—his own officers and Georgia civilians alike—with the belief that he really did not care how indiscriminately buildings were burned or how many other depredations occurred.

The offenses at Milledgeville were not, however, as grievous as they were painted by inflamed Southerners. The Augusta *Record* reported the arrival at that place of a man who had been in the Georgia capital while the Yankees were there. He told about "the most hellish deeds" charged to them. Those "incarnate devils ravished some of the nicest ladies in the town." One of the victims "was consigned to the asylum on Monday." Her sanity had "tottered beneath the load of wounded honor." She "is ruined forever."

Those crimes, it was revealed later, had not occurred. Early in January the Fayetteville *Observer* published a letter from a Savannah minister saying that he had seen letters from a number of Milledgeville women and from General G. T. Beauregard, who had visited the town after Sherman left. They stated unequivocally that there was no truth in the reports.

From newspapers which had accumulated in the Georgia capital from all over the South, Sherman gained valuable information about how the people were reacting to the march and what their leaders were doing about it.

On November 18, three days after the first units left Atlanta, General Beauregard, at his Corinth, Mississippi, headquarters, had appealed to the people of Georgia: "Arise for the defense of your native soil! Rally around your patriotic Governor and gallant soldiers! Obstruct and destroy all the roads in Sherman's front, flank, and rear, and his army will soon starve in your midst. Be confident. Be resolute. Trust in an overruling Providence, and success will soon crown your efforts. I hasten to join you in the defense of your homes and firesides."

A message from the Georgia delegation in the Confederate House of Representatives read:

> We have had a special conference with President Davis and the Secretary of War, and are able to assure that they have done and are still doing all that can be done to meet the emergency that presses upon you. Let every man fly to arms! Remove your

negroes, horses, cattle, and provisions from Sherman's army, and burn what you cannot carry. Burn all bridges, and block up the roads in his route. Assail the invader in front, flank, and rear, by night and by day. Let him have no rest.

In the effective carrying out of these urgent pleadings lay the South's best, and indeed only, hope of bringing the campaign to disaster. The Confederacy's weak, low-moraled and widely scattered armies were certainly unequal to the task. But hunger, cold and frustrating delays might easily have had the consequences in Georgia in 1864 that they had had in Russia in 1812. Had the South's "scorched earth" policy been as effective in execution as it was sound in conception, the dire possibilities hoped for by the Confederates, feared by the Yankees and viewed with judicial impartiality by those English editors, would almost certainly have eventuated. General Lee, who said he considered this scheme—to live off the country—Sherman's only really brilliant contribution to victory, praised it only because it worked out. Had the "scorched earth" policy been successful, Lee would have undoubtedly condemned the march as reckless and foolhardy.

November 24 was a sad Thanksgiving Day for Milledgeville. Overwhelmed and crushed by the enemy's failure to provide the protection he had asked for, Mayor DeGraffenreid turned for help to a city which had been lucky enough to get off with a mere threat of occupation, not the real thing. Because of the disruption of the normal means of communication, his message to Macon's Mayor Stephan Collins had to be sent by courier.

"Our citizens have been utterly despoiled by the Yankee army," he wrote. "Send us bread and meat, or there will be great suffering among us. We have no mules or horses. What you send must be brought by wagon trains. The railroad bridge and the bridge across the Oconee have been burned. The State House, Executive Mansion and Factory are still left to us. Send us relief at once."

"... Thanksgiving Day was very generally observed in the army, the troops scorning chickens in the plentitude of turkeys with which they have supplied themselves," the New York *Post* correspondent wrote three days later near Tennille Station on the Georgia Central Railroad. "Vegetables of all kinds and in unlimited quantities were at hand, and the soldiers gave thanks as soldiers may, and were merry as soldiers can be. In truth, as far as the gratification of the stomach goes, the troops are pursuing a continuous thanksgiving."

The troops, satiated with food and leisure, became bored, as armies do when they stop marching. So somebody suggested a mock session of the Georgia House of Representatives, using the seats, podium, gavel and other official paraphernalia left behind by the suddenly departed lawmakers. The suggestion caught on. A large assembly of "legislators" and spectators was on hand for the opening. One of the tasks assigned the newly appointed sergeant at arms was to take care of victims of "Bourbon fits," a condition described by a participant as "rather prevalent among the honorable members."

The session opened with a round of drinking. A "Committee on Federal Relations" was appointed and retired to a committee room. Its six members forgot all about Federal relations for a while and entered into an animated and noisy discussion of the comparative merits of various brands of whiskey. They drank and argued and drank and, after a while, they began singing, their barroom melodies ascending in a great wave to the legislative hall proper and to the rest of the building.

The "legislators" waiting for the "committee's" report were not idle. General Kilpatrick, whose cavalrymen had a reputation for heavy drinking and ruthless treatment of civilians and their property, kept them in high hilarity with recitals of his gallant campaigns against enemy wine cellars and whiskey storerooms.

"Though I am a very modest man, that never blows his own horn, like other gentlemen whom I might name, I must honestly tell you that I am Old Harry on raids," he shouted in alcoholic eloquence. "My men, too, have strongly imbibed the spirit, and are always full of it. I must confess that my fellows are very inquisitive. Having come so far to visit the good people of Georgia, who are famed for their hospitality, they live in the free and easy style among them; and if, perchance, they discover a deserted cellar, believing that it was kindly left to their use by the considerate owner, they take charge of it. It sometimes happens, too, that they look after the place and other little matters. Coming to my own particular raid, it was one of the handsomest and most brilliant assaults of the war. I—"

The speaker was interrupted by someone's raising a point of order: "I believe it is always the custom to treat the speaker." The presiding officer agreed, and a bottle was held to Kilpatrick's mouth. The attending cheers were interrupted by cries of "Order! Order!" as the six colonels comprising the "Committee on Federal Relations" returned, some singing "We Won't Get Home Till Morning," and the others "Marching, Marching Along."

They had managed to draw up some resolutions, which the chairman managed to read. The Georgia Ordinance of Secession was termed "highly indiscreet and injudicious,"—"a damned farce," which "is hereby repealed and abrogated." They promised that Sherman's men "will play the devil with the ordinance and the state itself," and proposed that a committee be appointed "to kick Joe Brown and Jeff Davis, and also to whip the state into the Union." The resolutions were adopted with a great shout. Then somebody stuck his head inside the door and yelled: "The Yankees are coming!" Imitating the real Legislature, they let up a yell and quickly emptied the hall. Major Hitchcock had not attended the "session" but concluded "from what I hear" that the whole affair was "pretty flat and not very creditable." And there were many who agreed with him.

IV

SANDERSVILLE, MILLEN AND EASTWARD

SHERMAN'S NEXT OBJECTIVE was Millen, near an important Confederate prisoner-of-war camp. He hoped to capture it before the prisoners could be transferred elsewhere.

He issued orders for the march on Millen November 23. Slocum's Left Wing was to move there by way of Sandersville, Davisboro and Louisville. Kilpatrick's cavalry was to swing north as though to attack Augusta, then swing south in a wide circle to Millen. Meanwhile Howard's Right Wing, which had struck the Georgia Central Railroad at Gordon, thirteen miles south of Milledgeville, about the same time Slocum's Left Wing entered Milledgeville, was to follow the railroad toward Savannah, tearing up tracks as it went.

Soon after leaving Milledgeville Slocum's XIV and XX Corps entered a new kind of country, altogether different from that between Atlanta and Milledgeville. Instead of expansive fields and great forests there were woods so thick that individual soldiers, let alone men in formation, could get through them only with the greatest difficulty. In desolated pine-tree areas women and children sat forlornly in front of miserable huts looking pale, enervated and sickly. The men had gone off to the war. "Dirt-eaters," the bluecoats called them.

Inevitably, the well-fed, ruddy-faced men in the dusty blue uniforms fell to contrasting their own condition with these people's. "We are living finely," Connolly wrote in his faithfully kept diary. He was sure "the whole army would have no objections to marching around through the State for the next six months." The trip thus far had been "a holiday excursion."

Around this time some prisoners of war escaped from the ill-reputed camp at Andersonville and succeeded in joining one of the Yankee columns. Their comrades greeted them joyously, but were appalled by their appearance. The escapees looked starved, terribly emaciated, haggard and weak to the point of collapse. One man who welcomed them commented on their "wild animal stare." When they were fed, they wept in gratitude and happiness. Their condition, according to Colonel Charles D. Kerr, "sickened and infuriated the men, who thought of them starving in the midst of plenty."

These prisoners and others who joined the long blue columns told of a phase of prisoner-of-war life theretofore unfamiliar to Northerners: pursuit by hounds. Those huge, powerful beasts were kept at or near every camp. When a prisoner escaped, they were turned loose on his trail and followed him, howling and snarling, until they overtook him or lost the scent. They were trained to be vicious man-killers, and many an escaped prisoner was chewed and torn horribly before being returned, bleeding and bruised, to camp. Savage dogs also came to be associated in the soldiers' minds with escaped slaves, who were tracked down and attacked in the same way.

The men of Sherman's army made a grim resolve: no large dogs would be left alive in the South. Whenever one would be sighted, around somebody's house, on the highway, in the woods, it would be shot or bludgeoned to death. Many were destroyed in that way.

Acting on Sherman's doctrine that any Southerner should be made to pay for acts committed by any other Southerner, the men who had seen and talked to escaped prisoners gave unrestrained vent to their anger in their usual way. They seized food and feed and carried them away in far greater quantities than were needed to keep the wagons filled. Looting was practically unchecked. The burning of private residences became commonplace. Orders or no orders, an officer of the 70th Indiana regiment observed, the men "think of the thousands of their imprisoned comrades, slowly perishing with hunger in the midst of wealth untold, barns bursting with grain and food to feed a dozen armies." Their anger caused them, he said, to be "swept by the besom of destruction."

The second day out from Milledgeville the XIV Corps ran into trouble at Buffalo Creek. "Fighting Joe" Wheeler's cavalry had destroyed all nine bridges over the wide swamp and was disputing the crossing with heavy fire. But a Federal regiment forded the stream, drove off the enemy and kept them at bay while engineers set up bridges.

Just before reaching the outskirts of Sandersville, the two Left Wing Corps again confronted Wheeler's cavalry. The Confederates, who, like most Confederate cavalrymen, had been trained to fight afoot as well as on horseback, dismounted and held their position courageously in the face of the furious assault that followed, then counterattacked so vigorously and successfully that the Federals were driven back two miles, with heavy losses in killed and wounded. Wheeler captured thirty prisoners and a large headquarters wagon, and at nightfall he showed his confidence by camping near the enemy. When the battle was resumed the next morning, however, the Federals' overwhelming numerical superiority began to tell. Yielding ground stubbornly but steadily, the Confederates were finally driven back to and beyond Sandersville.

Sherman would not concede that the enemy had put up a brave and strong fight against great odds. Instead, in his official report of the campaign, he merely mentioned his arrival there with the XX Corps, preceded by "skirmishing with Wheeler's cavalry." The Confederates, he said, "offered little opposition."

Major Nichols was as conservative as Sherman, conceding only that Wheeler had resisted the Federals from the place of their encounter back to and inside the town. And Major Connolly stated: "... the men [Federals] marched right into town loading and firing as they advanced: bands playing, flags waving, and Mr. Wheeler and his Rebels, of course, running almost without firing a shot."

The truth is that this was a more significant engagement than any of these men would admit. At Sandersville the Yankees encountered their first stiff resistance since leaving Atlanta. Their losses were fairly heavy, and their progress was slowed.

Just outside the town the Federal commander saw some Confederate soldiers who had stopped fighting long enough to set fire to fodder in the fields. This of course was in furtherance of the "scorched earth" policy which Secretary of War Seddon, General Beauregard and other Southern leaders regarded as perhaps their best hope of defeating the invaders. In retaliation, Sherman ordered his men to burn several houses in the neighborhood. Insuring that the full significance of the act was not lost on the local residents, he personally warned several of them: should any more food, corn or fodder be destroyed along his route, he would carry out a ruthless campaign of devastation and destruction.

Connolly reacted as violently as he did: "Let them do it if they dare. We'll burn every house, barn, church, and everything else we come to; we'll leave their families houseless and without food; their towns will *all* be destroyed, and nothing but the most complete desolation will be found in our track. This army will not be trifled with. If citizens raise their hands against us to retard our march or play the guerrilla against us, neither youth nor age nor sex will be respected. Everything must be destroyed ... We have gone so far now in our triumphal march that we will not be balked. It is a question of life or death with us, and all considerations of mercy and humanity must bow before the inexorable demands of self-preservation."

To prevent the two wings from becoming too widely separated, Sherman held the Left Wing at Sandersville until the Right Wing reached a point south of the town. They then moved forward along their parallel routes.

Meanwhile Howard's XV and XVII Corps had been moving along steadily and with terrible efficiency on the southern route. Following the right of way of the Georgia Central Railroad running from Atlanta and Macon to Augusta and Savannah, they did comparatively little fighting. But they worked hard at their number one job of keeping Confederate trains from running. None could be put into operation for months.

At the same time, Kilpatrick was heading northeast, feinting an attack on Augusta. His real objective was to destroy the trestle at Briar Creek, near Waynesboro, which would sever the railroad between Augusta and Millen at mid-point. To counter the anticipated attack on Augusta, Wheeler concentrated his forces there, which was exactly what Kilpatrick had expected. Kilpatrick's rapidly moving cavalrymen had turned east and were moving steadily away from Augusta before Wheeler recognized the threat as a piece of elaborate stage-setting.

Then Wheeler began looking for a chance to strike Kilpatrick a vicious blow. It came when the two regiments constituting Kilpatrick's rear guard dropped behind the main body. Attacking near Sylvian Grove in the middle of the night, Wheeler forced them to the main column and harassed the column itself. The chief advantage the Confederates gained from this foray was to prevent Kilpatrick from burning the important railroad trestle at Briar Creek. He did, however, succeed in destroying a mile or two of the Augusta-to-Millen-to-Savannah railroad.

Kilpatrick's weakness for taking risks caused his superior officers and the men he commanded considerable concern. It got him into trouble on the night of November 27-28. For reasons known only to himself, he decided to camp at a distance from the main body of his troops. Moreover, he had retained only a single regiment for protection. Striking in the early morning, Wheeler succeeded in placing his troops in that wide gap between Kilpatrick and his main forces. After some lively and brave fighting, Kilpatrick managed to join the others and was saved from paying dearly for his folly.

After these forays Wheeler fell back to Waynesboro, about thirty miles south of Augusta, with Kilpatrick in pursuit. There he ordered his men to dismount, turned suddenly and attacked. But again he was repulsed, not by Kilpatrick's superior generalship or by the superior fighting qualities of Kilpatrick's men but by Union musketry, manned by Sherman's infantrymen, and by greatly superior numbers. He lost about two hundred men. This defeat caused consternation in Augusta, where Kilpatrick's movements were still interpreted as preliminary to an attack upon the city. But while Kilpatrick's horsemen were making themselves as conspicuous as possible, all four corps of Sherman's army were well on their way to Millen and Savannah, getting farther from Augusta with every step.

Meanwhile, the XIV Corps was moving steadily toward Louisville, Georga's first state capital. This town on the upper Ogeechee, the seat of government of Jefferson County, received a rough going over in the manner of Madison and Milledgeville.

Kilpatrick rejoined the XIV Corps there, and remained a day or two to give his tired men and horses a rest. Then, fretting over his failure to burn the trestle at Briar Creek, he asked Sherman's permission to take another try at it, with the help of a division (Baird's) from the XIV Corps. Marching back toward Waynesboro, Kilpatrick's cavalry ran into a detachment of Wheeler's men. The Confederates put up such a stiff fight that the Yankees retreated toward Louisville. They were relieved, however, by the arrival of the division of XIV Corps infantrymen. Actually, the division took little, if any, part in the fighting. But its very presence, ready to be thrown into the fray at any moment, greatly strengthened Kilpatrick's troops. It also imposed a powerful psychological handicap upon the Southerners. Because of the increase in enemy strength, Wheeler, considering it unwise to continue fighting, withdrew. Following him to Briar Creek, Kilpatrick was able on this second try to burn the trestle, and to destroy two or three miles of track between Waynesboro and Millen on the Augusta-Savannah railroad. Continuing his semicircular swing and still supported by that strong detachment from the XIV Corps, he turned southward for a rendezvous several miles east of Louisville with the track-wrecking XX Corps and the rest of the XIV Corps, who had been marching together since their rendezvous at Davisboro.

Sherman, riding with XVII Corps, entered Millen December 3. Four miles north, near a community known as Buckhead Church, the XX Corps stood firmly astride the Georgia Central line to Augusta. North and a little east, in the neighborhood of Lumpkin's Station, was General Jeff Davis' XIV Corps. And considerably to the southeast of Millen and several miles south of the Ogeechee flowing to the sea at Savannah were General Howard and his XV Corps.

The men had heard reports about maltreatment of prisoners at Millen and were in no mood to be moderate in their treatment of the town. Nor did they differentiate between the residents who had had no connection with the prison camp and the camp officials and employes. Attending to the usual first order of business upon entering a town, they burned the railroad station, an unusually attractive structure. The blaze was so striking that even those fire-hardened veterans commented on it, one of them calling it "a superb fire, even at noonday." Years later Major Hitchcock remembered vividly the "densest black smoke in immense volumes—then broad sheets of flame licking the shingle roof and pillars and sucked in under the eaves like a sheet of blazing fluid."

59

After attending to this official chore, the men set out on a series of vengeance missions of their own. Without waiting for orders or authority, they fired the town's leading hotel, a large two-story building sitting back at a neat distance from the street and fronted by an attractive, well kept yard spotted with noble old trees and bushes. The wooden building made a quick, spectacular blaze. Others then warmed and flamed to the incendiaries' torch, and again the looters enjoyed a Roman holiday. Hitchcock looked on as well-clothed, well-fed troops carried away all the provisions in one of the houses, along with all the clothing, knives, forks and everything else they could find. He also heard about other depredations he did not see. And he did not like what he had seen and heard:

> Admit (as we must) the difficulty of preventing all lawlessness in a large army,—especially that of negroes and campfollowers, who cannot always be reached,—yet I am sure that a Headquarters Provost Marshall, if necessary, with a rigid system of roll-calls in every company required at every halt—severe punishment inflicted not only on men who straggle but also on officers who fail to prevent it—and the absolute prohibition and summary punishment even of legitimate foraging except by regular details,—would go far to prevent these outrages. The general orders contemplate and call for this,—but they are not enforced,—at least as I think they should and might be....

As soon as the troops had had their fill of looting and burning, they moved on to the abandoned prisoner-of-war stockade, buried in the heart of a dense pine forest, about six miles from Millen. Rimming it was a high log fence beyond the wall-scaling capablities of even the sturdiest and tallest. Within, no roof or other covering protected the prisoners from the weather. The Yankees were embittered by seeing hand-dug excavations which, they figured, were the work of the prisoners, following an animal instinct to burrow for protection. Major Nichols estimated that some seven hundred and fifty men must have died inside those grim enclosures.

Chaplain G. S. Bradley of the Twenty-second Wisconsin Regiment called the place "hardly fit for our swine to live in." He noticed near the entrance a set of stocks like those used in colonial times. They had "holes enough for seven persons." He noticed too that they "appeared to be well worn." Chaplain Bradley had been inclined to discount as propaganda the reports he had been hearing, but, after looking around a bit, he was ready to believe even the most improbable. And he did not rebuke the men when he heard them "muttering louder curses [than he had ever heard before] on Jefferson Davis and all his murderous crew."

General John White Geary of the XX Corps said that the "foul and fetid prison," gave eloquent and heartbreaking proof that "the worst sufferings of our prisoners at Andersonville, at Americus and Millen were by no means exaggerated."

Southern editors continued to discount the seriousness of Sherman's virtually uncontested advance into and through the very heart of Georgia. The picture they painted remained rosy.

The dire fate predicted for the Yankees when they set out from Atlanta was still held certain to befall them. Those who would admit that defeats had taken place proclaimed them as ground-layings for glorious Confederate victories to come.

"The fact that Sherman has been baffled thus far in his attempt to penetrate Georgia has been well known in this city for several days," the Richmond *Enquirer* declared November 29, a week after Slocum's troops entered Milledgeville, "and further reticence on that score is unnecessary He is floundering about now between the rapidly concentrating manoeuvres of the State troops and such portions of the regular army as were not otherwise more advantageously employed, it having been deemed imprudent and, perhaps, unnecessary, to draw off troops from any of our frontier armies ... "

The Savannah *News* exuded even greater optimism the next day:

> Sherman appears to be making no progress in his invasion of the State. He is no nearer the coast than he was several days ago. He appears to be hesitating and acting altogether as though he were caught in a bad box and don't know how to get out. Afraid to go forward and cannot go back, his men tired and hungry, with our forces rapidly closing in around him. All these things excite the liveliest hopes of his early destruction.

The Augusta *Constitutionalist* declared itself "strongly of the opinion" that "Sherman and his robbers are marching to doom . . . " Even if the Yankee commander should get through to the coast, "which is doubtful," the Richmond *Enquirer* predicted, "he will do so with the loss of half his army." The Richmond *Examiner* pretended to hope Sherman would attack Savannah, but "the hope is faint." Under the military leadership of Beauregard and his lieutenants, it contended, "we are not justified in only hoping for, but confidently expecting the most satisfactory results." The Savannah *Republican* called Sherman's "desperately jaded" men and animals "but little prepared for the trials to come." And the Richmond *Whig* interpreted as a boon to the South even a successful march to the Atlantic: "We contend that, even if successful in its immediate objective—that of getting through to the coast—the Confederate cause will be vastly the gainer, and the Yankee cause vastly the loser, in the general results of the campaign. . . . "

One who did not accept these sizings-up of the situation was an old man who had been a station master for the Central of Georgia Railroad before the Yankees wiped out his job by wiping out the railroad.

"They say you are retreating," he told a New York *Post* correspondent, "but it is the strangest sort of retreat I ever saw . . . Our army was allers whipping the Feds, and we allers fell back. I allers told 'em it was a damned humbug, and now, by God, I know it, for here you are on old John Wells' place; hogs, potatoes, corn and fences all gone . . . To bring back the good old times, it'll take the help of Divine Providence, a heap of rain, and a deal of elbow grease, to fix things up again."

With both Macon and Augusta now clearly behind him, Sherman ordered a bold march by all corps to Savannah. The XVII Corps was to turn southeast just after leaving Millen, following and destroying the Georgia Central as far as Ogeechee Church, about fifty miles from Savannah. It was then to continue on to Halley's Ferry on the Savannah river. The XV Corps was to march south of the Ogeechee to a point opposite Eden Station. Then it was to cross to the east bank. General Jeff Davis' XIV Corps was to follow the Savannah river road. The XX Corps was to take what Sherman called "the middle road" by way of Springfield. All routes were to approach the coast within a comparatively small area.

By this time Connolly, Hitchcock and others had become concerned over a practice which, they felt, held serious dangers. When the dusty columns would halt for the night, Negro girls and young women would put on their best and most alluring finery and start out in the direction of the campfires. These nocturnal visits soon became a part of every important overnight camp. A few months after the stalwart warriors had marched on to other adventures, many of those they had encountered were awaiting their progeny along the four main routes of Sherman's army. And, soon after marching away, men were having their initial experience with syphilis and gonorrhea.

Some of the women, interpreting their new freedom in their own way, traveled with the troops. And they traveled in great style, by army standards. While the men covered their allotted fifteen miles a day afoot, they rode in comparative luxury in the baggage wagons and other vehicles. Conyngham wrote: "I have even seen officers themselves very attentive to the wants of pretty octoroon girls, and provide them with horses to ride." Seeing their animals put to this use by their former slaves angered white Southerners, but they werent't able to do anything about it.

Another diversion was cockfighting. Lookout was kept for especially spirited roosters. It was a rare regiment that did not have its own stable. The cocks remained nameless until they proved their mettle in fights. But when one drove its antagonists off the field it was rewarded by being named for Sherman, General John Logan, Howard or some other Union hero. The losers were named Bob Lee, Beauregard, Jeff Davis and Joe Johnston. Worse than that, they would wind up the next day in the stew pan, while the Bill Shermans, the Johnny Logans and the Ulysses Grants were kept for other fights.

The men were generally well occupied after reaching camp. Cleanliness was not insisted upon to an unreasonable extent. But marching was more tolerable when men and clothing were fairly clean. So there was usually some washing to be done. Playing cards was popular. It made little difference that, by dint of much handling, grease and dirt, it was hard to distinguish hearts from clubs. They provided the men with entertainment. Regimental bands kept the martial spirit alive and furnished instrumental accompaniment for impromptu songfests. Many a Georgia community heard "John Brown's Body" so much and so often that it would have become thoroughly sick of it even if the tune had not been extremely distasteful *per se.*

Cockfights, card games, band concerts, songfests and woodland rendezvous with good-looking Negro women—all these and little fighting to speak of made the march through Georgia pretty much of a lark. It was so very different from the hard marching and bloody fighting which had marked their advance from Tennessee to Atlanta. The weather was excellent, except for occasional spells of rain. These men, who had been chosen because of their superior health, were still as healthy as when they started out. And rich plantations were providing them with better food than most of them had ever known before in their lives, in or out of the army. It is no wonder that, in later years, they remembered the march through Georgia as a great and gay adventure.

They also remembered, however, the exceptions: the corduroying which kept the wagons and ambulances rolling through those "no bottom" wildernesses of mud and over bad stretches of dry road. That was a job for the pioneers, the rugged work battalions brought along for tough tasks. The bugle would sound and the column would halt. The men would break ranks. The pioneers, tough, rough fellows of vast brawn but little brain or need for it, would go looking for strong pieces of wood. They might come back with fence rails that had been used by farmers to keep cattle off the highways. Or they might dive into a nearby forest and emerge with pine saplings or logs. The pieces would be placed crossways over the mudhole or washout. Then the wagons and other vehicles would be slowly eased over. While this was going on, the men would spend the brief fall-out period stretched out at full length on the soft, grassy ground of a nearby field or pasture, chewing away at the hardtack they always carried in their pockets and knapsacks. Some would snatch a few draughts on their pipes, and others would read books and newspapers picked up at the last town, or would lie flat-bellied lapping up water from a spring or pool. Two or three campfires would be started, and men would gather around, giving out lustily with "John Brown's Body" and other popular songs.

After the last wagon and ambulance had been taken across, the bugle would bellow again, and the men would fall back into ranks. There would be another bugle call, and the massive serpentine column would swing into motion, leaving behind gaping children and sad-faced adults, attracted by this passing vignette of army life.

This was one of a number of routines that became these men's habit as they gradually closed the wide gap between

Atlanta and the sea. Then there was the routine of beginning a new day's march.

In later years Sherman's veterans remembered vividly the watchfires burning dimly long before dawn on a late fall morning. Officers' horses, resting from the long march of the previous day, neighed restlessly in the corral. An occasional blast exploded from the mule sector. Except for these, the wooded hills were as quiet as though there had not been twenty thousand men within cannon shot, and tall pines sang softly in a fragrant breeze.

Then suddenly this peaceful panorama changed. Out of the sublime stillness came the nerve-shaking, penetrating first notes of reveille. Seconds later, like an echo of the first, came an identical call from a second bugle. Then came a third and fourth and on, until the shrill notes mixed and mingled with their echoes. By this time the drummers had gone to work with their heavy sticks, sending their own peculiar species of reveille to the ears and brains of suddenly awakened sleepers, still torn between slumber and wakefulness. Men wiggled into their uniforms and ran from their tents to get into the tasks that always marked a new day. There were lively shouts of greeting as comrade passed comrade in the company streets, and banter drove away the dregs of drowsiness. Campfires that had burned to near-extinction during the night were fueled and made to blaze anew. Ghostly shadows fell here and there as the troopers scurried about.

Soon pleasant odors began drifting cheerfully from pots and pans heated to redness over leaping flames. Potatoes that twenty-four hours earlier had been in some Georgia farmer's cellar fried and sizzled and spit hot grease. Chickens browned and withered amid red coals. Coffee pots, battered and worn from many a campaign and many a campfire, rumbled and puffed, sending out fragrant gusts.

The animal quarters leapt into activity. Even at this un-natural hour the sturdy horses and rugged mules knew it was feeding time and neighed and heehawed their demand that they be fed, emphasizing their impatience with energetic pawing. Cattle lowed gently as fodder was thrown into their corral. From nearby came the clatter of tools and the banging of metal against metal.

In a remarkably short time breakfast had been cooked and eaten. The horses and mules had been hitched to their wagons and ambulances. The meat animals had been nudged out of their corrals, and the men were standing in position, their weapons and knapsacks in place. Then the great engine of war began moving again at the command of a bugler. Renewed by sleep and food, it shoved ahead vigorously down the dusty road. The campsite, its fires still smoldering, dropped rapidly behind.

V

CONTACT WITH THE FLEET

As THOSE FOUR army corps edged their separate but parallel ways toward the sea, they found bleak expanses of dull pine forests. Rundown houses stood at the edges of barren fields. The people impressed them as tragically illiterate and backward. But most striking were those unending stretches of tall pines, where they had to be constantly on the alert lest they trip and fall on the slick carpets of pine needles or sink down through them into shallow pools or quagmires.

This country was conspicuously sandy. Sand permeated the men's shoes, clothing and hair. And it got into their food when they cooked in open pans in brisk breezes.

Foraging was not as rewarding as it had been in that rich, prosperous country to the west and north. The cellars, pantries and kitchens were not as large or as well filled. When the foragers went to barns, they found little to take. The animals grazing in the lifeless fields were puny. The more conscientious foragers were careful not to take too much.

But, as familiar food became scarce, an unfamiliar one became plentiful. They were now in the rice country, along the banks of the Ogeechee and Savannah rivers, and its novelty had great appeal. But after several days they longed for another thange.

This change was promised when they reached the coast, and the men looked forward to it hungrily. Major Nichols even attributed their uneagerness for battle to their hankering for "oysters roasted, oysters fried, oysters stewed, oysters on the half shell, oysters in abundance, without money and without price." Fighting would slow up their march to oysterland. And they "don't want to be delayed."

That country just west of Savannah was not all sand, although at times it seemed so. As the men approached the coast they encountered many marshes, which made the going hard. The Confederates added to their difficulties by stepping up their obstructive tactics. On the open highways and also along the narrow causeways leading across creeks and swamps, Sherman's men had to remove trees that had been felled across their routes. But these obstructions were annoyances rather than obstacles. For, as Sherman pointed out in his official report, his well-organized pioneer companies removed them "in an incredibly short time." They continued as a minor irritant until the troops were within fifteen miles of Savannah. From that point on "all the roads leading to the city were obstructed more or less by felled timber, with earthworks and artillery." However, these too "were easily turned and the enemy driven away."

A more effective enemy tactic was encountered December 8 about nine miles from Savannah. A torpedo—one of nine which had been placed along the roadway and camouflaged with a thin layer of sand—exploded. Several men were injured and a horse killed. Colonel Andrew Hickenlooper and a Lieutenant Tupper hurried to the spot and stooped over to scrape the dirt away. When Lieutenant Tupper stood up and started to walk off, he stepped upon another torpedo. It exploded and tore off his right foot, a piece of shell inflicted an ugly wound between the ankle and the knee, and another fragment inflicted severe damage to his hand.

When Sherman rode up to inquire what had happened a

blanket had been placed over Lieutenant Tupper, except for his face, which, Sherman noticed, had turned ghastly pale. The wounded man, in spite of his intense pain, was not complaining or groaning. He was just lying there as quietly as he could, waiting for the surgeon to come and amputate the leg. His horse had been killed outright. Several other men had been wounded less severely.

Sherman was furious. "This is not war, but murder," he wrote in his memoirs, "and it made me very angry." He sent for some Confederate prisoners, handed them picks and spades "and made them march in close order along the road, so as to explode their own torpedoes, or to discover and dig them up." The prisoners "begged hard." But Sherman was unmoved. He "reiterated the order," and "could hardly help laughing at their stepping so gingerly along the road." Sherman, Hitchcock tells us "didn't care" if they got blown up. And Hitchcock adds his own hearty approval: "He did exactly right."

Sherman's defenders have called up historical precedents to show that this was not the first time prisoners of war had been used for such a purpose. What Sherman did in Georgia, Wellington had done in Spain. McClellan had followed the same policy at Yorktown. Sheridan did not hesitate to use Confederate prisoners for highly dangerous work, and Sherman himself had done something similar near Chattanooga. Having heard reports that the Confederates had planted torpedoes along the route his troops were to travel, he ordered that a carload of prisoners or civilians be drawn over the area at the end of a long rope.

Precedents or no precedents, Sherman's act stirred furious criticism. He quite naturally went to his own defense when he wrote his memoirs:

> ... it was, I think, a much better show of tenderness for me to have the enemy do this work than to subject my own soldiers to so frightful a risk. ... They knew where the torpedoes were and could safely remove them while my men in hunting for

them would be blown to pieces. The fact that every torpedo was safely removed showed my reasoning was right.

Those prisoners of course were as ignorant of the location of the torpedoes as were Sherman's men. The detection and removal operation was of equal danger to them.

The army was now nearing the coast, and it was necessary to communicate with the fleet which was believed to be lying offshore. So on December 9 General Howard commissioned Captain William Duncan, an escaped prisoner of war and an exceptional officer, to lead a small party to effect liaison. Captain Duncan, accompanied by Sergeant Myron J. Amick and Private George W. Quimby, set off in a small boat on the Ogeechee. After a treacherous passage, traveling by night, and hiding out on shore by day, they were able to slip past Fort McAllister, the Confederate bastion defending the approaches to Savannah, and to reach the bay the morning of the third day. There they boarded the flagship U.S.S. *Philadelphia* and presented Rear Admiral John A. Dahlgren with the brief message from their chief:

> We have met with perfect success thus far.
> Troops in fine spirits and near by.
> > Respectfully,
> > O. O. HOWARD
> > MAJOR GENERAL COMMANDING

In a dispatch to Secretary of the Navy Gideon Welles, Admiral Dahlgren wrote:

> In view of his probable arrival, I had stationed several steamers at different points, and had come down the *Tilafinney* yesterday, in order to be at hand. I had not to wait many hours. . . . Captain Duncan states that our forces were in contact with the rebels a few miles outside of Savannah. He says that Sherman's army was not in want of anything. Perhaps no event could give greater satisfaction to the country than that which I announced, and I beg leave to congratulate the United States Government

on its occurrence. It may, perhaps be exceeding my province, but I cannot refrain from expressing the hope that the [Navy] department will commend Capt. Duncan and his companions to the Hon. Secretary of War for some marks of approbation, for the success in establishing communications between Gen. Sherman and the fleet. It was an enterprise that required both skill and courage.

The army continued to support its burden of Negro followers, determined to grab their freedom at once, despite Sherman's admonitions. Altogether, about twenty-five thousand—four Negroes for every ten soldiers—tagged along, but about three fourths of them became disillusioned by their new "freedom" and, a few days after starting out, began the weary trek back to their home places. When Sherman and his men came within sight of the coast, the horde had dwindled to sixty-eight hundred.

They did not expect a free trip. Most of them were glad to earn their keep in any way they could. They were fascinated by the guns and volunteered to "tote" them for the men. In camp they looked after the pots and pans and helped out with the cooking. At night they entertained their "liberators" with their plaintive plantation melodies. And the good-looking women peddled sex.

Sherman naturally was reluctant to take on these added appetites to be satisfied. And he had a strong personal dislike for colored people. ("Damn the nigger!" he once exploded.) Nevertheless, he looked tolerantly upon these hangers-on and the unsavory conditions they caused. He was touched by their poverty and ignorance, although often repelled by their actions and appearance.

Women with young children puffing and panting to keep up with the procession were particularly appealing. An officer of the 70th Indiana Regiment wrote his wife about the "vast numbers" of colored women following after the troops with infants in their arms. Many had "little ones like our Anna clinging to their tattered skirts." He saw one woman hide her two youngsters in a wagon, "intending, I suppose, that they should see the land of freedom if she couldn't." He told her about babies who "tumbled from the backs of mules to which they had been told to cling." Some fell off while the caravan was crossing swamps and were drowned.

A large number of Negroes lost their lives in a few minutes of horror and hysteria at Ebeneezer Creek. Upon approaching the creek General Jeff Davis of the XIV Corps issued orders for the Negroes to fall behind the troops, so that the latter would be unhampered in case of an enemy attack during the crossing. The Negroes paid little attention and continued marching in motley array alongside the columns. Becoming irritated, Davis double-timed the troops in order to get them across first. Then he ordered the pontoons taken up, leaving the Negroes on the west bank. In desperation the Negroes attempted a mass crossing. Even the few who could swim had great trouble making it, and although soldiers, distressed by their plight, went into the water and rescued as many as they could, many were drowned.

The nearness of the broad Atlantic and the crowning success of the campaign confirmed the childlike trust of the common soldiers Sherman commanded. They were as eager to follow him unquestioningly on the approaches to Savannah as in the environs of Atlanta. "I tell ye, boys, we should never ask where we are going, or what we are going to do," one of them said to a footsore comrade. "Obedience is the duty of a soldier; and whatever Old Billy says or does is right."

Even "Old Billy's" personal faults were "right" with most of his officers and men. But one Sherman weakness—his profanity—was anything but right with the deeply religious, ministerial-looking General Howard. The two close friends, with some other officers, were trying to keep themselves warm when the commander remarked that the weather was "damned cold." Howard agreed that it was "quite cold." Spurred on by this mild rebuke, Sherman winked at General Jeff Davis. Acting on cue, Davis started telling a yarn that was short on humor or interest but strong on profanity. Horrified and embarrassed, Howard did his best to interrupt the narrative and dam that Niagara of colorful words. But Davis kept on. Realizing he was defeated, Howard stalked out of the room.

Another Sherman characteristic that was not "right" with Howard and other reverent officers and men was his lack of interest in religion and Sabbath observance. When Howard suggested that fighting be avoided so far as possible on Sundays, he was pooh-poohed. When he began devoting as much of Sunday as he could to hymn-singing and visiting the sick, Sherman did not actively try to discourage him. However, when the Christian Commission asked Sherman to allow its agents —distributing literature and conducting religious services—to carry on their work among his troops, he shot back, "Certainly not . . . Crackers and oats are more necessary for the army than any moral and religious agency, and every regiment has its chaplain."

Sherman's associates found him extremely interesting to watch under the stress of a campaign. The New York *Herald* correspondent wrote of his impressions of the general at such a time. The tall, slender warrior, wearing a uniform "bordering on a hazy mellowness of gloss," rode up and dismounted not far from where the correspondent was standing. There was some cordwood nearby, and Sherman sat down on a piece of it. From a pocket he pulled a pencil and a sheet of note paper. Spreading the paper on his knee, he wrote rapidly, while long blue columns filled the road a few feet away. Beyond the road an entire infantry division rested, the dusty blue of the uniforms standing out in sharp contrast against the greenness of the fields. Undistracted by this pageant of war, because he had long been familiar with it and had made it a part of his life, Sherman filled several sheets of paper. From time to time a courier would poke a hand toward him, grab a sheet or two and ride off.

Someone arrived with dispatches. Sherman ripped open the envelopes and gave them a quick glance. Then he fell into conversation with some officers. A little later, with an abruptness characteristic of him, he leapt astride his horse and rode away alongside that long file of blue-coated men. His countenance was still "fresh and smiling."

The "Cump" Sherman of the sandy wastes and treacherous swamplands of east Georgia was blessed with an iron constitution, unaffected by wretched weather, fatiguing marches or loss of sleep. Many a night a sentinel would see his lean, tall hulk pacing rhythmically in front of his tent or poking at a dying campfire as he puffed silently on a cigar. "Old Billy" had awakened and knew he could not go back to sleep again for two or three hours. Instead of tossing about on his cot he was getting in some physical exercise and doing some quiet thinking. But the sentry and the general both knew that some of the sleep being lost tonight would be made up tomorrow. For Sherman needed no bed or blanket or a reclining position when drowsiness seized him. He could sleep erect in his saddle. He had even been known to sleep in battle.

VI

————————

FORAGERS AND BUMMERS

BY THE TIME the troops began sniffing the salty air which told
them they were nearing the coast, Sherman himself realized
that foraging, proclaimed as a legitimate and humane act of
warfare, had got out of hand. Grave crimes had been occurring
with disturbing frequency. Southern newspapers were charging
outrages and barbarities of the most repulsive nature. The
Macon *Telegraph* claimed that many Southern women had
been overpowered by the "lustful appetites of the hell-hounds."
The "cesspools of Northern infamy and corruption" had been
dredged, it said, "in order to collect the infamous spawn of
perdition sent out to despoil our country." Sherman, by the
acts of his men, had earned "the fame of the ravisher, the in-
cendiary and the thief." His was a "hyena soul that lurks in
the foul mass of corruption which has shaped itself into humanity." It was easy to dismiss such charges as enemy propaganda. But there was considerable fire with the smoke.

Sherman insisted that only rare cases of murder and rape
had come to his attention. In the postwar hearings to fix responsibility for the burning of Columbia he said army records
showed that only two women had been raped during the entire campaign. Those responsible for these crimes, as well as

those found guilty of murder, he insisted, had been properly punished. Actually, there probably were considerably more crimes of both kinds than he knew about or was willing to admit. On the other hand, investigations carried on in the milder atmosphere that followed the war failed to confirm most of the violent charges made by the Macon *Telegraph* and other papers. At the same time, the investigations strengthened the charge that a vast number of crimes just short of murder and rape did occur. Sherman not only made good his threat to "make Georgia howl" but also caused, by failing to prevent it, a vast amount of unjustifiable suffering.

"The foraging parties scattered over the country without any order or discipline, pounding like harpies upon the unfortunate inhabitants," the New York *Herald* correspondent with the army, certainly no Southern sympathizer, wrote. "Boxes were burst open—clothes dragged about—the finest silks belonging to the planters' ladies carried off to adorn some negro wenches around the camp—pictures, books, and furniture, all tossed about and torn in pieces. In most instances they burned down houses to cover their depredations and, in some cases, took the lives of their victims, as they would not reveal concealed treasure."

Although the regularly assigned foragers unquestionably committed many crimes that would have sent them to prison in civilian life, they were blamed for numerous outrages for which they were not responsible. For the "bummer" was as much an army institution as the forager. And, man for man, he was an infinitely worse character.

"Bummers" were the lawless element of the army. Though a part of it, they went off on long forays of their own. Being lawbreakers at heart and operating in a country where the civil authorities could provide little protection from them, they enjoyed a looter's Paradise. It gave them particular satisfaction to injure those they envied. In violent reaction to large plantations, beautiful homes and the other symbols of the Southern aristocracy, they delighted in causing fear and suffering among the rich while enjoying luxuries theretofore beyond their rosiest dreams. Fired by their antipathy, they often destroyed more than they could use or take away. Since they were at no pains to identify themselves as "bummers," they left the impression that they were members of regular foraging parties. So it was that regular foragers often were blamed for their crimes.

Some of the high-ranking officers made conscientious efforts, without much active encouragement from Sherman, to curb the lawless element. General Giles A. Smith lived up to his long-held reputation as a stern disciplinarian by setting the death penalty for any soldier caught burning an occupied house. German-born General Peter Joseph Osterhaus, with the German leaning toward preventing trouble, placed guards at every residence along his route. Though laudable in intent, this proved impracticable in execution, as the "bummers" did their worst work after the main columns had moved on. Osterhaus also fined his men a month's pay for looting, but this was rarely effective. When General Jeff Davis caught two men stealing women's clothing, he made them wear it in public, along with a placard identifying it as stolen property. Howard became so concerned that he ordered the shooting of any person—officer or man—guilty of looting or burning a building without proper authority. However, when one of his men was caught stealing a quilt, he relented after ordering the death sentence to be carried out, and the thief got off with a prison sentence. As more and more cases of indiscriminate burning and looting were reported, Howard issued these orders:

> The attention of the corps commanders and the commanders of unattached regiments and detachments is called to the irregularities existing in foraging, and the manner in which this privilege is often abused. It is noticed that many men not belonging to proper foraging parties are allowed to straggle from the ranks and forage for themselves without any authority

whatsoever. It is by such men that the greater part of the pillaging is done, and depredations committed, of which there is so much complaint. Officers in charge of foraging parties must be continually instructed to keep their men well in hand, never allowing them to precede the advance guard of the column, and to use more discretion in taking from the poor, being careful to leave them sufficient for their immediate subsistence....

The one or two officers and about fifty men comprising a foraging party would be briefed just before starting out at dawn on the route to be followed that day by its unit and the place where it would encamp for the night. Then the party would visit every farm within a five-mile or six-mile area along the unit's projected line of march. It would begin by confiscating wagons or carriages and animals to pull them. The next several hours would be spent loading the vehicles with foodstuffs and feed. After completing their circuit, they would return to the route of march at some point ahead of the column or at that night's campsite, where they would subsequently turn over to designated officers whatever they had collected. Sherman commented in his memoirs on the strange collections of articles, animate and inanimate, they brought in: "mules, horses, even cattle, packed with old saddles and loaded with hams, bacon, eggs, bags of cornmeal, and poultry of every character and description."

Sherman readily admitted that some members of these official foraging parties were not above committing reprehensible acts. He mentioned "jewelry taken from women," and "the plunder of articles that never reached the commissary." But these acts, he insisted, were "exceptional and incidental." Of course he stoutly defended foraging as an unchallengeable right in warfare. He claimed it was necessary in this case because his army was not able to carry along all the provisions needed for such a campaign. Having to live off the country, he contended, he had no choice but to forage: "The country was sparsely settled, with no magistrates or civil authorities who could respond to civil requisitions, as is done in all the wars of Europe; so that this system of foraging was simply indispensable to our success."

Major General J. D. Cox saw both regular foragers and "bummers" at work throughout the campaign. And this tall, erect, soldierly-looking soldier was certain that all the mischief was not done by the "bummers." The behavior of a regular foraging party depended largely, he said, upon the division or brigade which sent it out. The commanders of the best-disciplined units saw to it that the men acted with restraint and avoided hooliganism. Those who generally allowed discipline to disintegrate or tended to overlook misdemeanors sent out that kind of foraging parties. Some officers, he found out, not only openly countenanced outrages but even went into partnership with the men committing them and shared their loot. Kilpatrick's cavalrymen, Cox thought, were guilty of more crimes than any other unit of comparable size. They not only committed serious offenses themselves but set bad examples, which encouraged their comrades to acts of violence the latter would not have committed on their own. Kilpatrick himself was hardly a model officer and gentleman. Immoral and rapacious, he created an atmosphere of such ruffianry and irresponsibility that even the best disciplinarians among his subordinates had great difficulty in controlling their men.

Cox wrote of the reckless variety of things which were caught up in the foragers' copious net:

> Here would be a silver-mounted family carriage drawn by a jackass and a cow, loaded inside and out with everything the country produced, vegetable and animal, dead and alive. There would be an ox-cart, similarly loaded, and drawn by a nondescript tandem team, equally incongruous. Perched upon the top would be a ragged forager, rigged out in a fur hat of a fashion worn by dandies of a century ago, or a dress coat which had done service at stylish balls of a former generation. The gibes and jeers, the fun and the practical jokes ran down the

whole line as the cortege came in, and no masquerade in carnival could compare with it for original humor and rollicking
enjoyment.

Others have made their own catalogues of articles brought
in from a day's haul. Ornaments had been jerked off uniforms
worn by officers in Washington's army. A burly trooper wore
a white wig dating from the same period. Some of his comrades paraded three-cornered hats of the kind our country's
founders are often pictured as wearing. Swords of all sizes,
shapes and vintages dangled ludicrously from improvised
sheaths. Ladies' hats, grotesquely out of style, were more gro-
tesque above deeply ridged, rough-skinned masculine faces.
Here and there among the conventional blue uniforms were
white trousers, formal coats and fetching evening gowns that
had made Southern belles happy at their coming-out or birthday
parties. There were many articles of jewelry, including cherished
family heirlooms. Dirty, grimy, sweaty, heavily bearded troopers
thought it great fun to put on this finery and pirouette like
burlesque queens on a lighted runway. A soldier of the 70th
Indiana commented acidly that his foraging comrades showed
up at these daily rendezvous with "anything that had wheels,
drawn by anything that could pull." He saw horses, cows, goats
and donkeys hitched to farm wagons, family buggies, chaises,
sulkies and coaches. These vehicles, he noticed, were filled to
overloading with "every imaginable thing under the sun a
lot of fool soldiers could take it in their heads to bring away."
Major Conyngham wrote with disapproval about foraging
troopers "with pockets plethoric with silver and gold coin."
He saw troops "sinking under the weight of plate and fine
bedding material." There were "lean mules and horses, with
the richest trappings of Brussels carpets, and hangings of finest
chenille." Among the camp followers were "negro wenches,
particularly good-looking ones, decked in satins and silks, and
sporting diamond ornaments." Officers, who were supposed to

be above such pilferage, were wearing "sparkling rings that would set Tiffany in raptures." Having seen these things with his own Northern eyes, he could no longer lightly dismiss as propaganda "the stories of hanging up or fleshing an 'old cus' to make him shell out."

Conyngham recounted a few more of his observations:

A planter's house was overrun in a jiffy; boxes, drawers, and escritoires were ransacked with a laudable zeal, and emptied of their contents. If the spoils were ample, the depredators were satisfied, and went off in peace; if not, everything was torn and destroyed, and most likely the owner was tickled by sharp bayonets into a confession where he had his treasure hid. If he escaped, and was hiding in a thicket, this was prima facie evidence that he was a sulking rebel; and most likely some ruffian, in his zeal to get rid of such vipers, gave him a dose of lead, which cured him of his Sesech tendencies. Sorghum barrels were knocked open, bee-hives rifled, while their angry swarms rushed frantically about. Indeed, I have seen a soldier knock a planter down because a bee stung him. Hogs are bayoneted and then hung in quarters on the bayonets to bleed; chickens, geese, and turkeys knocked over and hung in garlands from the saddles and around the necks of swarthy negroes; mules and horses are fished out of the swamps; cows and calves, so wretchedly thin that they drop and perish on the first day's march, are driven along, or, if too weak to travel, are shot, lest they should give aid to the enemy.

Should the house be deserted, the furniture is smashed to pieces, music is pounded out of four hundred dollar pianos with the ends of muskets. Mirrors were wonderfully multiplied and rich cushions and carpets carried off to adorn teams and war-steeds. After all was cleared out, most likely some set of stragglers wanted to enjoy a good fire, and set the house, debris of furniture, and all the surroundings in a blaze. This is the way Sherman's army lived on the country. They were not ordered to do so, but I am afraid they were not brought to task for it much either.

At a farm known as Sam Hart's place some soldiers "committed inhuman atrocities," according to the Augusta *Contitutionalist*. They burned all his outbuildings, except the kitchen. They enticed away his male Negroes. They grossly insulted him. They pillaged his home and forced his wife, an elderly lady, to cook them dinner. After they had eaten, they knocked over the table, smashed the crockery, burned the family carriage and carried off the family silverware. The aged couple were left without a means of conveyance or an animal to pull any they might have been able to obtain.

The local correspondent of the Macon *Telegraph* cryptically told how he and his fellow citizens of Clinton had fared:

> ... Many of us are utterly ruined—hundreds of our people are without anything to eat—their stock of cattle and hogs are killed; horses and mules with wagons are all taken off—all through our streets and commons are to be seen dead horses and mules—entrails of hogs and cattle killed, and in many instances, the hams only taken—oxen and carts taken away, so that we are not able to remove the offensive matter—our school houses and most of the churches burned. Captain Bomer's beautiful residence in ashes, together with everything of his that could be found, destroyed. He was [away] from home. Atrocities most heinous were committed. Morgan's tannery, with a quantity of Government leather, destroyed, and his family, like many others, deprived of all food—clothes taken off the backs of some of the contrabands, and female servants taken and violated without mercy ...

The Macon *Telegraph* charged that, on two separate occasions in Burke County, no less eminent a member of the Sherman team than General Kilpatrick conducted himself in a manner usually ascribed to the lowest rank.

The youthful brigadier, reputedly the most licentious of Sherman's generals and perhaps the most lacking in physical courage, ordered elegant ladies to cook for him and his companions. At the first place his entourage consisted of three

Negro women. They ate with him, and during the meal the cavalry leader carried on with them "the most familiar and indecent conversation." At the second place, after finishing the meal, Kilpatrick encouraged the men in his party to make a shambles of the house. After they were finished indoors, they fired the corncribs and other outbuildings. When a Negro servant tried to extinguish the fire, one of the soldiers threatened to shoot him. Just then somebody shouted "Wheeler's men!" The visitors departed in all speed and the outbuildings were saved. Later the lady of the house found that sand had been poured into her sugar bowl and preserve jars.

A journalist representing the Augusta *Chronicle* and *Sentinel* told what he had seen on a trip through his home community:

> ... Many families have not a pound of meat, or a peck of meal or flour. Many negroes were enticed away from homes of comfort to share the uncertain fortunes of a Winter march to the coast, and then—freedom to starve. Families of wealth have not a house servant left, and those who were the most trusted were often the first to leave. The Yankees entered the house of my next-door neighbor, an old man of over three-score years, and tore up his wife's clothing and bedding, trampling her bonnets on the floor, and robbing the house and pantry of nearly everything of value. There was no provocation for any of these acts, for everyone treated them civilly, and offered all they wanted to eat....
>
> Those who, from any cause, chanced to be away, lost all. A lady on the Eatonton road, whose father is in the army, feeling afraid to stay at home, went to the house of a neighbor, and, on returning, found every plate broken, every knife and fork and spoon gone, and her clothes stripped to shreds and scattered about the lot.
>
> ... They have unquestionably caused great suffering, and tonight families who had an abundance last week, have scarcely a day's subsistence. The greatest inconvenience is horses. There is plenty in the country yet, but there are no horses to haul it. Our citizens are in distress for wood for the same reason.

The plight of Southern civilians was worsened by units of the Confederate army living off the country. Many a disgruntled Confederate soldier rejoiced in doing what he could to subjugate "the gentry." Confederate cavalry units seemed to have a particular attraction for a lawless order of men. Long before Sherman neared Savannah, Wheeler's troopers had committed so many acts of ruthlessness and general lawlessness that their appearance in a neighborhood spread as much fear as the arrival of Kilpatrick. Even the most chauvinistic complained of the depredations to newspapers and harried officials at Richmond. Southern pride in Southern warriors could find nothing to sustain it in letters like this one to Secretary of War Seddon:

> I cannot forbear appealing to you, in behalf of the producing population of the States of Georgia and South Carolina, for protection against the destructive lawlessness of members of General Wheeler's command. From Augusta to Hardeeville the road is now strewn with corn left on the ground unconsumed. Beeves have been shot down in the fields, one quarter taken off, and the balance left for the buzzards. Horses are stolen out of wagons on the road, and by wholesale out of stables at night ... Within a few miles of this neighborhood, Wheeler's men tried to rob a young lady of her horse while she was on a visit to a neighbor's, and would have succeeded but for the timely arrival of a citizen, who prevented the outrage from being perpetrated. It is no unusual sight to see these men ride late into camp with all sorts of plunder. Private houses are visited; carpets, blankets, and other furniture they can lay their hands on are taken by force in the presence of the owners ...

The Macon *Confederate's* correspondent told of Wheeler's visit to Laurens County:

> They stole horses, potatoes, turnips, chickens, sugarcane that was left for seed, pressed horses without authority, swapped horses without leave, killed fattening hogs they needed not, and broke open stores. Not content with this, they pocketed the silver spoons of their hospitable entertainers, stole watches,

knives and forks, tin pans and spiders, spun thread, which they peddled as they went along the road; leather, which they tried to sell—and indeed everything they could lay their hands upon; and in this community won the name of being the most unmitigated scoundrels that ever trod our soil....

The outrages became so serious that Governor Brown issued a proclamation appealing to local officials to organize their people for self-protection. Many men from Confederate cavalry units, who "should hang around and constantly annoy the enemy as he passes through our State, and cut off his foraging parties, and impede his march," were doing none of these things, he said. Instead, they had left their commands, formed small bands and scattered over nearly half the state. They were "robbing and plundering the citizens indiscriminately." And they were "taking from the wives and children of soldiers who are in service discharging their whole duty, the supplies of provisions which are their only means of support."

VII

FORT McALLISTER

WITH SAVANNAH just within Sherman's grasp, the enemy had stopped retreating and were preparing to fight under conditions highly favorable to themselves.

Of particular concern to Sherman were two swampy creeks lying athwart his path. One emptied into the Savannah river, the other into the Little Ogeechee. Not only were they marshy themselves, but adjoining them was a wasteland of rice fields, some flooded by tide water, others by ponds. The water level of the ponds could be raised and lowered by gates operated under the protection of the enemy's heavy artillery. To attempt to fight their way into the city by slogging through such a wide morass would be fatal. The men would be at the mercy of the enemy while bogged down in mud. It is true that there were five narrow causeways leading to the city. Two were railroads and the others highways to Augusta, Louisville (Georgia) and Ogeechee. But, like the floodgates, they were well defended by heavy artillery, considerably more powerful than Sherman's field guns. After weighing the situation Sherman ruled out a general attack against the city except as a final resort. "To assault an enemy of unknown strength at such a disadvantage appeared to me unwise," he wrote in his memoirs, "especially as I had so successfully brought my army, almost unscathed, so great a distance, and could surely attain the same result by the operation of time."

As plans for Savannah's gradual strangulation went ahead simultaneously with the army's steady march toward the city, Sherman heard the cheering sound of big guns. They presumably were being fired by naval craft offshore in Ossabaw Sound. The navy, there was good reason to believe, had a large fleet out there to assist the army in its final action of the campaign. Those deep, steady boomings were reminders that it was prepared for whatever its part might be.

The four army corps approached the Confederate defense lines guarding the city December 9th and 10th. Slocum's XIV Corps stood on the extreme left, pressing against the Savannah river. Next to it was the XX Corps. Howard's XV Corps was on the extreme right, along the route of the Savannah and Gulf Railroad. His XVII Corps was between it and the XX Corps thus, Sherman pointed out, "completely investing the city."

Sherman rode out with some officers on a personal reconnaissance. About eight hundred yards away there were a Confederate parapet and battery. Even at that distance, Sherman could see the movements of the men and realized they were about to fire one of their big guns. He ordered the party to scatter. Seconds later he saw the usual white puff of smoke and watched the cannon ball as it began its trajectory flight. Realizing that it was coming straight at him, he stepped aside and was not even scratched. However, a colored man nearby was not so fortunate. Somebody in the party—Sherman did not say it was himself—yelled for him to look out. But the warning either came too late or was misunderstood. The cannon ball, a thirty-two-pounder, hit the ground near the Negro and bounced. In that ricochet action it struck the colored man under the right jaw and beheaded him. A member of the party covered the body with an overcoat and the group, deciding there was nothing to be gained by taking any more risks, returned to the Federal lines.

Meanwhile, a division of the XVII Corps had crossed the canal to the right of the Louisville road. There it made an important and somewhat disconcerting discovery. Just ahead and extending as far as the city proper was an almost unbroken line of natural and man-made defenses peculiarly adaptable to this type of warfare. They consisted mainly of deep ditches, a baffling array of canals and a labyrinth of bayous. These would imperil any Federal troops lucky enough to escape enemy fire. Obviously, Savannah was in an excellent position to withstand the heaviest punches Sherman was capable of delivering. Reconnaissance reports and spies indicated that General William Joseph Hardee, the tough Confederate commander, was in a mood to fight. Forty-nine-year-old Hardee was a handsome, soldierly-looking officer with long hair, well-trimmed mustache and goatee. His presence on a battlefield always had a tremendous effect upon his men's fighting capabilities. He was an antagonist for whom Sherman had a great deal of respect. Now he would probably be a tougher opponent than ever before. For Savannah was his birthplace.

With such obstacles ahead, Sherman was convinced that he should link up with the fleet before trying to take the city. His men badly needed the fresh new uniforms, shoes and other articles of clothing that the fleet was presumed to have brought from army warehouses in the North. And, for the operation at hand, his army would need the heavy siege guns believed to be stacked away in the ships' holds. But, between the army and the fleet, stood firm, grim, formidable-looking Fort McAllister, powerfully watchdogging the Ogeechee's wide mouth. As long as McAllister remained in Confederate hands, the rendezvous would be extremely difficult, if not impossible.

Sherman had no assurance that the fleet was actually there, although those deep-throated boomings he had been hearing could hardly have come from anywhere else. And Negroes had been telling him about seeing strange lights in the sky at night over the water. But he had had no news about Captain Duncan and his expedition down the Ogeechee. He could only hope they had arrived safely and that the fleet was really at hand.

Kilpatrick turned hope into certainty. Taking his cavalrymen across the Ogeechee at Jenk's Bridge, he marched them rapidly along its south shore to Kilkenny's Bluff. There, lying quietly at anchor on the gentle waters of St. Catherine's Sound, they saw the U.S.S. *Fernandina*. Several officers went out to the craft in a small boat where Captain Lewis West, its commander, told them the fleet was indeed nearby.[3]

Kilpatrick begged Sherman for permission to throw his cavalry, reinforced by strong infantry support, against Fort McAllister. But Sherman had some doubts. He discussed the matter with Howard, and they decided to turn the job over to the Second Division of the XV Corps, commanded by 34-year-old Brigadier General William Babcock Hazen. Notwithstanding the danger, the men of the division, whom Sherman had personally commanded at Shiloh and Vicksburg and who had won his warm praise after the Battle of Missionary Ridge, were delighted. Indeed, one of their officers said, they were as happy "as if he had sent them a wagon load of brandy."

The assault would have to come soon. A large army remaining virtually immobile quickly exhausts its food supply, and its morale. However, an immediate attack was impracticable, because the Confederates had burned the highway bridge across the Ogeechee, known as King's Bridge, which was vital to the operation. The rebuilding job was turned over to the 58th Indiana regiment.

The Second Division started marching at daybreak December 13. After crossing King's Bridge, it continued down the Ogeechee's west bank. At 11 o'clock it halted about a mile from the fort, and Hazen began mapping his final plans and grouping the units for the assault. From some captured Confederates, he learned the location of torpedoes which had been planted along the road leading to the fort.

Unlike Sherman, Hazen had the location and removal of the torpedoes done by his own men. Then he divided his forces. A group were ordered to remain as a reserve force, the others to prepare for the assault. Advancing to within six hundred yards of the fort, they were again halted and skirmishers were sent ahead.

Few bastions have been attacked under greater natural deterrents. The wilderness of marshlands between the Federals and Fort McAllister made deployment of the troops slow and difficult. It was past 4:30 in the afternoon before Hazen was satisfied that everything was in order.

While these tense, tedious preparations were going on, Sherman and Howard were anxiously awaiting the outcome on the other side of the Ogeechee. After giving Hazen his final orders they, with their staff officers, rode downriver ten miles to a plantation owned by a Mr. Cheves. Howard had been there before. He had established on that site a signal station which provided an excellent view of the lower river and made it possible to keep on the lookout for any Federal warships that might help in the assault. From the observation station atop a rice mill, Fort McAllister was plainly visible across a three-mile sweep of salt marsh. Already, in anticipation of an attack, it was blasting away with its heaviest guns, some of the shells falling near where the officers were standing. They were being answered by two twenty-pound Parrot guns which had been set up at the rice mill.[4] Actually, however, the firing was lifeless and desultory on both sides. Except for that animated exchange, Sherman remembered, "everything about the place looked as peaceable and quiet as on the Sabbath."

The first indication Sherman and Howard had that the attack was about to begin came, not from Hazen but from Fort McAllister. From their high roost they saw "signs of commotion in the fort." Some of the heavy guns had been swung about.

They were no longer firing out into the bay but were aiming their shots inland, obviously to repel a land attack. At the same time there were sounds of musket skirmishing in nearby woods. That was something they had been waiting for. But it did not mean the attack was actually beginning.

Some time later the signal officer spotted a signal flag about three miles beyond the fort. The message was for Sherman: Hazen was *almost* ready to attack.

Sherman kept looking anxiously toward the west, and he was worried. The sun was not far above the horizon and, it seemed to him, was sinking rapidly. Time was getting short. He could not understand why Hazen was taking so long to get started. He admitted later that he was "dreadfully impatient." To speed things up, he ordered the signal officer to send a message to Hazen: it was essential that Fort McAllister be taken before nightfall. In a few minutes he had Hazen's reply: his preparations were going ahead rapidly, and the assault would get under way very soon.

About that time someone at the rice mill spotted a tiny wisp of smoke on the horizon. It gradually became larger, and underneath it they could dimly make out the outline of a ship. It entered the river's mouth and edged slowly toward the fort. And it was flying the Stars and Stripes. From then on, Sherman's and Howard's attention was divided between it and Hazen's men.

At last, about an hour before sunset, Hazen sent another message to the signal tower at the rice mill: he was now ready to attack. Sherman urged him to go ahead without delay.

Soon after that the signal officer picked up a message flagged from the ship:

"Who are you?" it asked.

"General Sherman."

"Is Fort McAllister taken?"

"Not yet," answered Sherman. "but it will be in a minute."

Hazen too had been worried over the delay in getting on with the assault. During the final anxious moments his normally placid countenance was a mask of gravity. The veins standing out from his face and neck revealed the tension inside. But at last the long waiting was at an end.

To a nearby bugler he gave the command to sound the *Attention*. The penetrating notes swept along the thin column and out to sea. "Sound it again!" he commanded, and again the familiar blast carried its lively message of anticipation to every tensely waiting soldier in the line. The command was given still again, and a third time the air was rent by the blast. Then Hazen shouted: "Sound the *Forward!*"

At the first notes the line sprang ahead like an unleashed animal. There was a furious burst of fire from the fort. It was aimed at the expanse of wasteland between it and them. As they moved ahead undisclosed torpedoes exploded, hurling mangled bodies into the air. They kept advancing on the double to the abatis, the felled trees, their tops, sharpened and trimmed, pointing like lances toward them. Pausing briefly to clear a passage through, they stormed into the ditch immediately surrounding the fort, firing their guns all the while. By now many of the fort's big guns had been silenced. But those with men left to operate them were in furious operation, and streams of lead poured from the smaller guns. The blue wave was held up only momentarily at the palisades to yank out enough stakes to make a wide gap, through which they swarmed. In a matter of seconds they had reached the parapets. There was desperate, heroic hand-to-hand fighting, mostly with bayonets, but it did not last long. There was no formal surrender. The Confederate flag was hauled down and the Stars and Stripes hoisted. All around were dead Confederates who had scorned surrender, and a few dead Yankees.

Meanwhile, Sherman and Howard had been having some anxious moments at the rice mill. Following the advancing line with field glasses, they had been tensely watching every move.

"How grandly they advance!" Sherman shouted exultantly.

"Not a waver!" He stopped talking a moment to concentrate upon that historic spectacle. Then: "Look, Howard! Look! Magnificent! See that flag, how steadily it advances! Not a man falters! Grand! Grand!"

Then came a moment of panic. That blue line had halted. It was wavering, or seemed to be. But it was only a preliminary to the final spurt and victory. The men were soon on the parapet and moving ahead again. Sherman was as excited as a boy: "There they go, right over it! See! See! There is a flag, and another, and another on the works! Hurrah, it's ours! The fort is taken! Howard, Savannah is mine!"

In that sudden lifting of the tension the commander's mind swept back to the Howell Cobb plantation near Milledgeville. There came to his recollection the remark of an old Negro who had come out to take a look at "Mr. Sherman." "This nigger," he quoted, "will have no sleep this night!"

Sherman was impatient and of overpowering impulses. That evening in the sweet afterglow of victory, he determined, in the face of the perils of unexploded torpedoes, enemy snipers and dangerous, unfamiliar waters, to go to see Hazen at once and then make personal contact with the fleet.

In the brilliant moonlight, Sherman could see the plantation wharf. Tied there, bobbing on the water's surface, was a skiff which Federal soldiers had been using for fishing and gathering oysters. He dog-trotted there, flanked by Howard and several other officers. Two of the latter volunteered to handle the oars.

It was no easy downstream journey but a stiff bucking of the incoming tide. Progress was slow and difficult. After a while they saw a soldier on the bank and pulled shoreward to talk to him. Sherman wanted to know the location of Hazen's headquarters, which he knew must be in that general vicinity. The soldier told him Hazen was staying in the house formerly occupied by the overseer of the McAllister plantation. He volunteered to take them there.

They tied the boat to a log and followed their guide through a wilderness of bushes to a frame house standing majestically in a grove of oaks. General Hazen and his staff were in jovial mood. They invited the visitors to join them at supper, which was just then being placed on the long table. Also at the table was Confederate Major George W. Anderson, who had been in command of Fort McAllister.

Sherman learned that the victory had been cheaply won. In his memoirs he gave Hazen's entire loss, dead and wounded, at only ninety-two. Other accounts set it somewhat higher, a hundred and thirty-four. In either case, Federal casualties had been extremely light, considering the terrain. The Confederate loss was about fifty killed and wounded, with about two hundred (the rest of the garrison) taken prisoner. Sherman heard warm praise for brave men on both sides, including a Captain Clinch, Major Anderson's chief of artillery. He had refused to surrender as long as he was physically able to stand and fight. At last— after the enemy had captured all the fort's big guns and he had received three serious saber wounds and two gunshot wounds— he had had no choice.

The victory had netted substantial booty: twenty-four pieces of artillery, many small arms and ten tons of ammunition, besides a quantity of food, numerous animals and a vast amount of personal property which had been carried inside the fort for safety.

Soon after supper Sherman, Howard and the officers who had accompained them from the rice mill set off on the mile walk to Fort McAllister. As they were about to enter, the sentinel cautioned them to exercise great care. The ground just outside was still planted with unexploded torpedoes; the slightest misstep might set off a blast. Just at that moment there was a thunderous noise a few yards away. A Federal soldier looking for the body of a comrade had struck one of the torpedoes with his shoe.

Inside the fort the visitors found many bodies, lying where they had fallen. All around them, so sound asleep that they were almost indistinguishable from the dead, were the victors, ex-hausted by the long march and the fighting. These two kinds of soldiers—the sleeping and the dead—and the beauty and quiet of the moonlight, made a deep impression on the battle-hardened general.

The water was as heavily mined with torpedoes as the land. The tide was high and the surface rough. But Sherman would not let himself be turned back. He was determined not to end the night's excursion short of actual contact with the fleet. Near the fort, tied to a stake, was a yawl, and there were some ex-cellent oarsmen among the troops. Sherman and Howard stepped gingerly aboard the bouncing craft as the crewmen tried to steady it.

Their immediate objective was the ship which had arrived so dramatically that afternoon. For six miles they followed the river's sharp elbow turns with extreme care before they saw the ship's lights.

It was the U.S.S. *Dandelion,* a tender of the gunboat *Flag,* which had been detached to guard the mouth of the river.

They learned that the *Dandelion* was a part of the South Atlantic squadron, charged with enforcing the blockade from Charleston southward. Rear Admiral John A. Dahlgren was the squadron commander. His flagship, the *Harvest Moon,* was then in Wassaw Sound. General J. G. Foster, commanding the Department of the South, had his headquarters at Hilton Head. Several ships carrying supplies for Sherman's men were lying offshore. They were ready to unload whenever they could safely do so. As for the seesaw war in Virginia, there had been little change. Grant was still trying to wear out the Confederates at Richmond and Petersburg and get them ready for the kill. Because of the relative inactivity in the Virgina sector and the silence which had swallowed up Sherman's troops between Atlanta and the sea, except for the conflicting reports published in Southern papers, there was a great deal more interest in his army than in the Army of the Potomac.

His appetite for news somewhat satisfied, Sherman asked his hosts for a pen and some paper. He was soon dashing off, in that jerky, nervous way of his, letters to General Foster, Admiral Dahlgren, General Grant and Secretary of War Stanton. Each message described the capture of Fort McAllister and outlined his immediate and long-range needs.

The capture of the fort had opened the way to Ossabaw Sound and the fleet, he told Stanton in a missive begun just ten minutes before midnight of that momentous December 13. His army had "completely destroyed all the railroads leading into Savannah" and had "invested the city." Its left was planted securely on the Savannah river three miles above the city. Its right was anchored firmly on the Ogeechee at King's Bridge. The army as a whole was "in splendid condition" and "equal to anything." The weather had been "fine" and supplies abundant. The march to the sea had been "most agreeable." He had had no trouble from guerrillas. He had arrived near Savannah three days before, but could not communicate with Washington or the fleet until Fort McAllister had been captured. However, "now that we have McAllister, we can go ahead." He had already seized two Confederate boats on the Savannah river and prevented others from coming downriver. He estimated the Confederate garrison at Savannah, probably correctly, at about fifteen thousand men. (A considerable proportion were Georgia militia, inferior to regular troops in fighting qualities.) His army had not lost a single wagon since leaving Atlanta. It had taken from civilians along the route many Negroes, horses and mules, and, as a result of being so well supplied, "our teams are in far better condition then when we started." Along that long march he had "utterly destroyed" more than two hundred miles of railroad and confiscated great stores of provisions and supplies badly needed by the Confederate armies in Tennessee and Virginia. As for Savannah, its capture would now be easy. Indeed he regarded it as "already gained."

Those dispatches finished and on their way, Sherman was ready to get moving again. The *Dandelion's* torpedo-shy Captain James C. Williamson agreed to tow the small boat as far upriver as he dared, and the two craft were within sight of Fort McAllister when the captain decided he had better not go any farther. After the towline was cut loose the oarsmen in Sherman's party went to work and were soon alongside the fort. From there Sherman and Howard walked back to Hazen's headquarters. They found Hazen and his officers asleep on the floor, and promptly joined them.

Sherman was soon awakened by an officer who had arrived with a message from General J. G. Foster. Foster was on a steamboat anchored below Fort McAllister and was anxious to talk to him as soon as possible but could not walk from the boat landing to Hazen's headquarters because of a wound he had received in the Mexican War. Could Sherman go to him?

Sherman had had very little sleep the night before and had thoroughly exhausted himself that day. He wanted to tell the messenger he would see General Foster the next day. But what he did was to shake off his weariness, get on his feet and get going. Striding for the third time that night along the road to McAllister, he found a small boat awaiting him. He and Foster's messenger were taken three miles down the river to Foster's steamer. Foster explained that he had made the trip from Port Royal to confer wtih Admiral Dahlgren. After the capture of Fort McAllister, he had decided to seize this opportunity to make contact with Sherman.

Sherman's and Foster's troops would probably be fighting alongside each other, or at least fighting in support of each other, in the campaigns ahead. So Foster gave Sherman an elaborate briefing regarding the status of his army. Realizing the importance of the railroad between Savannah and Charleston as a means of retreat for the Confederates should Hardee decide to evacuate Savannah, Foster had tried to wrest control of it from the enemy. But each attempt had failed. However, he had been able to seize and hold a strong position near the Broad river, which brought the railroad within range of his heavy guns.

Foster elaborated upon the news given Sherman a few hours earlier by the officers of the *Dandelion* regarding supplies. In addition to those already aboard ship, there were at Port Royal, he said, all the bread, sugar, coffee and other provisions they were likely to need, as well as large quantities of clothing.

Sherman could certainly use all those things. But his most immediate and most vital need was for heavy-caliber guns for the assault upon Savannah, to replace the light artillery pieces he had brought along. Foster promised him as many of these as he could spare, and also ample stocks of ammunition.

Since the Navy's help would be required to transport the provisions and equipment to the camps, off they went in Foster's steamer to Admiral Dahlgren aboard the *Harvest Moon* at anchor in Wassaw Sound. It was the first time Sherman and Dahlgren had met, but they got along like old friends. The shaggy-haired, strong-chinned admiral pledged his entire resources to the task not only of getting those supplies and guns to Sherman but of cooperating with the Army in its future operations.

VIII

HARDEE'S FAREWELL

SHERMAN RETURNED ON December 15 to Cheves' Mill, where he had left his horse two days before, and then rode to General Howard's headquarters about eight miles west of Savannah. Here he was able to relax and enjoy himself in the company of twenty-five or thirty congenial fellow officers quartered on a fine old plantation owned by an uncle of the Major Anderson who had led the gallant defense of Fort McAllister. The evening was spent relating adventures. A lively campfire blazed nearby and the landscape was bright by the moon. There was group singing to the accompaniment of a soldier guitarist, and in the background an army band played popular tunes. The war had briefly lost its harsher aspects.

While at Howard's headquarters Sherman wrote out for Howard and Slocum a detailed description of his movements since the capture of Fort McAllister. In an outline of future operations, he gave instructions concerning the use of the heavy guns coming from Port Royal in the assault against Savannah. That, he wrote, was to be carried out with all haste.

Sherman had good reason for wishing to begin operations as soon as possible. The terrain between his army and Savannah continued to favor the defenders. It was low and crisscrossed by many salt water creeks, swamps and rice fields. Only a few areas were firm enough to support marching troops and their equipment, and even they could not be used if the weather should turn rainy. At the moment it was pleasant and sunny, and the roads were in good condition. But, at that season especially, there would almost certainly be days of heavy, flooding rains which could immobilize the whole army.

It was important, too, to strike while Hardee's forces were still weak. After the losses they had suffered in the capture of Fort McAllister, they would have difficulty manning the defenses in the city proper and in the outlying forts—Beauliew, Rosedew, White Bluff, Bonaventura, Thunderbolt, Casten's Bluff, Jackson. But the Yankee commander feared they would soon receive heavy reinforcements from Lee's army in Virginia or from the Confederate garrison in Augusta.

Sherman set large work details to building a wharf and storage warehouse at King's Bridge to receive the guns, equipment and supplies from Port Royal. He ordered the roads leading to the area corduroyed, and had wreckage cleared from waterways and a fleet of shallow-draft boats assembled to augment his wagon trains.

Colonel A. H. Markland, absent from the command since leaving Atlanta for Washington in mid-November, arrived with mail. There was a friendly riot as the news-hungry men almost fought for the missives from families and friends. To Sherman, Markland brought a verbal message from Lincoln. "I was directed to take you by the hand wherever I met you," he told his general, "and to say to you for him, 'God bless you and the army under your command. Since cutting loose from Atlanta, my prayers and those of the nation have been for your success.'"

But less cordial and more to the point was written advice from Grant:

> ... I have concluded [Grant had written December 6] that the most important operation toward closing out the rebellion

will be to close out Lee and his army. You have now destroyed the roads of the South so that it will probably take them three months without interruption to reestablish a through line from east to west. In that time I think the job here will be effectually completed.

My idea is that you establish a base on the sea-coast, fortify and leave in it all your artillery and cavalry, and enough infantry to protect them and at the same time so threaten the interior that the militia of the South will have to be kept at home. With the balance of your command come here by water with all dispatch. Select yourself the officer to leave in command, but you I want in person. Unless you see objections to this plan, which I cannot see, use every vessel going to you for purposes of transportation.

Sherman saw objections to Grant's scheme, strong objections. He had long had his heart set upon the capture of Savannah. Now that it was almost within his grasp, he was reluctant to pull out and leave that climactic accomplishment to someone else. He was sure, too, that he could be of inestimably greater help in bringing about the collapse of the Confederacy by continuing the destruction of railroads, depriving the South of food and supplies vitally important to Lee's armies and striking more and stronger blows at Southern civilian morale than he could by adding his military forces to Grant's on the Richmond and Petersburg front. The march from Atlanta to the outskirts of Savannah had been the kind of war-making he liked. So would be the proposed sword thrust through the heart of the Carolinas. It was the kind to which he considered himself particularly suited. In truth, the whole Grant proposition was repugnant to him.

"Cump" Sherman had been too long steeped in military tradition to think of evading the faithful carrying out of any orders Grant might issue. But this letter was not an order. It was in the nature of a suggestion and asked for Sherman's reaction. It therefore was not only his right but also his duty to freely express his own views. This he did in letters to both Grant and Halleck.

His letter to Grant was dated December 16. It emphasized that he would cheerfully follow whatever orders he might receive. But he was firmly convinced, he wrote, that the cause of victory would best be served by carrying out his original intention of marching through the Carolinas. He felt "a personal dislike to turning northward" at this time. He had been planning, after taking Savannah, "to march to Columbia, South Carolina; thence to Raleigh, and hence to report to you." To strengthen his plea, he told his superior officer about some of the results accomplished between Atlanta and the coast:

> ... by liberal and judicious foraging, we reached the seacoast abundantly supplied with forage and provisions, needing nothing on arrival except bread. Of this we started from Atlanta, with from eight to twenty days' supply per corps, and some of the troops only had one day's issue of bread during the trip of thirty days; yet they did not want, for sweet-potatoes were very abundant, as well as corn-meal, and our soldiers took to them naturally. We started with about five thousand head of cattle, and arrived with over ten thousand, of course consuming mostly turkeys, chickens, sheep, hogs, and the cattle of the country. As to our mules and horses, we left Atlanta with about twenty-five hundred wagons, many of which were drawn by mules which had not yet recovered from the Chattanooga starvation, all of which were replaced, the poor mules shot, and our transportation is now in superb condition. I have no doubt the state of Georgia has lost, by our operations, fifteen thousand first-rate mules. As to horses, Kilpatrick collected all his remounts, and it looks to me, in riding along our columns, as though every officer had three or four led horses, and each regiment seems to be followed by at least fifty negroes and foot-sore soldiers riding on horses and mules.

Sherman's plea to the chief of staff, written several days later, was even stronger than that to Grant:

I attach more importance to these deep incisions into the enemy's country, because this war differs from European wars in this particular: we are not fighting armies, but a hostile people, and must make old and young, rich and poor, feel the hard hand of war, as well as their organized armies. I know that this recent movement of mine through Georgia has had a wonderful effect in this respect. Thousands who have been deceived by their lying newspapers to believe that we were being whipped all the time now realize the truth, and have no appetite for the repetition of the same experience. To be sure, Jeff Davis has his people under pretty good discipline, but I think faith in him is much shaken in Georgia, and before we have done with her South Carolina will not be quite so tempestuous.

Even if Grant and Halleck should remain firm in their decision to end the overland campaign on the Georgia coast, Sherman hoped his great prize would not escape him. It would require about a hundred steamers and sailing vessels to transfer his fifty thousand infantrymen. Assemblying so large a fleet would take considerable time. If he moved fast and luck was with him, he might take Savannah before his departure.

Notwithstanding his hope for a change in Grant's and Halleck's plans, he went ahead with preparations for carrying them out, should they be turned into definite orders. Fort McAllister, he decided, would be the best place to leave the artillery, cavalry and wagon trains which would not go with him to Virginia. So he sent his chief engineer, Colonel O. M. Poe, to prepare the fort for its new function.

Sherman's desire to resume the overland campaign was granted. But his epistolatory eloquence had had no effect on the decision. Before his letters had been received, Grant and Halleck had decided to leave Sherman's future actions to his own judgment. Thus the Carolinas were fated to feel the burning scourge that had been inflicted upon Georgia.

Sherman did not want to take Savannah by storm, if it could be gained in any other way. He was certain it was effectively blockaded. Inability to obtain adequate reinforcements, military supplies and food for the city's civilian population might force Hardee to give up without a fight.

"... the troops will continue to invest Savannah closely, making attacks and feints wherever we have fair ground to stand upon," he had written Grant in his letter of December 16, "and I will place some thirty thirty-pound Parrots, which I have got from General Foster, near enough to reach the center of the city, and then will demand its surrender. If General Hardee is alarmed, or fears starvation, he may surrender; otherwise, I will bombard the city, but not risk the lives of our men by assaults across the narrow causeways, by which alone I can now reach it ... "

Meanwhile the wily Confederate commander was laying his own plans. As his spies and scouts reported Sherman's day-to-day advance across Georgia, he kept in mind General Beauregard's instructions: " ... Whenever you shall have to select between the safety of your forces and that of Savannah, sacrifice the latter and form junction with General Jones." Two days after the fall of Fort McAllister, Beauregard sent him a reminder: "Under no circumstances" was he to allow himself to be cut off from retreat. The next day Hardee replied: "Sherman has secured a water base, and Foster, who is already nearly on my communications, can be safely and expeditiously reinforced. Unless assured that force sufficient to keep open communications can be sent to me, I shall be compelled to evacuate Savannah." When he learned that no reinforcements would be sent,[5] he disclosed his evacuation plans to his chief officers. They were to spike all heavy artillery. All pontoons were to be destroyed. All leftover ammunition was to be dumped into the river.

On December 17 Hardee received Sherman's surrender demand sent under a flag of truce:

You have doubtless observed, from your station at Rosedew, that seagoing vessels now come through Ossabaw Sound and up the Ogeechee to the rear of my army, giving me abundant supplies of all kinds, and more especially heavy ordnance necessary for the reduction of Savannah. I have already received guns that can cast heavy and destructive shot as far as the heart of your city; also I have for some days held and controlled every avenue by which the people and garrison of Savannah can be supplied, and I am therefore justified in demanding the surrender of the city of Savannah, and its dependent forts, and shall wait a reasonable time for your answer before opening with heavy ordnance. Should you entertain the proposition, I am prepared to grant liberal terms to the inhabitants and garrison; but should I be forced to resort to assault, or the slower and surer process of starvation, I shall then feel justified in resorting to the harshest measures, and shall make little effort to restrain my army—burning to avenge the national wrong which they attach to Savannah and other large cities which have been so prominent in dragging our country into civil war. I enclose you a copy of General Hood's demand for the surrender of the town of Resaca, to be used by you for what it is worth.

Hardee did not avail himself of the "reasonable time" Sherman offered, but answered immediately:

I have to acknowledge the receipt of a communication from you of this date, in which you demand "the surrender of Savannah and its dependent forts," on the ground that you "have received guns that can cast heavy and destructive shot into the heart of the city," and for the further reason that you "have, for some days, held and controlled every avenue by which the people and garrison can be supplied." You add that, should you be forced to assault, or to the slower and surer process of starvation, you will then feel justified in resorting to the harshest measures, and will make little effort to restrain your army, etc., etc. The position of your force (a half-mile beyond the outer line for the land defense of Savannah) is, at the nearest point, at least four miles from the heart of the city. That and the interior line are both intact.

Your statement that you have, for some days, held and controlled every avenue by which the people and garrison can be supplied is incorrect. I am in free and constant communication with my department.

Your demand for the surrender of Savannah and its dependent forts is refused.

With respect to the threats conveyed in the closing paragraphs of your letter (of what may be expected in case your demand is not complied with) I have to say that I have hitherto conducted the military operations intrusted to my direction in strict accordance with the rules of civilized warfare, and I shall deeply regret the adoption of any course by you that may force me to deviate from them in future.

Notwithstanding Hardee's peremptory rejection of Sherman's demand, he realized that it would be virtually impossible for him to hold Savannah. The two generals could argue on and on about the distance from Sherman's siege guns to the heart of the city, but there was no question about the Yankees' being able to do tremendous damage with those guns. Hardee knew too that his boast about being "in free and constant communication with my department" was an extremely tenuous and shaky one, based solely upon Confederate control of the Union causeway stretching into South Carolina. The control could be ended whenever Sherman felt inclined to commit enough men and guns to the causeway's capture. Indeed he probably would have already seized it had he not been under the impression that the Confederates could not use it. Once that weak link with the rest of the Confederacy was broken, surrender or annihilation would be inevitable.

Hardee therefore began setting into motion the evacuation plans he had formulated some time earlier. He ordered the destruction of the navy yard, the ironclad ships in the harbor and other government property in the city. Then, in the late afternoon of December 20, he ordered a fierce bombardment, one of the heaviest of the war. There was slight chance that this staggering mass of ammunition and metal would do much damage to the entrenched Federals, but it might fool them into thinking the small Confederate force of fewer than ten thousand able-bodied, well-trained men was much larger. In addition, the bombardment would dispose of the ammunition the men could not carry away with them.

About midnight Colonel Henry A. Barnum, commanding a regiment of General John W. Geary's Division of the XX Corps, advanced cautiously through the darkness beyond the Federal picket lines to within three hundred yards of the Confederate works. He could hear no enemy voices, nor could he see any figures silhouetted before campfires. Still, there was the steady boom of Confederate guns. Picking ten men to accompany him, he moved ahead and scaled the parapet rimming the extreme Confederate line. Still seeing nothing to indicate the presence of the enemy, the party advanced confidently into the fortifications. Fires burned, but there were no Confederates. Certain that the enemy had pulled out, the Yankees, including some additional troops sent to reinforce the party, entered and passed one earthwork after another, heading all the time toward the city. They entered it about dawn. In the distance they could see the rear guard of Hardee's men, hurrying up the causeway on the other side of the river. Sherman had Savannah, but he did not have Hardee.

Civilians in the besieged city had heard the steady tramping of feet during the night and knew what it meant. The following morning the Savannah *Republican* told them in a front-page editorial:

To the Citizens of Savannah:
By the fortunes of war we pass today under the authority of the Federal military forces. The evacuation of Savannah by the Confederate army, which took place last night, left the gates to

the city open, and General Sherman, with his army will, no doubt, to-day take possession.

The Mayor and Common Counsel leave under a flag of truce this morning, for the headquarters of Gen. Sherman, to offer the surrender of the city, and ask terms of capitulation by which private property and citizens may be respected.

We desire to counsel obedience and all proper respect on the part of our citizens, and to express the belief that their property and persons will be respected by our military ruler. The fear expressed by many that Gen. Sherman will repeat the order of expulsion from their homes which he enforced against the citizens of Atlanta, we think to be without foundation. He assigned his reason in that case as a military necessity, it was a question of food. He could not supply his army and the citizens with food, and he stated that he must have full and sole occupation. But in our case food can be abundantly supplied for both army and civilians. We would not be understood as even intimating that we are to be fed at the cost of the Federal Government, but that food can be easily obtained in all probability, by all who can afford to pay in the Federal currency.

It behooves all to keep within their houses until Gen. Sherman shall have organized a provost system and such police as will insure safety in persons as well as property.

Let our conduct be such as to win the admiration of a magnanimous foe, and give no ground for complaint or harsh treatment on the part of him who will for an indefinite period hold possession of our city.

In our city there are, as in other communities, a large proportion of poor and needy families, who, in the present situation of affairs, brought about by the privations of war, will be thrown upon the bounty of their more fortunate neighbors. Deal with them kindly, exercise your philanthropy and benevolence, and let the heart of the unfortunate not be deserted by your friendly aid.

Mayor R. D. Arnold and members of his official staff started out early that morning (December 21) to surrender the city. Just beyond the city limits they encountered a strong Federal force under General Geary. The mayor made to him the usual request for protection of the lives and property of private citizens. Geary treated him and the others with great kindness and courtesy and pledged his personal efforts to see that rights were respected.

Geary continued his advance into the city proper. Upon arrival there, he sent an officer with 400 men to take possession of Fort Jackson, one of the stronger Confederate outposts. Another officer was sent to General Slocum to inform him that Savannah was in Federal hands. By 8 o'clock the Yankees held all Confederate strongholds, and other units were pouring into the city.

From the time those troops marched out of Atlanta, November 15, until they marched into Savannah, December 21, ten officers and ninety-three men were killed. Twenty-four officers and 404 men were wounded, and one officer and 277 men were reported missing—a total casualty list of thirty-five officers and 774 men. The Federals captured seventy-seven Confederate officers and 1,261 men.

During that thirty-six-day march Sherman's men had passed through more than forty of the wealthiest and most progressive counties of the state. The Confederacy's transportation system had been grievously weakened by the destruction of about two hundred miles of vital railroad. Many cotton gins and cotton mills and great quantities of Confederate property had been destroyed. Sherman estimated the damage at about a hundred million dollars, "at least $20,000,000 of which has inured to our advantage." The rest he called "simple waste and destruction."

Many of the victors regarded Savannah as just another conquered city to be looted and pillaged, but General Geary made it sternly plain that he would not tolerate that. Provost guards were posted to protect private property and keep order. Civilians began moving about the city freely again. The stores reopened. Public transportation resumed. The people settled down to live as tolerably as possible under the new order.

Ironically, every private in Sherman's army knew about the

occupation hours before he did. He and Admiral Dahlgren left General Foster's headquarters at Hilton Head for Fort McAllister on the night of December 20, not knowing that Hardee had chosen that night to evacuate Savannah. A gale was stirring up, so the *Harvest Moon* followed an inland route leading to Wassaw Sound and the Ogeechee by way of a shallow waterway known as the Rommey Marshes. There the craft was caught by low tide and ran aground in the gummy mud. To avoid further delay, Dahlgren ordered the barge overboard, and he and Sherman resumed their journey in it. Late in the afternoon they were sighted by the Quartermaster's Department tug *Red Legs*, carrying letters from Colonel L. M. Dayton, Sherman's adjutant, telling of the arrival of Federal troops in the city.

Sherman transferred to the *Red Legs* and reached McAllister by nightfall but waited there until midnight for the tide, and arrived at the Cheves rice mill at 2:30 in the morning. After breakfast he, accompanied by his staff and an escort, began the nine-mile ride to Savannah.

IX

---~~---

THE OCCUPATION OF SAVANNAH

SHERMAN'S TRIUMPHAL RIDE into the heart of Savannah was in the nature of a homecoming, for he had been on duty there a number of years before. As he rode that frosty Thursday morning down aristocratic Bull Street to the custom house, it must have been with a feeling of irony that his eyes fell upon one spot after another intimately associated in his memory with those happy and peaceful days when he had been the popular Captain Sherman.

Dismounting at the custom house, he followed a stairway to the roof. Savannah now lay literally at his feet, and he enjoyed the sight. Just below him, it is true, was the river across which Hardee had escaped; an acid reminder of the incompleteness of his victory. And, on the other side, over in South Carolina, was a depressing expanse of marshland and rice fields, barren-looking in the wintry cold. But at hand was the intricate quiltwork of buildings, streets and parks that were now subject to his orders, and in the harbor lay the hulking wreckage of the Confederate ironclad ram *Savannah*, still smouldering.

The conquest of Savannah was the shining symbol of his success in one of the most spectacular and controversial campaigns in military history, the symbol of the wisdom of his judgment against strongly held opinions of the weightiest military brains of his generation. So, in spite of Hardee, he felt pleased with "the substantial fruits of victory." This was indeed a great day for him.

It was well that in his hour of triumph he did not know what an unfavorable view others would take of his failure to keep Hardee and his men in their trap. In later months and years newspaper writers, politicians and historians would take him severely to task for it. They would charge him with a failure to exercise due diligence. And in that failure, they would say angrily, he had handed Hardee a considerable moral and military victory. This was to become a sensitive point with him.[6]

During his earlier stay in the city, Sherman had lodged at the Pulaski House, and now he rode there to set up headquarters. The man in charge was a Vermont Yankee with a lame leg, who had been a clerk at the St. Louis Hotel in New Orleans.

The Vermonter was delighted at the prospect of a rich harvest of United States dollars for feeding and housing free-spending Yankee troops. But his enthusiasm cooled perceptibly when Sherman explained that he and his staff would not require any food: they had full mess equipment and would provide their own meals. However, they would require considerable housing space and rooms for offices—the equivalent, he figured, of about one wing. The rest of the building could be rented to officers and male civilians.

There was no stable near the hotel large enough to accommodate the horses of Sherman and his staff. He sent an officer to find one.

The officer was scarcely out of sight when visitors began arriving. Mayor Arnold, who had intended surrendering the city to Sherman personally the day before, was one of them. The mayor assured him that he and his fellow officials were anxious to cooperate with the military authorities in every way. The visit was pleasant all around, and Sherman treated his visitor with the rare graciousness which he displayed on occasion.

He was also most gracious to Mrs. G. W. Smith. He was some-what embarrassed, too. Mrs. Smith's husband was a Confederate general whom Sherman had known in 1850 while General Smith was on duty at West Point. Before leaving Savannah with the rest of Hardee's forces, he had written a letter to his enemy which Mrs. Smith delivered. Saluting the city's conqueror as "Dear Sherman" and pointing out that "the fortunes of war, etc., compel me to leave my wife in Savannah," the letter be-spoke "your courteous protection" for her. She had a particular request to make. The house where she was boarding had been taken over by officers. The landlady was expecting a baby, and the officers were extremely noisy. The woman was not able to get the rest she needed. Would General Sherman do whatever needed to be done to insure her getting it?

He promised her he would and took the matter up with General Slocum, whose troops were in immediate control of the city. Later, he made a visit to the house.

Soon after Mrs. Smith left, a brother of General Hardee arrived. The civilian Hardee was a Savannah merchant and had been for a long time. He brought a letter from his brother stating that he had never borne arms for the Confederacy, and asking protection for the Hardee family, its cotton and other property. Sherman assured the visitor that neither he nor any other law-abiding civilian would be molested. As for the Hardee cotton, that was a different matter. He could make no promises. The disposition of all cotton was still uncertain. Sherman was not even sure that it would be his responsibility.

Still another visitor arrived. Charles Green, a wealthy English-born banker with strong Union sympathies, offered Sherman his home, the city's most elegant. He had no use for it, he said, and would consider himself honored if the general would use it.

At first Sherman felt "strongly disinclined" to accept the offer. He preferred to use public buildings, such as governors' mansions and the residences of other officials. But Green insisted. At his urging, Sherman visited the place and found it to be just what he needed. He stipulated, however, that he and his staff would have their own mess and provide their own meals. Green reserved only two rooms for his own use.

A "most excellent house ... in all respects," Sherman called it. He was impressed by its roominess, its planning and arrangement, the expansive yard and the generous provisions for stabling horses. Major Hitchcock, one of those fortunate enough to rate this unaccustomed luxury, wrote his wife about it. He called it "a fine house, two-story double, larger than your Mother's." In the magnificent hall he and his fellow officers were surrounded by "some very handsome pieces of statuary." Nearby were "banana trees growing in tubs." In the bedrooms and other smaller rooms were "several fine pictures" and also "books of engravings." All in all, it would have been difficult to find more luxurious living quarters anywhere in the South, famed for its elegant homes.

The commander had been established there less than an hour when A. G. G. Browne, agent of the United States Treasury Department, arrived. His mission was to claim for the Department all captured cotton and rice and all public buildings. Sherman objected vigorously. That valuable property had been won by his troops. It therefore was military property and not subject to the control of any civilian agency. Moreover, he was certain the army could manage it more satisfactorily. However, he was in a conciliatory mood and willing to be generous. Without yielding his point that the army must retain possession and control, he nevertheless agreed to turn over to Browne whatever the army did not need. Since Browne was in no mood to quarrel either, the two men reached an agreement.

In the pleasant conversation that followed, Browne mentioned that a vessel was about to leave for Fortress Monroe and should be there by Christmas Day, three days off. Wouldn't Sherman like to send a Christmas gift to President Lincoln? Acting on an impulse, as he often did, Sherman seized a slip of paper. He wrote rapidly for a minute or two and handed the slip to his visitor, asking him to have it left at the telegraph office at Fortress Monroe for transmission to Washington. And on Christmas Day the President's sad, careworn face lighted up as he read:

SAVANNAH, GA., DECEMBER 22, 1864

To His Excellency, President Lincoln, Washington, D.C. I beg to present to you as a Christmas-gift the city of Savannah, with one hundred and fifty heavy guns and plenty of ammunition, also about twenty-five thousand bales of cotton.

W. T. SHERMAN, MAJOR-GENERAL

The message was widely published throughout the North, where it delighted millions of households.

Actually, Sherman's estimate of his booty was on the conservative side. General Foster reported to Grant and Halleck that the city contained, when captured, thirty-three thousand bales of cotton. A writer in *The New York Times* estimated their value at well in excess of eighteen million dollars. Foster's report also listed "eight hundred prisoners, one hundred and fifty guns, thirteen locomotives in good order, one hundred and ninety cars, a large supply of ammunition and materials of war" and three steamers. The prisoners presumably were Hardee's sick and wounded, unable to travel.

The day after Christmas President Lincoln wrote:

MY DEAR GENERAL SHERMAN:

Many, many thanks for your Christmas gift—the capture of Savannah.

When you were about to leave Atlanta for the Atlantic coast, I was *anxious*, if not fearful; but feeling you were the better judge, and remembering that "nothing risked, nothing gained," I did not interfere. Now the undertaking being a success, the honor is all yours, for I believe none of us went further than to acquiesce. And taking the work of General Thomas into account [the overwhelming defeat of Hood's army at Nashville], as it should be taken, it is indeed a great success.

Not only does it afford the obvious and immediate military

advantages, but in showing to the world that our army could
be divided, putting the stronger part to an important new
service, and yet leaving enough to vanquish the old opposing
forces of the whole—Hood's army—it brings those who sit in
darkness to see a great light.

But what next? I suppose it will be safe if I leave General
Grant and yourself to decide.

Please make my grateful acknowledgments to your whole
army, officers and men.

Yours very truly,
A. LINCOLN

Sherman showed he could be as generous with praise as the
President. After reading Kilpatrick's report of the cavalry's part
in the march from Atlanta, he wrote him an enthusiastic letter.
It called the cavalry's operations "skilful and eminently successful." Kilpatrick, it said, had "handsomely feigned" on Macon
and one or two other places, misleading and confusing the
enemy. He had done "all that was possible toward the rescue
of our prisoners at Millen," failing only because "the prisoners
were not there." On at least two occasions "you whipped a
superior cavalry force, and took from Wheeler all chance of
boasting over you." Kilpatrick's over-all accomplishment had
made possible "the march of four strong infantry columns, with
heavy trains and wagons, over 300 miles through an enemy's
country." This had been done "without the annoyance of
cavalry dashes on our flanks." That Sherman called "honor
enough for any military commander."

The colored people who flocked to see "Mr. Sherman" in
Savannah rivaled in both numbers and fervor those who had
hailed him on the march from Atlanta. Whenever he would
appear on the streets, he would be cheered. They would rush up
to him, seize his hand and shake it in a frenzy of jubilation, telling him they had long been waiting for him and praying for his

safe arrival. After he settled in the Green mansion they tramped in droves through the wide, elegant halls to his upstairs office.

Hitchcock, greatly impressed by these mass interviews, wrote in his diary:

> Frequently they come in a dozen or twenty at a time, to his room upstairs where he usually sits, and where, as my writing is done there, I have been in the way of hearing it all. He always has them shown in at once, stopping a dispatch or letter or a conversation to geer [greet] them in his off-hand—though not undignified way.—"Well, boys—come to see Mr. Sherman, have you? Well, I'm Mr. Sherman—glad to see you" and shaking hands with them in a manner highly disgusting, I dare say, to a "refined Southern gentleman!" Almost all of them who have talked at all have spoken of our success and their deliverance with an apparently religious feeling.—"Been prayin' for you all along, Sir, prayin' night and day for you, and now, bless God you is come," etc.

A colored preacher compared himself to the Biblical Simeon, who was promised by the Holy Ghost that he would not die until after he had seen Christ. Simeon had cried out in the temple after taking the infant Jesus in his arms: "Lord, now lettest Thou Thy servant depart in peace, for mine eyes have seen Thy salvation." Now, the visitor told Sherman, he would meet death calmly and happily. For he had seen the deliverer of his people.

To all those who trudged up those broad, luxuriously carpeted steps to his office, Sherman gave essentially the same advice: the millennium was not at hand. While they were free, they were not their former masters' masters. They had shed their obligation to work for the white people and do their bidding. But their former masters, by the same token, were no longer obliged to feed, shelter and care for them. From now on, they would be on their own. If they did not work, if they did not handle their money wisely or if they failed to meet the other responsibilities that came with freedom, they would go hungry, and in many ways they would be worse off than they had been as slaves.

This wise advice was dictated in part by Sherman's sincere interest in the Negroes' welfare. It was also motivated by his serious doubts regarding the wisdom of immediate, wholesale emancipation and his conviction that, slaves or free, the colored people of the South were incapable of assuming political equality with the whites.

". . . All the Congresses on earth can't make the negro anything else than what he is; he must be subject to the white man, or he will amalgamate or be destroyed," he had written as early as July 10, 1860. "Two such races cannot live in harmony save as master and slave. Mexico shows the result of general equality and amalgamation, and the Indians give a fair illustration of the fate of negroes if they are released from the control of the whites. . . . "

This was not a transitory view. Sherman felt as strongly on the subject after the war as before it. He said practically the same thing in 1867:

> . . . I have my doubts as to the propriety of giving them [the Negroes] all the political rights of the white race as long as they live commingled. My opinions have been more influenced by what I observed in Brazil, in Chile and in Mexico. The cause of constitutional liberty in those countries had been retarded by the mingling of the races, and I am not certain the same result may not unsue [sic] in this country. . . .

While Sherman was giving his throngs of Negro callers sound advice tinctured by his personal views on the black man's place in American life, Secretary of War Stanton had come to Savannah with another motive, to assure the Negroes of full political equality with their former masters and to remind them that they owed it all—their freedom and their vote—to the Lincoln administration. Although Sherman had little stomach for this noisy beating of the political drums, he had no choice but to go along.

To get a firmer grip upon the Negro vote, the short, pudgy Stanton, whose disheveled appearance and generally disagreeable manner Sherman found repulsive, arranged a meeting at Sherman's headquarters of the Negro ministers of the city. He questioned them about the treatment they had received under the occupation and urged them to air grievances. That they might express themselves more freely, he asked Sherman to leave the room. Then he asked them point-blank what they thought of him.

Their replies were all Sherman could have desired. He was friendly, they said, and a model of courtesy. Without exception, they thought no other person could have handled the complicated problems of occupation better.

But Stanton and other politicians wanted more positive action on Sherman's part to impress upon the vote-conscious Negroes that he was bubbling over with friendliness for them. Under their pressure he set aside certain areas, consisting largely of rice fields, for settlement by former slaves. Every freedman was entitled to forty acres. At the same time, able-bodied Negroes were encouraged to enlist in the army. The enticements of the military life were increased by a proviso that a volunteer could claim his forty acres at the time of enlistment. The land could be cultivated by his family until his return, and enlistment bounties and other stipends would be paid to the family.

Stanton discussed with Sherman the reports he had heard that General Jeff C. Davis was in favor of slavery. He was especially disturbed over the tragedy at Ebeneezer Creek, where the Negroes traveling with the XIV Corps had drowned when Davis ordered the removal of the pontoon bridge. There were ugly rumors, he said, that Davis had deliberately given the order in the expectation that they would drown or be captured by Wheeler's cavalry. Sherman assured him the rumors were pure poppycock. Whatever might be Davis' personal views on slavery, he said, he was one of the ablest generals in the army, far too big to vent his dislikes in such a vindictive way.

Sherman was no less emphatic in his defense of Davis in a letter to Halleck. The charge was just a "cock-and-bull story" and "humbug." Nobody had been turned back at Ebeneezer Creek for any reason. Davis had taken up the pontoon bridge "not because he wanted to leave them, but because he wanted his bridge." Both Davis and Slocum had assured him that, so far as they knew, not a single Negro left behind had been killed by Wheeler's men.

During his stay in Savannah the perpetually tired-looking Stanton complained frequently that he was a sick man.[7] His bad health, he told Sherman, would probably force him to resign from the cabinet soon. He also painted a gloomy picture of the general state of the country. He was especially pessimistic about the economic outlook. Disaster, he seemed to think, was near unless the war ended soon. This cabinet officer who had panicked after the appearance of the Confederate ironclad *Merrimac* and predicted she would be shelling the Capitol at any moment, urged Sherman to push ahead with his campaign as rapidly as possible and to do everything else he could to win that grim race between national bankruptcy and victory. Sherman was to recall that plea a few months later, when that same Stanton would be publicly excoriating him for trying to get the war over with in a hurry.

Sherman enjoyed his stay, and was pleased with the people's adjustment to the occupation.

His troops and the public were told what to expect in Special Field Order No. 143, issued the day after Christmas. In wartime, it stipulated, "the military is superior to civil authority." Whenever there is a clash between the two, "the civil must give way." Insofar as possible, "every encouragement should be given to well-disposed and peaceful inhabitants to resume their usual pursuits." The army's chief quartermaster and commissary would give employment to suitable persons, black and white, and would transport others to places where jobs could be had. Commerce with the outer world would be resumed "to an extent commensurate with the wants of the citizens, governed by the restrictions and rules of the Treasury Department."

Mayor Arnold and his fellow officials, who had conscientiously lived up to their pledge to cooperate with the occupying forces, were authorized to continue their normal functions. They, "in concert with the commanding officer of the post and the chief-quartermaster," would keep the fire-fighting organizations in efficient operation and the streets clean and well lighted at all times. They would also encourage "a good understanding between citizens and soldiers." Worthy families in distress would be reported to the chief quartermaster of subsistence, who would help them according to their needs. The people of the city would have to decide whether they would remain there "and conduct themselves as good citizens" or "depart in peace." Those choosing to leave would receive transportation beyond the Federal lines.

Two newspapers were permitted to continue publication. Their editors and proprietors would be held to strict accountability for their contents. Severe punishment "in person and property" would be inflicted for "any libelous publication, mischievous matter, premature news, exaggerated statements" or "any comments whatever upon the acts of the constituted authorities."

Only a few, about two hundred, chose to leave the city. They were for the most part relatives of Confederate soldiers. They were placed aboard a steamboat flying a flag of truce and carried to Charleston, where a Confederate officer took charge of them.

As Geary's division of the XX Corps had been the first to enter the city, he was chosen as its military commander, or military governor. The choice was a most fortunate one. This tall, black-bearded, hearty and friendly soldier had a genius for getting on pleasant, hospitable terms with the people he dealt with. Far from being a "softie" or sentimentalist, he nevertheless had a strong sense of humanity. When difficult situations arose, he dealt with them with rare diplomacy and tact, and in a very short time even the most ardent Yankee-hater had to concede that he was doing an excellent job. Guards assigned to the protection of private property were carefully screened to eliminate toughs, drunks and rowdies. The city quickly developed a sense of contentment and security. The daily mounting of the guard and the frequent parades became important social functions, witnessed by ladies from all over the city. Schools reopened and operated without untoward incidents or friction. The churches were well filled every Sunday. (When a minister asked Sherman if he might continue to pray for President Davis, the commander replied: "Pray for Jeff Davis? Why certainly! You ought to pray for him every day, for Jeff Davis and the devil need praying for very much.") Business establishments carried on as they had done before the occupation. The destitute received supplies from army stores. Sherman was probably right when he wrote in his memoirs: "I doubt if Savannah, either before or since, has had a better government than during our stay."

This policy of leniency and friendliness was, of course, strongly based on practical considerations. A contented, well-fed Savannah would serve as a powerful force in the breakdown of morale in the rest of the Confederacy. Military authorities encouraged the writing of letters telling how much better things were than they had been before the occupation. Such letters to hungry, frightened and distressed kinsmen and friends and especially to Savannah men in the Confederate Army were highly effective. The hardships of the march and the battlefield were harder to endure after reading letters describing pleasant conditions at home, along with statements that the Confederate cause was doomed and further resistance meant only the fruitless sacrifice of lives. Many letters were outright pleas to the men to quit and return home.

"They produced a wonderful effect," *The New York Times'* Savannah correspondent wrote. "Applications are registered hourly by those who have abandoned the rebel service and come within our lines, to be admitted to the benefits of the amnesty proclamation."

George Ward Nichols left in his diary his impressions of the city after being there several days:

> Ladies walk the streets with perfect confidence and security, and the public squares are filled with children at play; the stores and theatres are open; soldiers are lounging on the doorsteps of the houses in cheerful conversations with fair damsels; carriages whisk by, wherein the blue coat and brass buttons are in close proximity—anything but warlike—to jockey hats and flowing ringlets. In truth, there is a delightful *entente cordiale* between the officers and ladies, which would never be disturbed, perhaps, could many of them be consulted.

Major Hitchcock was also greatly impressed. He paid his own tribute to the good conduct of the soldiers and the way in which General Geary and his aides were looking after the well-being of the people:

> ... I am glad to say that the perfectly unexceptionable conduct of our army here is not only apparent in the streets, but most favorably remarked upon by the citizens. Since we came, a week today, I have seen but two drunken soldiers, and both of these were on their way to the guardhouse at the time. I meet ladies and children on the street whenever I go out, and tonight at dinner the General was speaking with great pleasure and feeling of the number of children he saw in the park playing, etc., this afternoon.

Nevertheless, Savannah by no means was a Utopia. There was a serious food shortage, especially of bread.

"Savannah is suffering, just now, from a deplorable scarcity of provisions," *The New York Times* correspondent wrote a few days after Christmas. "There is an absolute want of the necessary means of subsistence. Rice abounds in immense quantities, and is almost the only kind of food within the reach of the great mass of citizens. Of course they cannot subsist entirely on rice; and they propose, I understand, to send an agent [a prominent Savannahan, Colonel Julian Allen] to New-York to barter a quantity of this commodity for other articles of food. . . . It is hoped that he will be successful in his mission. Meanwhile, the military authorities are doing their utmost to alleviate the sufferings of the poor of the city, among whom the commissary stores left behind by the rebels, in their hasty evacuation of the city, will be judiciously distributed."

Prominent individuals and newspapers in the North launched a campaign for money, food and clothing. "The move to relieve the suffering people of Savannah deserves the support of every patriotic and every humane man," *The New York Times* said in an editorial headed "The War to Restore Fellowship."

> The simple statement of Gen. Sherman is proof enough that great need exists. The military authorities are doing what they well can to abate it, but their available means are very limited. Something will be realized from the shipments of rice made by the municipal authorities of Savannah to be exchanged for other articles of food. But much will yet remain to be supplied from other sources. It is an opportunity which not only appeals to every Christian feeling, but which can be turned to most excellent advantage.
>
> It is fortunate that the people of Savannah are manifesting a spirit that we can respect and easily fraternize with. Considering how their pride must have suffered from the almost bloodless victory gained over them, it is indeed, remarkable that they should adapt to their changed fortunes with such good grace. . . . Let us meet them like brothers, and make them a standing illustration before the Southern people of the brotherhood we would extend to all of them, if they would but cease resistance to the Constitution and the laws. . . .

The appeals made by the *Times* and many others were effective. By mid-January, the Philadelphia *Bulletin* reported, approximately twenty-one thousand dollars had been contributed by the residents of that city alone, with other contributions still to come. Generous gifts were made also by people in such faraway cities as St. Louis and Chicago. Before long ships shuttling between northeastern ports and Savannah began unloading vast amounts of food, clothing, blankets and other necessities at the newly renovated docks.

The alert *New York Times* correspondent was on hand when the distribution got under way:

> ... Rome, in time of the carnival, can exhibit no such spectacle. There are two doors to the store, one on Bay and the other on Barnard street, affording entrance and exit. Several hundred persons of both sexes, all ages, sizes, complexions, costumes; gray-haired old men, with canes, with bags, bottles and baskets; old "Uncle Neds," who just before death gives them liberty from hardship and suffering, are made freemen by the mighty march of events; well dressed women wearing crepe for their husbands and sons, who have fallen while fighting against the old flag, with pale and sunken cheeks, stand there patiently awaiting their turn. There are women with tattered dresses—old silks and satins, which were laid aside as useless, but which have become valuable through destitution. There are women in linsey-woolsey, demi-white women wearing negro cloth, negro women dressed in gunny cloth; men with Confederate uniforms, men with butternut clothes. There is a boy in a crimson plush jacket, made from what was once the upholstering of a sofa. There are old men in short jackets, little boys in long ones—the cast-off overcoats of soldiers, the rags which have been picked up from garrets—wearing the boots and shoes which have been kicked off and thrown aside, down at the heel, out at the toes, open on the instep. There are old bonnets of every description, some with white and crimson flowers, some with ribbons once bright and flaming, but faded now and worn. There are Shaker bonnets, "sugar scoops," "coal

scuttles," hats of every description, size and shape worn by both sexes—women wearing men's hats of palm-leaf or felt, men wearing stove-pipes battered and bruised, felt, slouched and torn, ventilated by accident and not by patent ventilators. There is one which had no crown, worn by a man who had red hair, reminding one of a chimney on fire and flaming out at the top. It is the ragman's fair—rather the ragman's jubilee and day of rejoicing, for Charity, like a kind angel, has suddenly stepped in to ward off the wolf which is howling at their doors.

... There are teams in the street—old, dilapidated wagons—weak, broken down horses—sorry mules, with rope harness. It is a collection of odds and ends.... It is literally a distribution of the bread of life. In no profane sense, but in truth and reality, it is a sacrament, given freely, and I doubt not thankfully received. The recipients, at any rate, are eager to partake of it—so eager that the sentinels at the door at times are compelled to present their bayonets to the crowd to keep the passage clear.

There will be some who will fail to receive the aid they need—persons who have never known want, who will suffer silently rather than mix in the crowd which throng at the door. Others will obtain provisions when they have an abundance at home.

Sherman regarded the march to the sea as only a phase in a larger operation: not a major objective in itself. "I simply moved," he wrote in his memoirs, "from Atlanta to Savannah as one step in the direction of Richmond. ..." He considered the post-Savannah campaign a ten times more important contribution to winning the war.

He had been in Savannah only two days when he wrote a long letter to Grant saying he expected to "sally forth again" in about ten days. He had pondered his plans so much that "they appear as clear as daylight." He had purposely bypassed Augusta, although feinting at it, so as to leave the Confederates uncertain as to his route after leaving Savannah, trying to decide whether he would head for Charleston or Augusta. The resulting confusion and uncertainty would again keep the enemy's forces divided, some at one place, some at the other. He would bypass both of them, of course, moving toward Columbia and destroying railroads along the way. There would be brief halts at Columbia and Camden. Then he would strike for the Charleston & Wilmington Railroad at some point between the Santee and Cape Fear rivers. Then, perhaps after affecting another rendezvous with Admiral Dahlgren somewhere along the coast, he would move on Wilmington, assuming of course that the North Carolina port city had not been captured in the meantime.

He was forthright about his decision to leave Charleston alone. It was "a mere desolated wreck" and "hardly worth the time it would take to starve it out." From Wilmington he favored a move straight to Raleigh. With Wilmington and Raleigh in Federal hands:

> The game is then up with Lee, unless he comes out of Richmond, avoids you and fights me; in which case I should reckon on your being on his heels. Now that Hood is used up by Thomas, I feel disposed to bring this matter to an issue as quick as possible. I feel confident that I can break up the whole railroad system of South Carolina and North Carolina, and be on the Roanoke, either at Raleigh [8] or Weldon, by the time spring fairly opens; and, if you feel confident you can whip Lee outside of his entrenchments, I feel equally confident that I can handle him in the open country.

As Sherman plotted his next military move, he was also thinking of vengeance. South Carolina, he vowed, would suffer and suffer for leading the parade of states out of the Union. The treatment that had made Georgia howl would be too lenient. Knowing what their sister state had undergone, South Carolinians awaited the next move with anxiety.

Three days before Federal troops entered Savannah, Sherman had written Grant about its anticipated capture. After that, he added, "we can punish South Carolina as she deserves." That very same day Halleck wrote him: "Should you capture Charleston, I hope that by *some accident* the place may be destroyed." Moreover, "if a little salt should be sown upon its site, it may prevent the growth of future crops of nullification and secession." Sherman replied December 24. As he had written Grant, he planned to bypass Charleston and head for Columbia and Wilmington. But he might possibly change his route. In that case, "I will bear in mind your hint as to Charleston," but "do not think 'salt' will be necessary." In such an operation, "the Fifteenth Corps will be on the right of the right wing, and their position will naturally bring them into Charleston first." If Halleck had kept up with that corps' history, "you will have remarked that they generally do their work pretty well." His entire army "is burning with an insatiable desire to wreak vengeance upon South Carolina." Indeed his troops were so vindictive that "I almost tremble at her fate" but felt "she deserves all that is in store for her." As for Columbia, he regarded it as "quite as bad as Charleston," and "I doubt that we shall spare the public buildings as we did at Milledgeville."

As the move on Columbia neared, General Slocum turned over control of Savannah to the physically handicapped but capable General Foster. To fill the vacuum caused by the withdrawal of Slocum's troops, Foster selected Major General Cuvier Grover's division of the XIX Corps. It had just arrived from the Virginia theatre of operations.

Sherman and his aides started rumors about the city that Charleston was to be his next objective, at the same time having it said that he would head straight for Augusta. These conflicting reports served their purpose well.

Cheering news came on the eve of the army's departure. General John M. Schofield and his XXIII Corps, which had played a gallant part in crushing Hood's army at Nashville, were en route to North Carolina and would be on hand to give Sherman powerful support in the later phases of the campaign.

X

"HELLHOLE OF SECESSION"

CONSISTENT with his over-all plan, Sherman ordered Slocum's Left Wing to march out of Savannah along both banks of the Savannah river as though headed for Augusta. At Sister's Ferry, about forty miles upriver, those troops on the south bank were to join the rest of the Wing on the north bank and to march toward a rendezvous with Howard's Right Wing, moving inland from their feint on Charleston at Beaufort. The reunited army would then wheel sharply and march rapidly on Columbia.

The new campaign began easily enough. In a nine-day ferrying operation that began early in January, transports carried the XVII Corps of Howard's Right Wing from Savannah to Beaufort without a serious hitch. But soon after the XV Corps began to move, heavy rain and high water made the embarkation so hazardous that the water movement had to be abandoned. The remainder of the XV Corps were forced to a mean march in gummy mud, biting wind and slashing rain through southeast South Carolina to rejoin their Right Wing comrades.

On January 13 General Blair's XVII Corps of the Right Wing moved westward out of Beaufort and without a fight the second day. The Confederates had quietly withdrawn across occupied Pocotaligo, twenty-five miles away, on the morning of the Salkahatchie, or Salk, river during the night, on orders from the commander, whose military judgment is said to have been dulled by whiskey. The Corps remained at Pocotaligo until the evening of January 29, then resumed the westward march, reaching the Salkahatchie at River's Bridge February 3. General John A. Logan's depleted XV Corps left Beaufort the 30th and reached Buford Bridge, a few miles to the west, at about the same time.

The Salkahatchie was a rampaging torrent at both points. It had flooded the surrounding countryside, and its bridges, though of doubtful value under the circumstances, had been destroyed by the Confederates. Enemy troops were strongly entrenched on the other side, waiting to fight off any attempt to get across.

Preparing for such a crossing was normally the work of the pioneers, but there were not enough to cope with the present need. So every man fell to. Trees were cut down, jerked out of the icy water and axed into suitable thicknesses for corduroying. Amateurs became adept at laying pontoons, in a hurry and under heavy fire. Some cleared out underbrush obstructing the advance. Others "toted" fence rails several miles, placed them under stalled, bogged wagons and pushed the vehicles into motion. Hours were spent in the ice-caked river. Many were in there all night steadying themselves against trees, their skins blue, almost unconscious from numbness. Alligators and poisonous snakes struck as they passed. How they advanced under such conditions is one of the miracles of nineteenth century war-making. But advance they did.

The Confederate leaders were so certain that such a movement could not possibly be made in February that they dismissed the possibility that Sherman would be foolhardy enough to attempt it. General Joseph E. Johnston, who had been relieved of command of the Confederate forces in Tennessee and Georgia on the eve of the Battle of Atlanta, was awed. He had been assured by his engineers, he said, that "it was absolutely impossible for an army to march across the lower portion of the state in midwinter." He "took it for granted," therefore, that Sherman "would not attempt to advance unless across the upper hill section of the state." Hardee agreed without reservation, calling the Salkahatchie in midwinter "entirely impassable." When Sherman's army continued "marching through them [the Salkahatchie swamps] at the regular pace of ten or twelve miles daily, making corduroy roads for his train nearly every mile of the way," General Cox heard the Southerner say, he "made up his mind that there had been no such army since the days of Julius Caesar."

After leaving the Savannah area on January 20, Slocum's Left Wing was contending, none too successfully, with South Carolina mud and floods. The steady downpour kept the men's clothing saturated with a freezing icy mixture. At times the roads were altogether impassable, so sticky and oozy that all movement had to halt. The entire XIV Corps was bogged down in mud for twenty-four hours, as immovable as if it had been frozen in solid ice. The rains, which old-timers in that part of the country called the most torrential they had ever seen, sent streams over their banks, turning lowlands into rampaging floods and keeping highways under several feet of water. Vicious cold added to the discomfort of wet clothing. Many of the troops, unable to go forward or backward toward Savannah, had to be supplied by boat. Crossing streams over pontoon bridges became more hazardous than battles, the flimsy structures being swept away like planking. When Slocum at last reached Sister's Ferry, the designated crossing-over point, the river was nearly three miles wide, and wild. Trying to cross would mean risking the lives of thousands of his best troops. So there was nothing to do but wait. A message was sent ad-

vising Sherman, then with the Right Wing. Anxious as he was
to get ahead with the campaign, he had no choice but to post-
pone the rendezvous of the wings.

With the Salkahatchie at its rear, the Right Wing began
advancing toward the Charleston-Augusta railroad, intent upon
breaking that important Confederate communications link.
Knowing how important it was to the enemy to keep the railroad open, Howard expected a tough battle at Midway. But it
did not come.

As the XVII was approaching Midway February 7, Howard
saw a forager racing toward him astride a white horse.

"Hurry up, general!" the forager shouted as he pulled his
horse to a halt, forgetting in his excitement that privates do
not advise generals. "We've got the railroad!"

He was right. While Sherman, Howard and the other high-
ranking officers were laying elaborate plans for a big battle,
a handful of foragers, looking, not for glory or military conquest but for plunder, had actually captured an important
railroad. They were now waiting for the combat troops to show
up and take possession.

At the time the XVII Corps was taking Midway, the XV
Corps struck the same railroad at Bamberg, a small town a
few miles to the west. That placed it about equidistant from
Charleston, Augusta and Columbia, in position to advance
rapidly on either place.

Howard's men did a more painstaking job than usual of
destroying the tracks for a distance of fifty miles. It kept the
men busy and high in morale while they waited for Slocum's
Left Wing troops to close the gap between them.

Slocum struck that Augusta-Charleston railroad February
9 at Blackville, west of Bamberg, after enduring the same kind
of body-torturing swamp-crossing that had proved such a trial
to Howard's men. Sherman, giving him and his men no rest,
ordered him to resume the march toward Columbia immediately. Howard's Right Wing received the same orders. Kil-

patrick, however, was ordered to move on Aiken, between Blackville and Augusta, and then swing his cavalrymen around and protect Slocum's Left Wing against Wheeler's cavalry.

There was sound logic behind the orders to Kilpatrick. Reports had reached Sherman that troops from Hood's defeated and disorganized army in Tennessee had already arrived in Augusta. It was important that they be kept there, instead of moving on to Columbia. By diverting Kilpatrick's cavalry toward Augusta, Sherman was sure he could keep them there, seventy-five miles away from the impending battle.

So, on February 11, the day the two wings resumed their northward swing, Kilpatrick and his cavalrymen started marching toward Aiken. Learning of this movement, Wheeler concentrated a large force there. But he kept his troops hidden to enable him to strike a powerful surprise blow.

Here again the cocksure Kilpatrick demonstrated his peculiar recklessness and unawareness of danger. He had been warned that Aiken would be strongly defended. His scouts reported large numbers of Confederate cavalrymen in the area. A woman near the town told him that Wheeler had been at her house a short time before. But these reports appear to have made little impression. He took no precautions against surprise, continuing the jaunty march as though he were on a parade field in Washington. Soon after his advance unit entered the town without encountering enemy troops, Kilpatrick himself rode in. The Confederates kept themselves hidden until the Federals were well inside. Then they began firing, exploded with a terror-inspiring rebel yell and closed in. A tough man-to-man fight erupted. It ended with the Federals scurrying away like chickens, led by the swift-riding Kilpatrick. Some forty or fifty of Wheeler's men pursued them, three or four almost within grabbing distance of Kilpatrick. They were halted short of success by the near-presence of Federal pickets.

It was a victory for Wheeler and his men, although Kilpatrick's escape diminished the glory. Wheeler's plans had miscarried because the premature firing of a few of his troopers warned the enemy of the trap before it was quite ready to be sprung.

Two days after the drive north was resumed at the Charleston-Augusta railroad, the XV Corps reached Holman's Bridge on the South Branch of the Edisto. At about the same time the XVII Corps reached that same stream at Binneker's Bridge.

There both corps halted again. All the bridges had been destroyed. The Confederates were in strong position on the other side. Choosing a spot considerably upriver from where the main force was marking time, the 55th Illinois of the XV Corps waded into the frigid stream and moved ahead toward the north bank on trees and floats. After getting across the river proper, it had to wade a mile through a treacherous swamp, much of it four feet deep, before solid ground was reached. This small force then swept down upon the Confederates and forced them to retreat. No longer harassed by the enemy, the XV Corps' pioneers felled trees to use as makeshift bridges for the main body.

After that slight delay, those two Right Wing corps again started moving. As the XVII Corps neared Orangeburg on the Charleston-Columbia railroad, it found the North Branch of the Edisto, on the approaches to the town, also in flood and the bridge severely damaged. Again the men had to wade waist-deep through icy water, peppered by enemy artillery fire from the other side. But they were not to be stopped. Again the Confederate troops were driven back. The Yankees met little opposition when they entered Orangeburg on the morning of February 12.

The first troops to arrive celebrated their victory—bringing a break in railroad communications between South Carolina's capital and its chief seaport—by firing one of the town's largest stores. This was a cue for other troops, and they spread the flames to other buildings. Their efforts were aided by high winds.

Before Sherman and his high-ranking officers arrived, bummers and foragers had their way, looting stores, invading homes, and raiding smokehouses, cellars and pantries. Some threatened rape; however, so far as is known, no crimes of this kind were actually committed.

"When I reached the city," Captain Conyngham wrote, "it was in flames. Our men say that they found several houses, in which cotton was stored, on fire when they entered it. Be that as it may, the whole town was soon in flames, and by the next morning one heap of ashes.... old women and children, hopeless, helpless, almost frenzied, wandering amidst the desolation."

Rapid movement away from devastated Orangeburg began on the morning of February 14. Thanks in part to the confusion Sherman had created among the Confederate leaders and to the destruction of the only direct railway link between Charleston and Columbia, Confederate forces at Augusta, Charleston and Branchville had been prevented from uniting for a stand. The XVII corps, even with time out for tearing up railroads en route, averaged about fifteen miles a day. On February 15 it was at Harrel's Branch, less than nine miles from Columbia.

The effects of Sherman's efforts began to be felt in distant parts of the Confederacy. Communications especially suffered. Mail that formerly had required a few days to reach its destination now required weeks. The Richmond *Whig* complained on February 13 that the latest Columbia papers to reach it were dated February 7. Its latest Charleston exchanges had been en route since February 4. Those from Augusta had been published February 5, those from Macon February 2, and those from Columbus (Georgia) and Atlanta February 1. No February issues of any Montgomery, Mobile or Selma papers had been received at all. The *Whig* editor satirically called the Confederate postal system "a great institution—worthy of the days of Noah." *The New York Times*, which reprinted the *Whig* editorial, appended its own editorial comment: "In other words, it takes longer to travel to Richmond from Mobile or Mont-

gomery than from New York to London or Paris." The additional railroad destruction carried out since the *Whig* editorial
was published, the *Times* writer went on, had caused even
greater delays: it now required more than a month for mail to
reach Richmond from any place south of the Savannah river.

And as soon as the distractions of bad weather and marching
conditions decreased, the troops were free to resume with intensity the wholesale burning and devastation that had marked
their march through Georgia.

"Poor South Carolina must suffer now," Chaplain John J.
Hucht, of the 58th Indiana, wrote in his journal as that flaming
march got under way. "None of the soldiers are storing up mercy
for her. Her deluded people will reap the full reward of their
folly and crimes." He had heard the rumor that, upon leaving
Savannah, Kilpatrick had filled every cavalryman's saddlebag
with matches. He could not verify its authenticity. But of one
thing he was certain: Kilpatrick's men—and also Slocum's men
and Howard's men—had matches in apparently inexhaustible
supply. And they used them with the profligacy of a millionaire
spending pennies. "Sometimes the world seemed on fire," the
chaplain observed. "We were almost stifled by smoke and
flames."

"As for wholesale burnings, pillage, devastation, committed
in South Carolina," the keen-eyed Conyngham observed,
"magnify all I have said of Georgia some fifty fold, and then
throw in an occasional murder, 'just to make an old, hard-
fisted cuss come to his senses,' and you have a pretty good idea
of the whole thing."

This extra measure of destruction reserved for South Carolina
Conyngham attributed to the "extreme bitterness" among the
men. He had heard "threatening words" from many who had
not been disposed toward destruction in Georgia. Officers had
been predicting since before they left Savannah that the South
Carolina campaign would be "a wicked one."

"Hellhole of Secession"

In Georgia, he remembered, "few houses were burned." In South Carolina "few escaped." The wide area through which the bluecoats passed was converted into "one vast bonfire." The pine forests, the resin factories, public buildings, private dwellings—all were reduced to hot ashes. Noontime of a bright, sunshiny day was made to look "black and gloomy" by the thick smoke rising slowly heavenward. After dark, flaming pine trees became "huge pillars of fire." The raging flames "hissed and screeched" as they ate hungrily into the rich resin and dry branches. The fiery antics as a whole gave the forests "a most fearful appearance."

Conyngham saw looters dash out of a house they had just fired, loaded down with their pilferage. The old woman and her grandchildren who lived there looked on in helpless dismay as the brilliant flames shot upward and dark smoke poured from the windows. Her pleas to get her furniture out before the roof fell in were treated with complete unconcern or scornful amusement.

Conyngham, who had expressed soldierly disapproval of earlier depredations, protested. "Boys," he said, "look at that poor, crazy woman and those helpless children. You all have mothers, some of you children. Think of them, and any of you that are men will follow me."

Several, shamed to action, helped him drag furniture out. And Conyngham rescued the picture of her husband from above the mantel of a flaming room.

At another farmhouse a bummer demanded a jar of sorghum from a woman. He complained that it was too heavy and filled his canteen from the jug. Then, taking a wad of tobacco from his mouth, he pushed it inside the jug. The woman protested against this wanton ruining of food which he could not use. "Oh," he replied coolly, "some feller'll come along and taste that sorghum, and think you've poisoned him. Then he'll burn your damned old house."

At Hardeeville one of the town's most beautiful churches was

141

destroyed plank by plank. First to go was the pulpit, then the benches; then the sides of the building were knocked down. Finally the men removed the columns, sending the roof and the majestic steeple crashing. Somebody shouted derisively to townspeople standing nearby: "There goes your damned old gospel shop!"

The other buildings met a quicker and more dramatic end by fire. Few towns have so completely ceased to exist after visits by hostile armies.

Lexington, some twenty miles west of Columbia, was another South Carolina town that practically disappeared. Kilpatrick's cavalrymen, the first to enter, set fires with raucous glee. A visitor from Columbia, two weeks later, found no town at all. Only a "blackened ruin" marked the site where the friendly, prosperous community had been.

Considerable ingenuity was shown in the hiding of valuables. People gathered up silver, gold, expensive chinaware and family heirlooms and took them to the swamps, to nearby rivers and ponds, to flower gardens, even to cemeteries, to be buried. But the rampaging troops were wise in the ways of concealment. Their visits to community burial grounds and family cemeteries were fruitful.

An officer stayed behind in a beautiful mansion until all the troops had left the neighborhood in order to protect it. That night some of the men sneaked out of camp, walked back three miles, and set it afire. "Their dreams would have been troubled," the officer said in a letter to the Chicago *Tribune,* "had that building remained as a monument to their oversight or neglect."

Before the troops arrived in her community, Mrs. Rachel Pearsall put her choice sides of meat in a big crate, buried it in the garden, and planted vegetables on the site. Her absent husband's gun she wrapped in a buggy robe and hid in a hollow tree. She hid a set of double harness under the planks of a Negro's cabin, and wrapped her husband's watch and the silver in a waxed cloth which she placed in a stone jar and buried in the hen house.

The rest was sacrificed to disloyalty and greed. When the Yankees came the Negro cook opened the smokehouse and invited them to help themselves. She cooked bountiful meals for them. Under her guidance, they raided the pantries and denuded the shelves of preserved vegetables and fruits. They pillaged the house from cellar to attic, jerking open every drawer, invading every closet and exposing the contents of every trunk. What they took a fancy to, they took. What they did not, they left behind in a mess. Why the cook did not reveal her mistress' hiding places, no one understood.

Living in a nearby house was a sick relative of Mrs. Pearsall's. The men pulled her out of bed, threw her on the floor and turned the bed upside down. They threw the beautiful quilts on the sore-infested backs of runty horses and mules for saddles. They pulled the family carriage out of the shed, loaded it with meat, hitched a pair of mules to the rig and drove off. These same soldiers had taken the carriage horses the day before.

William Gilmore Simms, one of South Carolina's outstanding men of letters, wrote about the nervous queues of refugees he saw lining the roadways, with their pitiful accumulations of wagons, household goods, cows, horses and mules. Some, half-naked, "cowered from the winter" under bush tents. Others sought protection beneath the eaves of houses, under railroad sheds and in dilapidated old railway cars. Flaming buildings "lighted the winter and midnight sky with crimson horrors."

He saw grain "strewn to waste under the feet of the cavalry or consigned to the fire which consumed the dwelling." Roads were littered with hogs, mules, furniture and butchered cattle. The bluecoats hacked fine cabinets and pianos to pieces and poured ink, turpentine or oil—"whatever could efface or destroy"—on the wreckage.

Widespread and devastating as this destruction of private property was, its accomplishment retarded the troops' progress but little. Spurred on by the need to get to Columbia ahead of Confederate reinforcements, they kept up the pace set between Atlanta and Savannah.

Sherman's anxiety regarding the reinforcements was relieved by accident. On the night of February 13–14, his aide, Colonel Joseph C. C. Audenried, overhauled a rider and began talking to him. In the darkness, this uniformed stranger, a Confederate soldier privy to important military secrets, did not recognize his companion as an enemy officer. Becoming garrulous, the Southerner discussed freely any matter that was brought up. And the Yankee made it a point to bring up several subjects having to do with Confederate military dispositions. Instead of the expected heavy concentration of troops at Columbia, he told him, the city actually was defended by only a comparatively small force, mainly Hampton's cavalry. Hardee and his troops were in Charleston, braced for an attack there. Another sizable force had been concentrated in Augusta in anticipation of a strike there. Beauregard and Hampton, he said, had heard so many rumors and seen so many Federal troops in so many places that they "seem to have lost their heads."

Columbia was doing its best to prepare for the blow.

As early as January 4, when Sherman was still in Savannah and was regarded as much more likely to move on Charleston or Augusta than Columbia, seventeen-year-old Emma LeConte, daughter of a former professor at South Carolina College, wrote in her journal that she was "constantly thinking" about how Columbia would fare when attacked and captured. That "horrible picture" was "constantly before my mind." Her mother wanted to get her out of the city while there was still time. But "of course I would not leave her." Emma hoped the Yankees' conduct there "will not be as shocking as it has been through the country."

She could find little to keep up her spirits. Her under-clothing was of a material much coarser than the slaves'. Her stockings she had knit herself. Her shoes were of coarse calf-skin. Her two comparatively new calico dresses and the few other dresses she had had before the war hung on her "in a dilapidated condition," a "reminiscence of better days." They would have looked shabby indeed alongside brand new frocks. But there were none with which to compare: everyone else's dresses "are in the same state of decay."

Only two meals a day were the rule in the LeConte household. Just before Professor LeConte left for his day's stint as consultant to the Confederate States Nitre and Mining Bureau, a breakfast consisting of two plates of bread was served. Hours later, at what was optimistically called dinner, there would be a tiny piece of meat, some hominy and some corn bread. Wood was selling at a hundred dollars a load. So fires had to be built sparingly, usually a single one in the living room. But, strained as they were, the LeContes were far better off than many of their neighbors. Calico was selling for sixteen dollars a yard, so not every girl could have two calico dresses. Few families were lucky enough to have milk and butter from their own cows, which was the only way they could be had. And there were many who had not had meat for months. Emma was philosophical: "We have no reason to complain. So many families are so much worse off."

On February 14 Emma wrote: "What a panic the whole town is in! I have not been out of the house myself, but Father says the intensest excitement prevails in the street. The Yankees are reported a few miles off on the other side of the river. . . . It is true some think Sherman will burn the town, but we can hardly believe that. . . . I have been hastily making large pockets to wear under my hoopskirt, for they will hardly search our persons. . . . I do not feel so frightened as I thought I would. Perhaps because I cannot realize they are coming. . . . Alas, what may we not have gone through with by the end of this week! Ah me, I look forward with terror, and yet with a kind of callousness to their approach."

145

With the enemy making long strides toward the city and the air heavy with rumors of disaster, nerves were jumpy. An accidental explosion at the depot emptied the streets and sent people rushing to shelter, thinking that it signaled Sherman's entry into the city. "How," the frightened but courageous Emma wrote in her journal, "is it possible to write amid this excitement and confusion?"

Columbia's streets "are lined with panic-stricken crowds, trying to escape." All around her were "confusion and turmoil." The Government "is rapidly moving all stores—all day the trains have been running, whistles blowing and wagons rattling through the street. All day we have been listening to the booming of cannon—receiving conflicting rumors of the fighting. All day wagons and ambulances have been bringing in the wounded over the muddy streets and through the drizzling rain. . . ."

Soon the city took on the aspects of a besieged garrison. Even the slight luxury of that single fire did not last. The wood gave out, and there was little chance of getting any more. The rural people were afraid to bring it to town, lest Confederate authorities seize their horses. And all the time, as they waited in the cold, Emma could hear the sound of cannon more and more distinctly.

Her father, who had also turned diary keeper, was ordered to send his chemical equipment to Richmond and spent all day February 14 in a vain and disheartening effort to get the packages aboard a train. Early the next morning he was back at the depot. By "much entreaty and considerable threatening," he got the packages loaded and found room in one of the suffocatingly crowded coaches for his assistant, who was to accompany them. Later in the afternoon he returned to the station to assure himself that neither had been shoved off at the last moment.

On his way home in a "gloomy and anxious state of mind," he heard, even more distinctly than he had been hearing it these past few days, the steady booming of Yankee cannon. It was rumored that Hardee was on his way with enough men to beat off the attack. But he wondered if these rumors could be depended upon—there had been so very many of them before, and they had all turned out to be false. His anxiety deepened when he met a long Confederate wagon train heading for the depot he had left a few minutes before. Obviously it was getting out of town. That meant just one thing: there would be no real fight to hold Columbia. It "smote painfully upon my heart." For the first time since the war began, he "utterly lost hope."

When the bitter truth—that no sizable reinforcements would arrive and the city was doomed—reached the people, the chaos rose to a frenzy. Officials were in a dither to get government records and materials, as well as themselves, out of the city. Those who had not taken the danger seriously until now added to the crush at the depot: they took along as many of their possessions as they could get packed, and bid, and even fought, frantically against each other for train space. "Hurry, excitement and confusion," wrote the Richmond *Whig's* Columbia correspondent, "became the order of the day."

He saw trains loaded to absolute capacity pull out of the stations, complete their runs and return for other loads, with no regard for schedules. The straining locomotives "shrieked their signal notes morning, noon and night." Activity around the station was "ceaseless." The depot was as crowded with packages as with human beings. Many people who had lost the fight for train space got away in wagons, drawn by tired animals driven by tired Negroes.

Wednesday, Feburary 15, the enemy was only three miles away. Martial law was declared, but it did little good. The tiny Confederate force dropped back after a skirmish to the city limits and reformed for another stand. Army wagon trains moved through the streets—in the wrong direction—making it plainer than ever that the city was to be given up without a fight. Stores closed, and people huddled in their homes.

There was wholesale looting, much of it the work of Confederate soldiers. The Richmond *Whig* correspondent, writing afterward from Charlotte, told how men supposed to be defending the city became its merciless pillagers:

> ...A party of Wheeler's cavalry, accompanied by their officers, dashed into town, tied their horses, and as systematically as if they had been bred to the business, proceeded to break into the stores along Main-street and rob them of their contents. A detachment of detailed men fired on one party and drove them out. Captain Hamilton, the Provost Marshal, with another officer, drew swords and pistols on another party, and succeeded in clearing several establishments but the valiant raiders still swarmed like locusts, and today, a hundred miles away from Columbia, you may see men smoking the cigars and wearing on their saddles the elegant clothes stolen from the merchants of that city. It is said that two of the "cavalry" drew pistols on Gen. Hampton, who was attempting to protect a store, and threatened his life.

Wheeler's men were feared even more than "the Yankees or old Satan himself." *Frightful* was the word that correspondent used to describe their conduct.

On Thursday morning, February 16, the female members of the LeConte family who had scraped up a little wood somewhere, were huddled in front of a fire in the dining room. Somebody suggested the possibility of the city's being shelled. But Mrs. LeConte replied positively: "They would not do that, for they have not demanded its surrender." Just then a servant rushed in with exciting news: shells were falling all about the city. Hurrying to the front door, they heard one whistling past and also heard it a few seconds later when it exploded with a deafening thunder in a nearby block. Emma recorded her emotions: "... I leaned against the door fairly shivering, partly with cold, but chiefly with nervous excitement. After listening to them awhile, this wore off and I became accustomed to the shells. ..."

Sherman's men were shelling Columbia from the Lexington Heights across the river. They could be seen from the campus gate, "drawn up on the hilltops." Negroes had been grabbing what they could find "after the government stores were thrown open to the people," and "there was a general scramble." But they had been sent back to their homes in fright by the shells. After a while the shelling stopped "for an hour or two." Then it was renewed with such intensity that "we unanimously resolved to adjourn to the basement and abandon the upper rooms." She went up to get some things from her room. Standing in front of her bureau with her arms full, she heard a tremendous noise. A shell passed directly over her head. She "stood breathless, really expecting to see it fall in the room." But it didn't. Seconds later she heard a terrible detonation nearby.

The shells were coming from a battery of twenty-pound Parrot guns commanded by Captain Francis De Gres. Sherman asked him why he was shelling a city which had not been called upon to surrender. De Gres replied that he had seen Confederate cavalry moving about at street intersections. It was his belief, he said, that the enemy had concealed a large infantry force on the opposite side of the river to repel any attempt to cross at that point. This explanation did not completely satisfy the commander. He ordered the general shelling to stop. However, he authorized De Gres to fire shells at certain specified targets, including the depot and the uncompleted State House.

Columbia was now within easy artillery range. It could have been pounded severely by heavy guns from across the Congaree. That would seem the logical place to launch the attack. But the Congaree was much broader than either the Broad or the Saluda, which coalesced a few miles upstream to form it. It was also much swifter, making pontooning difficult; and enemy resistance would logically be stronger there than anywhere else. So Sherman decided, instead, to stage the main attack in the Saluda area, west of the city. This would involve crossing the Saluda, racing across a narrow neck of land and crossing the Broad. He would then have a fairly easy route directly into the heart of the city.

To Howard's XV Corps went the distinction of taking over Columbia. The rest of the army was ordered to bypass the city. Slocum's XIV and XX Corps and Kilpatrick's cavalry were to march northward toward Alston, while Howard's XVII Corps, after crossing the Broad river, was to continue eastward to the Winnsboro road.

Late in the afternoon of February 16 Howard's men were temporarily halted at the Saluda river by a destroyed bridge. They crossed on pontoons and rushed ahead, hoping to get to the Broad in time to prevent the retreating Confederates from burning that bridge too. That river-to-river race was lively and close, and the Confederates won. Having previously prepared the bridge for burning, they sent it up in flames as soon as they were across.

The Federals remained on the west bank that night with the exception of two regiments of the XV Corps which crossed over on rafts and boats. The next morning, the position strengthened by the force already on the Columbia side, General John A. Logan's engineers went to work building a pontoon bridge over the narrowest stretch of the river.

They were still at work when Sherman arrived at mid-morning. Impatient and impetuous as usual, he started pacing in uneven circles, an unlighted cigar pressed between nervous, tight lips. Every now and then he would stop to shoot a question at someone. Occasionally he would sit down and whittle a stick. General Howard sat on a log reading a newspaper as calmly as if he had been a country storekeeper on a slow day.

At about 11 o'clock a messenger arrived with a dispatch from Colonel George A. Stone, commander of the troops who had made the crossing during the night. A group of them had moved in to about two miles from the city, the message said. Mayor T. J. Goodwyn and three members of the city council were coming out in a carriage to surrender it. Colonel Stone asked for instructions.

Howard's reply, dictated by Sherman, ordered Stone to take his troops into the city. The two generals would follow as soon as the bridge was ready.

The messenger also bore a penciled note from the Lady Superioress of a convent in Columbia. She had been a teacher, it said, in a convent in Ohio attended by Sherman's daughter. Would he not see that her institution received special protection?

Sherman handed the note to his brother-in-law, Colonel Charles Ewing. See her in person, he told him, and rest her fears: he had no intention of destroying the convent or any other private property in the city.

Colonel Stone met Mayor Goodwyn and his fellow officials in the white-flagged carriage. He greeted them in friendly fashion. So far as his authority extended, he assured them, their request for protection of private property would be scrupulously respected. Then, without further ceremony, Stone and several officers rode back with the official deputation to the city, where the mayor made a formal surrender.

When the bridge was completed, Sherman walked across, leading his horse. Just behind him were the members of his staff. Then came General Howard, with his staff, followed by General Logan and General C. R. Woods. Behind them marched the entire XV Corps, many of the men chanting prophetically:

> "Hail Columbia, happy land
> If I don't burn you, I'll be damned."

Soon the majestic caravan was on a broad, wind-swept highway flanked on both sides by large cotton and corn fields. A little before noon they entered the outskirts. Leaning from

windows and balconies were handkerchief-waving and flag-flut-
tering women, Unionist sympathizers who had been caught in
Columbia at the outbreak of war and were now able to shout
their sentiments to the world. Jubilant, grinning Negroes
poured from cabins, their masters' houses, workshops and stores.
They were singing, cheering and dancing. This was their day of
jubilation. The air was alive with the rousing music of regimental bands, spotted here and there along the line of march.
"Hail, Columbia," "Yankee Doodle" and other tunes not played
in the old city for years were heard by some with thrilling
pleasure, by most with heartsickness, humiliation and dark
foreboding.

While Columbia stared at this pageant of miltary triumph,
many among the conquerors, as they swung jauntily through
the residential section and into the business district, were plotting their own personal revenge. This capital city of "the hell-
hole of Secession" would know they had been there. And it
would be very glad indeed when they left.

XI

ONE NIGHT IN COLUMBIA

SIDE BY SIDE, Sherman and Howard rode slowly down State Street to Market Square. A roaring crowd of white people and Negroes had gathered there. As soon as the two generals had pulled their horses to a halt, Mayor Goodwyn approached and, shouting to make himself heard above the tumult, told them that the people of the city were greatly disturbed. They were afraid that their property would be destroyed, their personal possessions taken away, their lives endangered. Sherman quickly assured him that there was absolutely no cause for concern. The occupation would be for a short time only, and lives and private property would be fully protected.

Soon after Mayor Goodwyn left, Sherman saw some men pushing through the crowd toward him, and called to some Negroes to open a passage for them. They said they were escaped prisoners of war, all officers, and would like to return to active duty. He told them to report to General Howard. Before leaving, one of the men handed him a piece of paper, asking him to read it at his leisure.

Sherman and Howard watched that milling crowd a while longer, then rode off to look over the city. After stopping briefly at the site of the Charleston depot, which had been burned, they continued along the railroad track until they came to a large foundry. Someone warned them that Confederate cavalry were still in the neighborhood and advised them not to go any farther.

On their way back Sherman noticed what had been obvious to others for some time. The troops were drunk. Both Negroes and white, anxious to curry favor with the conquerors, had greeted them upon their arrival with outstretched arms holding liquor in cups, bottles and pails. Many of the troops had had neither sleep the previous night nor breakfast, and the strong liquor had sent them reeling, stumbling and falling all over town.

Back at Market Square, Sherman again saw Mayor Goodwyn and asked him for a suitable house for his headquarters. The mayor told him he had in mind a beautiful residence belonging to Blanton Duncan, whose plant had been turning out Confederate currency, and who had left the city on the eve of Sherman's arrival. The two men rode out to look it over. Finding it satisfactory, Sherman moved in.

When the Federals arrived, Emma LeConte was in a room near the back of the house. The blare of the bands brought her to the front door on the run. About that time Jane, a family servant, showed up all excited. "Oh, Miss Emma," she shouted, "they've come at last!" The bluecoats were marching down Main Street, she said, and just ahead of them were a crowd of women and children. All were frightened and panicky. Emma hurried upstairs to get a better view, and what she saw made her sick: the United States flag was being run up atop the State House. She closed her eyes.

"Oh, what a horrid sight!" she wrote in her diary. "What a degradation! After four long bitter years of bloodshed and hatred, now to float there at last! That hateful symbol of despotism! I do not think I could possibly describe my feelings. I know I could not look at it." She "left the window and went downstairs to mother." A little later she looked out again. Some guards stationed at the nearby entrance to the college campus were cooking their dinner. "This is the first sight we have had of these fiends except as prisoners. The sight does not stir up very pleasant feelings in our hearts. We cannot look at them with anything but horror and hatred—loathing and disgust."

Several who witnessed that triumphal entry commented on the men's splendid discipline. It was generally agreed that they had been under excellent control—until they stacked their arms and were dismissed. At that very moment, William Gilmore Simms tells us, "whether by tacit permission or direct command, their whole deportment underwent a sudden and rapid change." What followed he called "the saturnalia."

Guards were provided for those asking for them. But they did not insure protection. Some, it is true, were gentlemen. But many were hoodlums, hungry for excitement, loot and revenge. Many a gentle housewife or timid young girl looked up while dressing to find a burly, beetle-eyed bluecoat in her bedroom. But while the women were in constant fear of rape, they were in greater danger of being robbed. Few houses escaped the looters. Those in search of food would invade kitchens and take away whatever happened to be on the stove. The more ruthless pushed their way through room after room, threatening the occupants with pistols and other firearms.

They had a particular liking for watches, which they would demand upon entering a house. They also collected rings, bracelets and other jewelry. A pair of eyes would light up. A dirty, sweaty hand would lash out. There would be a ripping of cloth or a tinkling of gold chain, and a prized family heirloom would be gone forever. Anyone showing resistance risked a beating, if not worse.

Nor were these depredations confined to homes. Watches and other jewelry were seized on the streets by roving bands. It was a common experience to be accosted by a soldier and asked the time of day. When the accommodating civilian pulled out his watch, the hoodlum would jerk it away from him. He might yell back as he hurried away: "This is such a pretty little watch that I'll take it myself."

One of Columbia's leading doctors lost his prized timepiece that way. But his reaction to the loss was different from most. When the soldier started away with it, he called to him: "Stop! The watch will be of no use to you without the key; won't you take that also?" And he did.

Many people, having heard how watches were being stolen, left theirs at home when they went out. Others, when asked the time, would reply that they did not know and keep on walking. One retorted: "You are too late, my good fellow. I was asked that same question by one of your parties at the other corner."

Rivaling watches in popularity was liquor. There was a tremendous amount of it because of imports from Charleston and other places considered more likely than Columbia to be on Sherman's itinerary. It was guzzled in vast quantities. Afraid of being poisoned, many of the troops forced householders and servants to drink some first. One teetotaler was forced to sample several barrels which made him so drunk and sick that he was not able to stand on his feet for a week.

More galling than the seizure of valuables was the brutal destruction and waste. Lonely women and old, crippled men, having no choice, would take the intruders into their bedrooms and attics, drag out trunks and chests and hand over the keys. Scorning the keys, the soldiers would smash them open with axes and gun butts. What they could not take away they would ruin beyond use.

"All the precious things of family such as the heart loves to pore over in quiet hours when alone with memory—the dear miniature, the photograph, the portrait—these were dashed to pieces, crushed under foot," William Gilmore Simms recounted angrily, "and the more the trembler pleaded for the objects so precious, the more violent the rage which destroyed it. Nothing was sacred in their eyes, save the gold and silver which they bore away. . . ."

One Night in Columbia

The claim has often been made that vandalism and theft in Columbia were the work of privates and N.C.O.'s who had got out of control. The officers, reportedly, made every effort to curb them. However, Simms insists:

> ... Nor were these acts of common soldiers. Commissioned officers, of rank as high as colonel, were frequently among the most active in spoilation, and not always the most tender or considerate in the manner or acting of their crimes. ...

The churches and the Ursuline Convent and Academy, for which special protection had been requested, were far from safe from the marauders. The units composed primarily of Irish Catholic troops were for some reason kept outside the city, but there were Catholics among those on duty and at liberty inside. Many attempted to protect Catholic property and institutions. A Catholic saw another soldier drinking liquor from a chalice which he recognized as a sacred vessel. Assuming that it had been stolen from a Catholic church, he wrested it from him and took it to a priest. It turned out that the chalice actually had been taken from an Episcopal church, to which the priest returned it.

A woman awaiting momentarily the birth of her child was roughly carried outside the house by soldiers who laughed at her pleas that such treatment might kill her baby and do serious injury to her. Troopers invaded the bedroom of another woman who had just had a baby and jerked her rings off her fingers and her watch from beneath her pillow. Her theretofore normal recovery took a turn for the worse, and she died a day or two later. A courageous old man stood by his daughters with a knife poised, ready to stab anybody attempting to ravish them. Another father warned his daughter's assailant to keep his distance: the soldier could take anything he wanted, but the father would kill him before he would allow his daughter to be ravished. Still another drew a pistol on two men holding young women in forced embraces.

157

While these outrages were going on all over the city, there were ominous hints of worse to come: "This is nothing. Wait till tonight, and you'll see Hell."

At his headquarters in the Blanton Duncan mansion Sherman went through his pockets, as he did periodically, for memoranda, notes and other bits of paper that might have collected there. He found the sheet handed him at Market Square by the escaped prisoner of war. It contained the words of a song. Their author, Adjutant S. H. M. Byers, of the 5th Iowa Infantry, had entitled it "Sherman's March to the Sea." It had been sung many times, Sherman learned later, in the prisoners' quarters in Columbia, and some of the city's young beauties of the most ardent Confederate sympathies had listened. Its five stanzas and chorus pleased the Yankee general so much that he sent for Adjutant Byers and made him a member of his staff. The spirit and theme are reflected by the chorus:

> *Then sang we a song of our chieftain,*
> *That echoed over river and lea;*
> *And the stars of our banner shone brighter*
> *When Sherman marched down to the sea!*

Later that afternoon Mayor Goodwyn called upon Sherman to tell him about a Columbia woman who said she once had been a good friend of the general's. Her name was not familiar, but when the mayor told him her maiden name, he recalled that some twenty years before, as a lieutenant stationed at Fort Moultrie, he had visited the Poyas family in their home about fifty miles from Charleston. He had gone hunting with young James Poyas. James had several sisters, one of whom, Sherman recalled, had been unusually gifted in doing watercolors, and he had given her a book on the subject. So it was probably she or one of her sisters in Columbia. He asked Mayor Goodwyn to take him to her.

The house, in one of the city's pleasant residential districts, was typical Southern middle class. Of simple frame construction, it was situated on a large lot, its porch some distance above the ground. Ducks and chickens were strutting and squawking in the yard. Sherman was impressed by the "general air of peace and comfort . . . really pleasant to behold at that time of universal desolation." This was in sharp contrast to other property in that part of town, which had been roughed up considerably. He wondered by what magic it had been spared.

The former Miss Poyas greeted the general and the mayor at the door and led them into the parlor. Sherman inquired about her family. Then he asked the question that had been in his mind since coming within sight of the house: why had it and the grounds escaped the treatment received by her neighbors' homes?

She reached for a book and handed it to him. On the flyleaf was the inscription: *To Miss ——— Poyas, with the compliments of W. T. Sherman, First Lieutenant, Third Artillery.*[9]

When the troops arrived, she explained, she thought of the little book. She showed it to one of the men, who seemed to be the leader, and he recognized the handwriting, having seen the Sherman signature several times. Impressed, he ordered the others to do no damage there, and left someone to protect the house until a regular provost guard could be provided. The guard supplied had been most courteous and helpful. Indeed, at that moment he was caring for her baby in another part of the house.

Next, Mayor Goodwyn took Sherman to see a Mrs. Harris Simons, sister-in-law of another person whom the general had known at Charleston. This visit would have been pleasant if Sherman had been more discreet. The Rev. A. Toomer Porter, former Confederate army chaplain and now rector of a large Episcopal church, was also present. Just before the little gathering ended the minister asked Sherman to spare the South Carolina College library. Sherman so promised, but instead of taking leave on that gesture of courtesy and consideration, he remarked that if the library had been put to better use, the people of South Carolina would have known enough history not to secede and plunge the nation into war.

In the early evening, after the busiest and most trying day Mayor Goodwyn had ever known, Sherman noticed that he was thoroughly worn out. He told him to go home and get some rest, assured that "not a finger's breadth" of the city would be harmed: "You may lie down to sleep, satisfied that your town shall be as safe in my hands as if wholly in your own." It was his duty as military commander, he said, to destroy government property and certain public buildings. But that would be done later—the next day, if the weather was favorable, some other day, if not.

Sherman was thoroughly exhausted and went to bed soon after the mayor left. Before he had time to fall asleep he noticed flashes of light playing gayly on the walls of the room. Calling a member of his headquarters staff, he ordered him to investigate. The aide, not greatly concerned, told him a house near Market Square was on fire. Sherman sent him to find out more. The soldier reported that a block of buildings was aflame and the flames were spreading. He said, however, General Charles R. Woods had taken personal charge of the fire-fighting. His troops were doing everything they could to put it out or, failing in that, to keep it confined within a small area. It was obvious after a while, though, that a major conflagration was under way, fanned by a strong wind. From Sherman's headquarters "the whole heavens became lurid."

The rapidly rolling flames soon threatened the Simons home. Sherman invited the ladies to spend the night in the Blanton Duncan residence, and his headquarters wagon was hitched up to move their possessions. By this time the air was alive with flying sparks, as one old wooden building after another caught. In a short time the very heart of the city was burned out.

GENERAL JOSEPH JOHNSTON

GENERAL WILLIAM T. SHERMAN

THE SIEGE OF ATLANTA—CONFEDERATE ATTACK ON GENERAL LOGAN'S
CORPS, JULY 28, 1861

EXODUS OF CONFEDERATES FROM ATLANTA

SHERMAN'S FORAGERS ON A GEORGIA PLANTATION

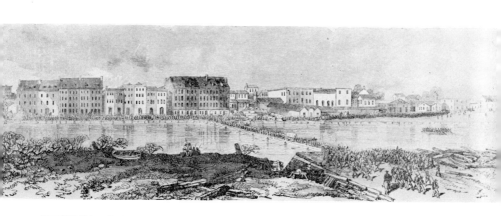

PONTOON BRIDGE ON SAVANNAH RIVER, OVER WHICH THE CONFEDERATES
CROSSED ON THE EVACUATION OF SAVANNAH, DECEMBER 21, 1861

SHERMAN'S ARMY ENTERING SAVANNAH

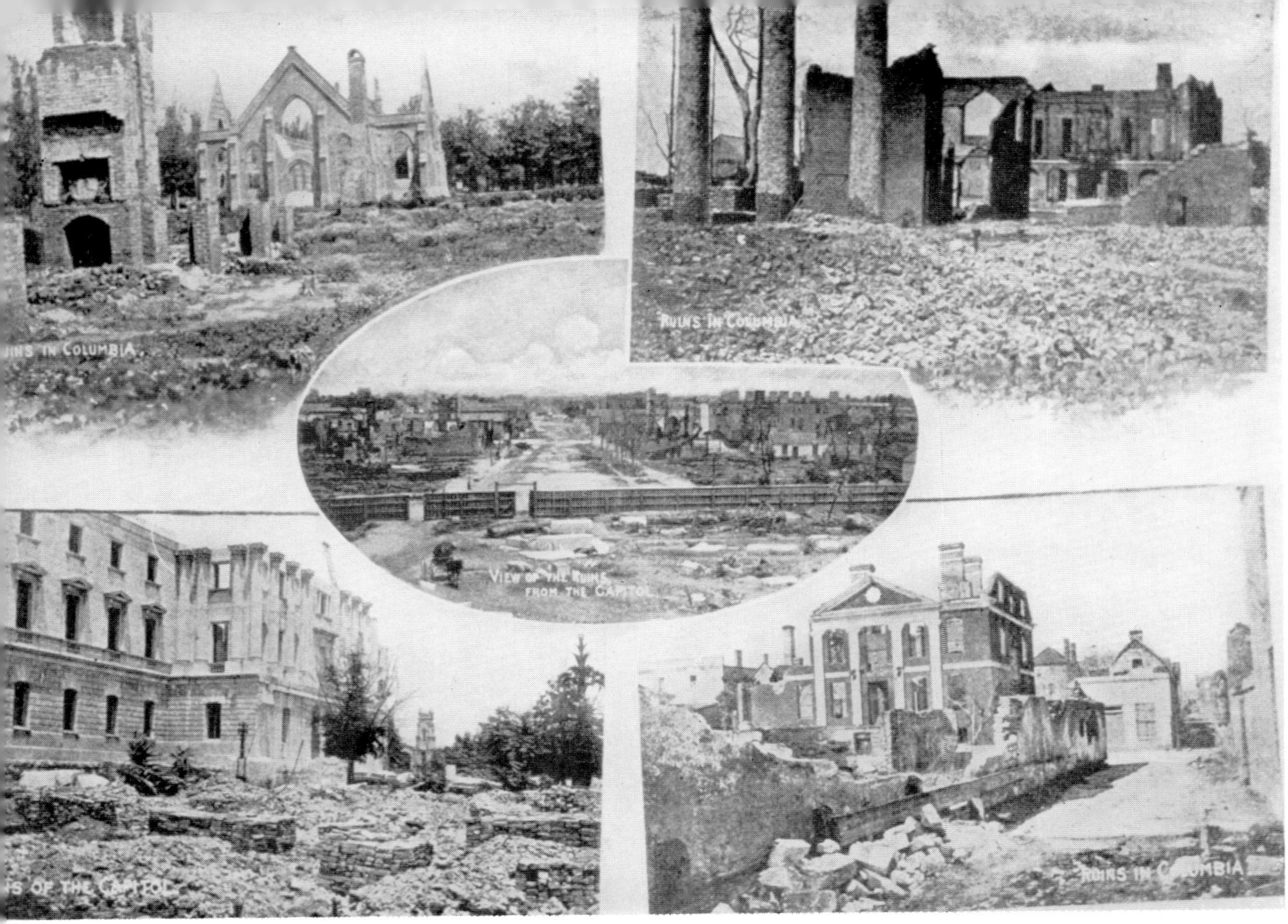

CITY OF
COLUMBIA, S. C.

THE BATTLE AT BLACK RIVER, NEAR AVERYSBOROUGH, NORTH CAROLINA,
MARCH 16, 1865 (SKETCHED BY W. WAUD)

BATTLE OF BENTONSVILLE, NORTH CAROLINA, MARCH 20—FIFTEENTH CORPS ENGAGED ON THE RIGHT.—[SKETCHED BY W. WAUD.]

BATTLE OF BENTONVILLE, NORTH CAROLINA, MARCH 20: FIFTEENTH CORPS
ENGAGED ON THE RIGHT (SKETCHED BY W. WAUD)

SCENE OF THE NEGOTIATIONS BETWEEN GENERALS SHERMAN AND JOHNSTON, APRIL 18, 1865: JAMES BENNETT'S HOUSE, WHERE THE INTERVIEW WAS HELD; GENERAL KILPATRICK, WITH CONFEDERATE GENERAL HAMPTON AND STAFF, DISCUSSING THE CAMPAIGN

One Night in Columbia

The fire on Market Square had been only one of fifteen or twenty that had appeared simultaneously throughout the city. The fire department and the few soldiers making a real effort to keep it under control fought in vain. Pitted against them were the onsweeping waves of flame driven by a wind of near-hurricane force and constantly fed by roving mobs of drunken, faggot-tossing Negroes, former prisoners of war and soldiers. Simms saw how terribly efficient they were:

> ... The men engaged in this were well prepared with the appliances essential to their work. They did not need the torch. They carried with them, from house to house, pots and vessels containing combustible liquids, composed probably of phosphorous and other similar agents, turpentine, etc.; and with balls of fire saturated in this liquid, with which they also overspread floors and walls, they conveyed the flames with wonderful rapidity from dwelling to dwelling. Each had his ready box of Lucifer matches, and with a scrape upon the walls, the flames began to rage. Where houses were closely contiguous, a brand from one was the means of conveying destruction to the other.

The men of Colonel Stone's brigade were so drunk by 8 o'clock that Howard ordered them relieved. Those able to stand were marched out of the city, and Colonel W. B. Wood's brigade took over. Rounding up the drunks, the fire-spreaders and the looters proved more of a task than he was capable of. But he did the best he could. His men arrested three hundred and seventy, killed two and wounded thirty. His task was greatly magnified by his own men's fondness for liquor. Many became as drunk as those they had relieved, and there were not enough sober officers to keep them under control.

Conyngham, who had seen many a fire and a great deal of suffering since leaving Atlanta, wrote:

> I trust I shall never witness such a scene again—drunken soldiers, rushing from house to house, emptying them of their valuables, and then firing them; negroes carrying off piles of

booty, and grinning at the good chance, and exulting, like so many demons; officers and men revelling in the wines and liquors, until the burning houses buried them in their drunken orgies.

I was fired at for trying to save an unfortunate man from being murdered.

The frequent shots on every side told that some victim had fallen. Shrieks, groans, and cries of distress resounded from every side. Men, women, and children, some half naked, as they rushed from their beds, were running frantically about, seeking their friends, or trying to escape from the fated town. A troop of cavalry, I think the 29th Missouri, were left to patrol the street; but I did not once see them interfering with the groups that rushed about to fire and pillage the houses.

The wind kept blowing at a terrific rate. Flakes of loose burning cotton, ignited in burning buildings, would be picked up and dropped on old, wooden roofs. Then the flaming shingles and boards would also be caught up and swept on to other buildings, starting fresh fires. Those driven from their homes drew little sympathy and almost no help from the war-hardened troops. But a few, like Sergeant Theodore Upson, were deeply touched:

> ... We soon began to help the women and children. Poor souls! They did not know what to do. All we could do was to hustle them out, and, if they had any valuables, help them get them to a safe place. Many of them were in their night clothes. They had no time to get anything else. Where we could get blankets we gave them without asking to whom they belonged. Some of the women we had to carry as best we could, and the little children too. I do not doubt, with all our help, some were burned in their houses. We could hardly get some of them to leave; in fact had to carry some of them out. Even the men— what few there were of them—seemed to lose their nerve and some of them were abject cowards and of course some of them were very old and like children ...

One Night in Columbia

Simms saw enough that night to haunt his memory forever:

> Throughout the whole of this terrible scene the soldiers con-
> tinued their search after spoil. The houses were severally and
> soon gutted of their contents. Hundreds of iron safes, warranted
> "impenetrable to fire and the burglar," it was soon satisfactorily
> demonstrated, were not "Yankee proof." They were split open
> and robbed, yielding, in some cases, very largely of Confederate
> money and bonds, if not of gold and silver. Jewelry and plate
> in abundance was found. Men could be seen staggering off with
> huge waiters, vases, candelabra, to say nothing of cups, goblets,
> and smaller vessels, all of solid silver. Clothes and shoes, when
> new, were appropriated—the rest left to burn. Liquors were
> drank with such avidity as to astonish the veteran Bacchanals
> of Columbia, nor did the parties thus distinguishing themselves
> hesitate about the vintage... In one vault on Main Street,
> seventeen casks of wine were stored away, which, an eye-witness
> tells us, barely sufficed, once broken into, for the draughts of a
> single hour—such were the appetites at work and the numbers
> in possession of them. Rye, corn, claret, Madeira, all found their
> way into the same channels, and we are not to wonder, when
> told that no less than one hundred and fifty of the drunken
> creatures perished miserably among the flames kindled by their
> own comrades, and from which they were unable to escape...
> Sherman's officers are reported to have said that they lost more
> men in the sacking and burning of the city (including certain
> explosions) than in all their fights while approaching it....

In a number of places "parlors, articles of crockery, and even
beds were used by the soldiers as if they were water closets."
At one house someone used pieces of china for that purpose,
then "put them on the bed, fired at and smashed them to pieces,
emptying the filthy contents over the bedding."

Fortunately, Columbia was a city of wide streets. Many of
the refugees were able to walk to the parks between rows of
burning buildings without coming too close to the flames. Once
there, they would drop on the cool grass. Some carried mat-

tresses and feather beds, which were a great comfort when they found places to put them.

Simms told about women's being "hustled from their chambers—their ornaments plucked from their persons, their bundles from their hands." Anguished mothers begged piteously for the scanty clothing they had saved for their children, only to see it torn from their grasp and thrown into the flames. A young girl clinging desperately to her only dress "had it rent in fibres in her grasp." Mobsters set upon old people carrying trunks between them. They burst open the trunks and exposed their contents, appropriating choice articles and throwing the others into the fire. Simms watched the owner of a burning house, "standing woe-begone, aghast, gazing at his tumbling dwelling." There was "a dumb agony" on his face that was "inexpressibly touching." He heard home owners shouting "wild blasphemies assailing the justice of Heaven." Still others were "invoking, with lifted and clenched hands, the fiery wrath of the avenger." And in this flaming world of misery, frustration and blasphemy, "the soldiers plundered and drank, the fiery work raged, and the moon sailed over all with as serene an aspect as when she first smiled upon the ark resting against the slopes of Ararat."

Relying upon Sherman's promise that no religious buildings would be destroyed, the Lady Superioress of the Ursuline Convent and Academy kept her two hundred charges in the convent until it became apparent that the building was doomed. Then she told the frightened children to go to their rooms, put on their warmest clothing, roll up their sheets and blankets and collect as much of their personal property as they could carry. Calmly and unhurriedly, she and the nuns led them out of the building. Marching slowly in single file, they walked through an inferno of cascading roofs and walls and flaming wood that burned ugly holes in the nuns' robes to St. Peter's Catholic Church. The bedding was rolled out on the floor, and they lay down. A few volunteers, including two Irish Catholic officers, watched over them.

Some soldiers set fire to the church, but the volunteers put it out. Later there were other fires, presumably set by the same men. They too were extinguished before they could do much damage. But the Lady Superioress decided it would be dangerous to remain, and the sleepy girls were again lined up and marched out into the cold night air. That is where they spent the rest of the night—in the churchyard shivering from the cold and from fright, surrounded by tombstones.

Match-wielders were frustrated in two attempts to fire the Washington Street Methodist Church. Both times the pastor, who lived next door, put out the fire before it had gained any headway. But their third attempt was successful. They set the parsonage afire, and while the minister was carrying his child from the burning building, they set fire to the church itself. By the time the child was out of danger the benign old building was a holocaust. A soldier jerked off the blanket which the father had placed around the youngster and threw it into the flames. "Damn you!" he shouted, "if you say a word, I'll throw the child after it."

Emma LeConte recorded that by 4 o'clock in the morning the old State House was nearly gone. The college library opposite the LeConte home "seemed framed by gushing flames and smoke," while "through the window flamed the liquid fire." Several buildings on the South Carolina College campus serving as a hospital for the sick and wounded of both armies had now leapt into flames. Nurses, doctors and others fought the fire in any way they could. Emma was close enough to see the semi-bedridden crawl and stumble out. She thought of the patients who, unable to leave their beds, "waited to be burned to death." The campus was "crowded with homeless women and children, a few wrapped in blankets and many shivering in the night air." These wretched people and, nearby, "the drunken, fiendish soldiery in their dark uniforms, infuriated, cursing, screaming, exulting in their work," gave her a more realistic preview of Hell "than I ever expect to see again."

A few hours before dawn of Saturday, February 18, the wind shifted and the fires eventually died down. Howard called the city "a blackened surface." It contained little but naked chimneys and a few houses that, "as if by a miracle," had been spared.

Simms, who loved Columbia passionately, lamented that never in all the tragic history of war and devastation "was ruin more complete." When the sun appeared it wore "a wan countenance, peering dimly through the dense vapors which seemed wholly to overspread the firmament." Fanning out in all directions was a wide, heart-sickening spectacle of human misery. Wherever he looked there were "smoking masses of blackened walls" and "towers of grim ghastly chimneys." In between were "desolate groups, reclining on mattress or bed, or earth."

Sherman reported that that sun rose "bright and clear" over a "ruined city." About half its total area, he estimated, had been laid waste. Other estimates differed considerably. A few days after the fire Mayor Goodwyn told the people of Augusta, in an appeal for help, that two thirds of the city "is in ashes."

Conyngham wrote:

> There the city lay wrapped in her own shroud, the tall chimneys and blackened trunks of trees looking like so many sepulchral monuments, and the woe-striken people, that listlessly wandered about the street, its pallid mourners.
>
> Old and young moved about seemingly without a purpose. Some mournfully contemplated the piles of rubbish, the only remains of their late happy homesteads.
>
> Old men, women and children were grouped together. Some had piles of bedding and furniture which they had saved from the wreck; others who were wealthy the night previous, had not now a loaf of bread to break their fast.
>
> Children were crying with fright and hunger; mothers were weeping; strong men, who could not help either them or them-

selves, sat bowed down, with their heads buried between their hands.

Major Nichols forecast its future:

> Columbia will have bitter cause to remember the visit of Sherman's army. Even if peace and prosperity soon return to the land, not in this generation nor the next—no, not for a century—can this city or the state recover from the deadly blow which has taken its life....

Looters and vandals resumed their orgy with the new day. Operating mainly in the sections that had escaped total destruction, they descended like frenzied birds of prey upon frightened, unprotected old women and men, demanding jewelry, money and other valuables. Slipping their loot into cavernous pockets they moved on to other conquests. Some found articles of value in the still-warm ashes of burned buildings. Boastful displays of their grabbings were accompanied by recitals of personal adventures in fire-setting.

Vandals became interested in the majestic new State House, or Capitol, which had been left unfinished after the outbreak of war. They smashed the Corinthian capitals, topping stately columns on the four sides of the building, and sent them crashing to the ground. The bases upon which the columns rested were smashed to rubble. Using workmen's ladders, they climbed up to batter the ornamental figures and scrolls above the entrances. The bronze statue of George Washington, an excellent copy of the Houdon original in the rotunda of the Virgina State Capitol, they scarred with maliciously hurled brickbats. Busts of John C. Calhoun, Andrew Jackson and the Genius of Liberty were completely ruined. And as a parting gesture names, regiments and obscenities were scribbled on the walls.

As thorough as the great fire had been, there were some buildings still standing which, according to the Sherman code, should not be left behind when his troops moved on. For the better part of two days Howard's men toiled away at completing that task. They damaged beyond repair the smokestacks of six factories, demolished ten tons of machinery belonging to the Confederate Army, and tore up railroad tracks leading out of the city in several directions. Two thousand bales of cotton, nineteen locomotives, and twenty box cars; all railroad stations, two large freight sheds, about five tons of railroad machinery, six hundred and fifty cart wheels and twenty-five powder mills— they immobilized or completely destroyed.

The destruction of the State Arsenal was a dangerous operation. To reduce the risk, Sherman ordered the explosives to be loaded onto wagons, carried to the Saluda river and dumped. A workman dropped a box he was carrying, and the flame resulting from the explosion ran along a trail of powder, which had sifted from an imperfectly sealed package, to the wagons. The second blast killed twenty men and wounded a number of others.

On Sunday, a delegation headed by Mayor Goodwyn asked Sherman for food to hold off starvation. He sent them to Howard who issued them five hundred head of inferior cattle, army rations, medicine (in a quantity far from sufficient to meet the need), salt, wire and miscellaneous necessities. He also provided a hundred muskets, with ammunition, to be used in preserving order after the army left.

In partial restitution for the burning of the Ursuline Convent and Academy, Sherman turned over to the Lady Superioress the luxurious mansion of Confederate General John S. Preston, Wade Hampton's brother-in-law. When she and her students, accompanied by Colonel Ewing, arrived to take possession on the eve of the troops' departure, they found they had come just in time. General Logan, its current occupant, was about to give the order for its destruction. Husky troopers were already rolling barrels of highly inflammable pitch into the cellar. Logan burst into profanity when Ewing handed him his orders, but he had the barrels removed, and the nuns and children moved in. They found the troopers had mutilated the fine paintings and other works of art; portraits had acquired penciled mustaches. Nude statues had been covered over.

The demolition work was completed February 19. The next day the march was resumed in the direction of Winnsboro. The crowds lining the streets booed, spat at and cursed the blue columns—but it was Sherman whom they held responsible.[10]

XII

WINNSBORO, CHERAW AND UNWELCOME NEWS

ON THE FORTY-TWO-MILE march from Columbia to Winnsboro, the troops, assisted by their comrades who had bypassed the city, resumed their less spectacular work of tearing up railroads; the XV Corps on the Charleston Railway, the XVII Corps on the Charlotte, and Slocum's Left Wing and Kilpatrick's cavalry on the branch line to Abbeville.

To isolate Columbia from the rest of the Confederacy was only one of Sherman's several aims in concentrating north of the city. Others were to hamstring the concentration of Confederate forces in northern South Carolina, and to mislead the enemy into thinking he was on his way to Charlotte.

North of Columbia the land became rolling, and the streams were few and easily crossed. The prosperous farms yielded an abundance to the forage wagons. Night marching, normally risky because of the danger of surprise, was safe by the light of the flaming pine woods. And the resultant smoke effectively screened the rear.

As the Left Wing, led by General John W. Geary's XX Corps division, approached Winnsboro, Geary saw ahead the familiar coils of black smoke pointing to the sky. He knew it meant foragers had already entered the town and started firing buildings. He ordered the advance regiments to move ahead on the double. They attacked the flames vigorously, and so did other units as soon as they arrived. Every officer, from General Slocum down to the youngest second lieutenant, and many enlisted men fought them actively and personally, singeing their whiskers and their uniforms. Damage estimates varied widely, but a total of thirty buildings is probably accurate.

While Christ Episcopal Church flamed and crashed, soldiers carried the organ outside and played popular tunes on it. In a nearby churchyard, vandals are said to have dug up a recently buried body. The casket was knocked open with an axe and stood on end so that the dead person might face the burning structure.

The young son of the rector, Rev. M. W. Lord, said troops arrived loaded down with loot collected in the nearby country-side. They tied their horses to convenient fences and hitching posts and started looting the town and destroying property. They "played snowball along the firelit streets with precious flour." They "made bonfires of hams and sides of bacon." They "set boxes and barrels of crackers afloat on streams of molasses and vinegar." And they "fed horses from hats full of sugar." The food they destroyed would have kept the whole town supplied a year or longer.

Other Southerners were looking ahead apprehensively to similar experiences. Charlotte, almost directly north, and pre-sumably Sherman's next objective, was under martial law. The Charlotte *Daily Bulletin* warned of the severe penalties awaiting "the unfortunate wight" caught on the street after the ringing of the 9 o'clock curfew. In spite of the imminence of Sherman's expected arrival, the city was choked with refugees from other cities and towns, just as Columbia had been. Officials appealed to them to stay away from Charlotte. It would be impossible for them to find shelter and food, and they would make things much harder for the residents.

But when the columns marched out of Winnsboro their direction veered eastward and northeastward toward Cheraw. This did not necessarily mean that an attack on Charlotte was not coming. A sharp swing to the left could be made at any time, and it would place Charlotte in as much danger as when the troops left Columbia. Sherman kept reminding them of this by having Kilpatrick make dramatic feints in that direction. But there was comfort in the knowledge that the immediate danger had apparently passed.

Marching was not easy. Rains beat the roads, pocking the route with gullies, and turned small streams into big ones and big ones into major engineering problems. Corduroying had to be resorted to time and again in order to make any headway at all. At one crossing Hazen was obliged to corduroy more than three hundred yards to get to and leave the two-hundred-yard bridge his engineers had built. Pontooning at a more favorable site was made impossible by tree stumps and snags.

The rains had swollen the Wateree far outside its banks, and the heavily loaded wagons sank down and down into the oozy morass until it seemed they would be completely swallowed. After crossing the river proper they had to be pulled up a steep, slippery incline. Any wagon that sank through the mud into a hole remained bogged for hours. For, as Nichols found out, "no effort of man or beast can extricate it from the tenacious grip of the mud." The XX Corps spent two days getting over.

The XIV Corps lost three days at the Wateree when its pontoon boats were washed downstream by flood waters. Since it was necessary to keep the four corps fairly close together for mutual protection, the delay affected the whole army. To avoid further loss of time, Sherman ordered Slocum to get his huge machine moving again regardless. The troops still stranded west of the river were to destroy their wagons, shoot their horses and mules, spike their guns and cross on rafts. That night Slocum rode through twenty miles of enemy country, accompanied by only two orderlies, to deliver Sherman's orders to General Jeff Davis, the XIV Corps' commander. Distressed at the thought of leaving so much valuable material behind, Davis begged Slocum for delay in carrying out the order. The two men, aided by some high-ranking comrades, went to work and, in one way and another, succeeded in getting the wagons, guns and animals across. The enterprise's success was due primarily to Brigadier General George F. Buell. He urged upon his unenthusiastic comrades his plan to anchor improvised pontoons to the forks of trees and keep them manageable by loading them down with heavy rocks.

The Right Wing, moving to the east of the Left Wing, had fewer problems with terrain; however, its XVII Corps was under constant threat from Wade Hampton's cavalrymen. Although the Confederates did not actually attack the main force, they did capture some of Logan's XV Corps foragers, and some wagons. Logan personally led a counterattack and drove them off. He ordered two Confederate prisoners executed in retaliation for the death of the two Federal foragers who, he claimed, had been shot after they were captured. He released a third prisoner after telling him to spread the word among his fellow soldiers that he intended to shoot five Confederate prisoners for every Federal prisoner killed.

At Liberty Hall, just east of the Wateree, General Logan split his XV Corps into two units. One continued toward Cheraw. The other, considerably smaller, wheeled sharply for a raid on Camden. Easily overcoming the weak resistance offered by a small detachment of Confederate cavalry, these raiders, under Colonel R. N. Adams, brigade commander of the XV Corps' Fourth Division, entered the town in the early afternoon of February 24. Camden was a pleasant community on the Wateree about thirty-five miles east of Columbia and a hundred and forty from Charleston. The raiders destroyed government buildings, the freight and passenger depots of the South Carolina Railroad, some two thousand bales of cotton and vast quantities of meat, flour, soap, rice, wheat and corn. They also freed fourteen Federal prisoners.

The mayor and city council had planned to surrender the town in an elaborate ceremony, and had prepared an eloquent speech. But the bluecoats were too occupied with demolition to listen.

The solemn bonds of Freemasonry, which had not deterred Masons in the army from burning and looting the homes of Masons in Columbia, or from allowing the beautiful Masonic Temple to be destroyed, proved stronger near Camden. When a party of raiders from the XV Corps approached a grist mill owned by W. C. S. Ellerbe, the old Negro running the mill in the absence on war service of the owner decided to appeal to the mystic brotherhood to save his master's property. Hobbling into the house, he returned in a few minutes with Mr. Ellerbe's Masonic apron. He stationed himself at the door of the ramshackle old building and waved it with all the energy and fervor of a frightened woman flagging down a train. The officer in charge of the troops was a Mason and considered his obligation to help a brother Mason, even an enemy brother Mason, to be stronger than his obligation to destroy property. He ordered his men to bypass the mill. It still stands, probably the oldest water mill in South Carolina.

From time to time, Sherman's soldiers would find dead bodies wearing uniforms like theirs. Pinned to them were sheets of paper proclaiming "Death to all foragers." Sherman, ever jealous of the safety of every one of his men, became furious. He wrote Howard:

> I have ordered Kilpatrick to select of his prisoners, man for man, shoot them, and leave them by the roadside labeled, so that our enemy will see for every man he executes he takes the life of one of his own. . . . If any of your foragers are murdered, take life for life, leaving a record of each case.

Sherman took the matter up directly with Wade Hampton. In a letter dated February 24, he told the Confederate cavalry leader about some of the incidents reported to him and about ordering the execution of a Confederate prisoner for every executed Federal forager. He had, he said, about a thousand Confederates "and can stand it as long as you." However: "I hardly think these murders are continued with your knowledge; and would suggest that you give notice to the people at large that every life taken by them simply results in the death of one of your Confederates."

> Of course you cannot question my right to forage on the country. It is a war right as old as history. The manner of exercising it varies with circumstances, and if the civil authorities will supply my requisition, I will forbid all foraging. But I find no civil authorities who can respond to calls for forage or provisions, and therefore must collect directly of the people. I have no doubt this is the occasion of much misbehavior on the part of our men, but I cannot permit an enemy to judge or punish with wholesale murder.
>
> Personally, I regret the bitter feelings engendered by this war, but they were to be expected, and I simply allege that those who struck the first blow and made war inevitable, ought not in fairness to reproach us for the natural consequences. I merely assert our war right to forage, and my resolve to protect any forager to the extent of life for life.

The letter reached Hampton three days later on February 27. He replied immediately.

Sherman's execution of Confederate prisoners in retaliation for the killing of Federal foragers, he wrote, was an act of murder. For every Confederate executed "I shall have executed at least two of yours." [11] Moreover, he would give "in all cases, preference to any officers who may be in my hands."

The Confederate commander declared that no orders of his "authorize the killing of prisoners after capture"; moreover, "I do not believe that my men killed any of yours except under circumstances in which it was perfectly legitimate and proper they should kill them."

There was a difference, he contended, between foragers engaged in their normal tasks of collecting food and supplies for the army and rascals "whom you designate as foragers." Soldiers who "fire the dwellings of those whom they have robbed" were not foragers but outlaws. The "inhuman system" Sherman was defending "is justly execrated by every civilized nation." To combat it, Hampton had directed his men "to shoot down all your own who are caught burning houses." That order "shall remain in force as long as you disgrace the profession of arms by allowing your men to destroy private dwellings." Referring to Sherman's contention that "you cannot question my right to forage on the country," the South Carolinian told his enemy he did not question it at all. But:

> ... there is a right even older than this, and one more inalienble—the right that every man has to defend his home, and to protect those that are dependent upon him. And from my heart I wish that every old man and boy in my country who can fire a gun, would shoot down, as he would a wild beast, the men who are desolating their land, burning their houses and insulting their women.
>
> You are particular in defining and claiming "war rights." May I ask if you enumerate among them the right to fire upon a defenseless city without notice; to burn the city to the ground after it has been surrendered by the authorities, who claimed, though in vain, the protection which is always accorded in civilized warfare to non-combatants; to fire the dwelling houses of citizens, after robbing them, and to perpetrate even darker crimes than these—crimes too black to be mentioned?

Now boldly on the offensive, Hampton struck out again and again at his accuser:

> You have permitted, if you have not ordered, the commission of these offenses against humanity and the rules of war. You fired into the city of Columbia without a word of warning. After its surrender by the Mayor, who demanded protection of private property, you laid the whole city in ashes, leaving among

its ruins thousands of old men and helpless women, who are likely to perish of starvation and exposure. Your line of march can be traced by the lurid light of burning houses, and in more than one household there is an agony far more bitter than that of death.

The Indian scalped his victims, regardless of sex or age, but with all his barbarity, he always respected the persons of his female captives. Your soldiers, more savage than the Indians, insult those whose natural protectors are absent.

The Hampton missive ended with the pert request that Sherman keep him informed regarding the execution of Confederate prisoners. He needed this information, he said, "in order that I may know what action to take in the matter." In the meantime, "I shall hold fifty-six of your men as hostages for those whom you have ordered executed."

In calling Sherman's attention to sex offenses against Southern women, Hampton may have been thinking of an incident related by Confederate Brigadier General James Chestnut, Jr.

The second day after leaving Columbia, General Chestnut arrived at a place which he identified only as belonging to "the M's." Mr. "M" was not at home. His very handsome daughter was sitting beside her mother, and General Chestnut wondered about her safety, with both Federal and Confederate armies nearby. But, when he suggested that she be sent away, she replied quickly that she wished to stay with her mother.

A few hours later a party of Joe Wheeler's cavalrymen arrived at General Chestnut's campsite with tragic news. Mrs. "M" had been tied, held or otherwise restrained. Then they had ravished the daughter. The seven Federals had ridden off just a short time before Wheeler's men arrived, leaving the older woman "raving." The Confederates had followed and overtaken them, cut their throats and written on their breasts: "These are the seven!"

When asked about the daughter, General Chestnut replied that she was dead.

The Right Wing, progressing at a more comfortable pace than the Left, lost its luck when it struck Lynch's Creek, several miles from Cheraw. Crossing the stream itself was no serious problem. The engineers were able to span it with a timbered bridge as they had spanned many another since leaving Atlanta. But it was deep in the swampy country. The banks were imaginary lines. Stretching for miles on either side were expanses of mud that, to the exploring engineers, seemed bottomless. The pioneers and axmen resorted to cutting down large trees, anchoring them to long timbers placed at right angles to them and piling them one atop the other. These layers kept rising until the top of the pile protruded above the surface. This type of operation was tedious and long; the enemy was winning priceless time for the strengthening of defenses and collection of scattered forces.

The mud was encountered everywhere in that part of South Carolina. Sherman's only hope of rapidly crossing the Great Pee Dee at Cheraw and hastening on toward eastern North Carolina was to seize the bridge there. Its capture intact became a major objective.

As the XX Corps approached Chesterfield, twelve miles from Cheraw, on Friday, March 2, its progress was challenged by Butler's cavalry. The opposition did not amount to much, and the march into the town continued. There the Yankees found about a score of dwellings, a typical county seat brick courthouse, a few stores and a hotel. Soon after his arrival Sherman received a dispatch from Howard telling him the XVII Corps had arrived within a very short distance of Cheraw. He expected to enter the town the next day. The XV Corps was also near.

To nobody's surprise—for Cheraw was the logical place for the Confederates to make a strong stand—Howard found the approaches to that town strongly defended. Working against time,

General Hardee had constructed formidable defenses, which might have been effective if he had had sufficiently strong forces to man them. Just west of Thompson's Creek, near the town's west perimeter, the oncoming Yankees clashed briefly with Confederate cavalry. The latter, lacking infantry support, were forced to retreat across the bridge, which had been previously soaked in tar, oil and other combustibles. It burst into flames when ignited by the Confederates as soon as they were across. But the rapid approach of a division of the XV Corps and quick work in dousing the flames prevented it from being completely destroyed, and they marched across without any trouble, delayed slightly but not stopped.

The Confederates made another stand between the creek and the town. They had no hope of preventing the Federals from entering Cheraw but wanted to allow their comrades time to saturate the bridge over the Great Pee Dee with turpentine. Then they retreated eastward across the river and fired the bridge. When the Yankees got there, the structure was too badly burned to be of any use.

That quick withdrawal across the river left the town wide open, and the Right Wing's advance units marched in. A strong force consisting of mounted infantry and foragers continued on to Society Hill, fourteen miles away, and drove the enemy out. A train, the depot and a mile of track were destroyed.

A similar expedition to Florence, forty miles from Cheraw, was less successful. Mounted infantry sent there to destroy depots, railway trestles, bridges and other strategically important structures encountered stronger opposition than expected. The Confederate cavalry made such a stubborn stand in fact that the bluecoats had to return to Cheraw with their objective unattained. The only accomplishment they could report was the destruction of sections of the branch railroad running between Florence and Cheraw. It had served Hardee handsomely a few days before in getting his troops and supplies from Charleston to Cheraw.

After Sherman got the news that Howard was near Cheraw he ordered Slocum and Kilpatrick to take the Left Wing and cavalry to Sneedsboro, about ten miles north of Cheraw, where there was another bridge across the Great Pee Dee. He would rejoin the Right Wing at Cheraw. Early on the morning of March 3 he rode out of Chesterfield with the XX Corps and forded Thompson's Creek. From the pleasant eminence of a hill, he saw a road leading off to the right. This, as far as he could tell from his map, was the one leading to Cheraw. Accompanied only by his staff, he followed it for about two hours and rode into Cheraw in a drizzling rain. Howard's engineers had laid a pontoon bridge across the river to replace the one destroyed by the Confederates, and Federal troops had been skirmishing with the enemy about two miles east of the town.

General Francis P. Blair established his headquarters in one of the town's most luxurious homes, built with fabulous profits earned in blockade running. The XVII Corps' commander invited Sherman and some others to have lunch with him. It was served family style in the basement dining room, and the long, wide table sagged under the weight of the food and beverages piled on it. Sherman and the others relished the dozen bottles of old Madeira beside their plates. It was a part of eight wagonloads recently shipped from the cellars of Charleston aristocrats, which Blair's men had confiscated. Sherman, no novice as a judge of wines, called it "the finest Madeira I ever tasted."

In high spirits over this latest conquest, stimulated by the wine and food and relaxed after a strenuous campaign, Sherman, Blair and the other guests were in a jovial and convivial mood. Logan turned songbird, playing his own violin accompaniment, and Adjutant Byers, without too much insistence, consented to recite his "Sherman's March to the Sea."

After lunch Blair asked Sherman if he could use some carpets and showed him several he had found under a stairway. Like the wine and many other things in Cheraw at that time, they

181

were recent imports from Charleston. Sherman, who had always maintained that he did not benefit personally from looting, picked out those he wanted and, later in the afternoon, sent his orderly for them. They were made into rugs for his tent, saddle-cloths and blankets.

With Savannah, Charleston and Columbia lost, the Confederates had turned Cheraw into a vast arsenal. The twenty-five captured Blakely cannons had beat off every attempt by the Federal fleet to capture Charleston from the sea. Now, the day after the bluecoats entered Cheraw, Abraham Lincoln made his second inaugural address in Washington, and those captive Blakelys made the surrounding countryside resound in thunderous salute.

In addition, the Yankees found small arms by the thousands, a tremendous quantity of fixed ammunition and twenty tons of gunpowder. Also captured were enough commissary stores to fill every wagon of the XVII Corps and some of the XV Corps, twelve railway cars, a locomotive and several thousand bales of cotton. This great treasure fell into the invaders' hands as a direct result of Sherman's success in making the enemy think his next objective after Columbia was Charlotte.

To dispose of the explosives without endangering lives, wagons hauled them to a ravine near the town, to be buried under a thick blanket of sand. A guard was posted at the site to prevent the soldiers' smoking and other acts which might trigger an explosion. However, someone was careless, and a terrific blast was set off. Shell fragments were hurled into the air and burst far from the site of the explosion. Several persons were killed. Houses were crushed, and the very earth was scorched and blackened within a radius of nine hundred feet.

Sherman's first reaction was to blame the blast on the Confederates. He threatened to retaliate by burning every building in Cheraw. Later he calmed down when an investigation placed the responsibility with a careless soldier.

During the three days the Federals were in Cheraw they burned and looted and committed other depredations similar to those which had stirred so much bitterness in other communities.

The Rev. Dr. John Bachman, the Lutheran minister who had led the prayer at the South Carolina secession convention, was unfortunate enough to be at Cash's Depot, about six miles from Cheraw. He saw soldiers accost women and tear off lapel watches, wedding rings and earrings. A personal friend of his was forced to undress in their presence; they pretended she was hiding jewelry under her dress. Property owners and servants reluctant to reveal the hiding places of prized china, silver and other valuables were tortured.

Somebody told the bluecoats that the family Dr. Bachman and his daughter were visiting had a hundred thousand dollars in gold and silver hidden about the place. When they asked him where it was, he told them, quite truthfully, that he did not know. They carried him behind a stable and threatened that if he didn't talk they'd send him "to hell in five minutes." To give potency to their threat, they cocked their pistols and held them to his head. Dr. Bachman coolly told them to fire away. One of his tormentors, "a square-built, broad-faced, large-mouthed, clumsy lieutenant," with "the face of a demon," kicked him in the stomach, sending him in a helpless heap to the ground. He staggered to his feet. Again the soldiers asked him where the silver and gold were hidden, and again he told them he did not know. That lieutenant, who "did not utter five words without an awful blasphemy," struck him in the back with his "heavy, elephant foot," and he fell again. In all, he was knocked down seven or eight times.

The lieutenant tried another tactic: "How would you like to have both your arms cut off?" Before Dr. Bachman could answer the officer swung at his left arm near the shoulder with his heavy sheathed sword. The minister "heard it crack." It "hung powerless by my side," and "I supposed it was broken."

The lieutenant then struck the right arm. The pain was "most excruciating." About that time Dr. Bachman's daughter arrived and appealed to them to show some humanity to this Christian soldier, who, she told them, had served the same church for forty years. The lieutenant replied scornfully: "I don't believe in a God, a heaven or a hell." However, concluding there was nothing to be gained by torturing his victim any more, he released him.

A few weeks later Dr. Bachman was in Florence on a pastoral errand. There he learned that some recently captured Federal prisoners were in town on their way to Sumter. Among them, his informant told him, were believed to be the men who had committed outrages in the Cheraw community. Would the minister take a look at them and say whether one was the officer who had mistreated him?

He promised to do so but insisted upon their remaining behind and letting him see the prisoners alone. As soon as he entered the railway car several of them recognized him, "held down their guilty heads, and trembled like aspen leaves." One of his arms was still in a sling. He used the other to lift one man's hat after another. One man made an obvious effort to avoid his eyes by looking steadily at the floor.

> I approached him slowly, and, in a whisper, asked him: "Do you know me, sir—the old man whose pockets you first searched, to see whether he might have a penknife to defend himself, and then kicked and knocked him down with your fist and heavy scabbard?" He presented the picture of arrant coward, and in a trembling voice implored me to have mercy: "Don't let me be shot; have pity! Old man, beg for me! I won't do it again. For God's sake, save me! Oh, God, help me!"
>
> "Did you not tell my daughter there was no God? Why call on Him now?"
>
> "Oh, I have changed my mind; I believe in a God now."

The militiamen in charge of the prisoners had become impatient and were moving in on the group. Chilling clicks were heard as they cocked their pistols. Again he begged for mercy. The militiamen moved closer. One asked Dr. Bachman to point out the guilty man. But the minister merely walked slowly to the end of the car, got into his carriage and drove away.

People in that general area were also subjected to outrages not blamable upon Sherman and his men. On the day after the Federals entered Cheraw, Mr. S. S. Jackson wrote from Asheboro, across the line in North Carolina, about a raid by Confederate deserters:

> Night before last about 50 deserters went to Mrs. I. H. Foust's house, broke open the safe with axes, and got about $1,000 in Specie—about $7,000 in Confederate money, about $9,000 in Bank notes and a good deal in State Treasury notes —1 Barrel of Sugar, leather and various other articles. Locked Mrs. Foust and Sallie up in a room while the plundering was going on. They took off all the keys. They went to Alfred Smith same night and took 70 pieces of meat; Smith got 2-pieces back by giving some Brandy.
>
> Robbing us this way is becoming a daily occurrence. I learn this morning that there are about 700 troops at High Point from Gen. Lee's army headed by Col. McAllister, supposed to be coming this way for the purpose of shooting down and capturing them.

While in Cheraw Sherman obtained a copy of the New York *Tribune* containing an article that disturbed him greatly. It stated that he and his army would soon be in Goldsboro: his supply vessels from Savannah were "known to be rendezvousing at Morehead City." This was not news to him of course. But its disclosure by the press was most disconcerting. Now every *Tribune* reader in the Confederacy knew his plans. Kilpatrick's feints in the direction of Charlotte were useless. Knowing that Charlotte was safe, the enemy would be relieved of the necessity of keeping substantial troops there. To the exasperated commander the article was "extremely mischievous."

Sherman received more unwelcome news. At General Lee's insistence, Jefferson Davis had appointed General Joseph Eggleston Johnston as commander of all troops in the Carolinas.

Sherman, who had faced the astute Johnston in the relentless drive on Atlanta and had been tremendously pleased when he was replaced by Hood, had great respect for his adversary. The going would be tougher with him in command. The long march over hundreds of miles without encountering anything more formidable than swollen streams, skirmishes and brief shows of resistance was at an end. Johnston would not long avoid a battle. And Sherman knew enough about his capabilities and resourcefulness to know it would be a big and bloody one.

Johnston's appointment, sobering and depressing as it was to Sherman, had an entirely different effect upon the Confederates. To those who had followed him from First Manassas to Atlanta without once suffering a defeat, although forced into some costly retreats, he was one of the war's top strategists. They remembered his human qualities—how lightly, for one thing, he had treated his serious wound at Fair Oaks. ("It's nothing, gentlemen . . . If a surgeon is within call, and not too busy, at his convenience, perfect convenience, he might as well look me over.") And they loved him for his passionate interest in their welfare. Civilians, resentful of his dismissal on the eve of the Battle of Atlanta, were delighted at his new opportunity to display the brilliant qualities of generalship they were sure he possessed.

So, from one end of the Confederacy to the other, there was a tremendous revival of morale in civilians and soldiers alike. Desertions dropped sharply. The long, unbroken series of defeats, retreats and fruitless skirmishes had left a trail of hopelessness and defeatism. But there came a feeling that perhaps all that would end now. The Raleigh *Progress* reported that thousands of soldiers absent without leave had returned to fight under their old chieftain. "Instead of demoralization," the Richmond *Whig* observed hopefully, "the Army of Tennessee is now buoyant and follow with pride the standard of their former commander, whom they seem to love and revere as children do a father."

"There will be rejoicing round many a hearth in the Confederacy when this news is heard," the Richmond *Examiner* declared the day after the appointment was made. "Especially there will be jubilee in the army, and that gallant remnant of that once fine army of Tennessee . . . will now feel equal to double duty."

As for the man who had been recalled from humiliating retirement to achieve a miracle, he did not share their optimism. He was under no illusions. He made that clear at his final conference with his predecessor, General Beauregard, in Charlotte. He could see no prospect of defeating and crippling Sherman's forces, sending them reeling back into the North or causing them to surrender en masse. Nor could he see any chance of saving Lee from eventual defeat in Virginia. The South's brave, gallant gamble had been lost. The best he could hope to do was to prevent a final and complete military defeat and win an honorable peace. He was not sure he could do that, but he set himself grimly to the task.

XIII

KILPATRICK IN NIGHTSHIRT

THE XVII CORPS began moving across the Great Pee Dee just east of Cheraw on the evening of March 4; this movement was completed the next morning. The XV Corps crossed on the night of March 5 and the morning of March 6. The XX Corps left the XIV Corps at Sneedsboro, after accompanying it there from Chesterfield. Turning south, it marched parallel to the river and crossed at Cheraw behind the XV Corps. With that formidable barrier at their back at last, they headed toward Fayetteville, some seventy miles away.

Even before Howard's infantrymen and artillerymen had reached Cheraw, Kilpatrick's cavalry crossed the state line and began making violent stabs at small towns and rural communities in North Carolina. The first sizable raid was at Monroe, only twenty-six miles from Charlotte. It was sharp and brief. No buildings were destroyed. But the raiders took what they wanted, and the residents had good reason to know the war had at last come to their community. The hardest hit were a party of refugees fleeing from the Federals in Chester, South Carolina. They had the misfortune to reach Monroe about the same time the raiders did. The ten wagons carrying their hastily assembled possessions were captured. A day or two later

189

there was the first of two raids on Wadesboro, twenty-five miles east of Monroe. Striking furiously, a party of Kilpatrick's men invaded and terrorized the town and nearby rural community.

The Rev. Thomas Atkinson, Episcopal Bishop of North Carolina, gave up his watch, clothing, jewelry and horse under the threat of being killed if he refused. A raider shot down one of the oldest and wealthiest residents of the county in his own house when the old man did not surrender his money and watch, which he could not do because another raider had already taken them. Another wealthy Anson County resident stood by helplessly while the bluecoats fired his cotton gin, burned more than two hundred bales of cotton and destroyed his well-filled corn crib, his granary, wheat, oats and field peas.

The raiders, according to General William A. Smith, broke into one place and "cut into fragments with an axe" every piece of furniture. They "opened the tick and scattered the feathers over the floors of the chamber," and they filled buckets with molasses "and mixed it with the feathers by thoroughly stirring."

While this was going on, the lady of the house, Mrs. Jane Bennett, and her two daughters were in a locked room, which the raiders tried to enter. After shaking the door and demanding that it be opened, they threatened to break it down. When it was unlocked and pushed open, the older of the girls held a gun in her hands. Cowed by her cool courage and obvious determination to shoot, if necessary, the men slunk away. Before they left the plantation, however, they hooked up the family's team of bay horses to "the finest carriage in Anson County" and loaded it with hams from the smokehouse and other choice foods. Then they either shot or drove off every horse, mule, cow, sheep, goat, duck and chicken around the place.

The second raid on Wadesboro came the next day. About a hundred of Kilpatrick's men suddenly appeared and worked fast, reducing to rubble, among other things, a tannery, a grist mill, a saw mill and stables for Confederate army horses.

Things did not go easily at Phillips Cross Roads, where there was a clash with Wheeler's cavalry March 4. It lasted all day and showed the Yankees that the Southerners still had plenty of fight left. Wheeler's men captured fifty prisoners and seemed about to win a clear-cut victory, but the heavier Federal artillery drove them back at last.

Wheeler followed up three days later by personally leading a party of his scouts in an attack upon the Federals near Rockingham. They killed and captured thirty-five. While the raid was underway another struggle was going on inside the town between foragers from Sherman's Right Wing and a party of Calbraith Butler's cavalrymen. The Confederates acquitted themselves well. But, like Wheeler's men at Phillips Cross Roads, they were obliged to yield to superior force; large units of Kilpatrick's cavalry.

Foraging became easier and more productive for the main columns after they entered North Carolina. Crops had been good. Great quantities of food and feedstuffs were on hand. Even flour, something of a luxury in Georgia and South Carolina, was to be had in abundance, as the numerous streams in that part of the country provided excellent power for grist mills, many of which lay along the army's route.

The weather was pleasant and sunny for a while. Nichols' diary of March 7 describes a sight he had not witnessed since leaving Savannah: lively clouds of dust were being stirred up by the men's boots and the horses' hooves. When they marched through wooded country their noses would pick up the pleasant perfume of pine and cedar. North Carolina, they decided, was vastly superior to South Carolina in every way. Moreover, if current reports could be believed, they would find many North Carolinians opposed to Secession and friendly to the Union.

To fan pro-Union sentiment, Sherman made some gestures of conciliation. He even decided to call in his foragers but changed his mind under the practical necessity of feeding a large army. As an alternative, he ordered his officers and men to make requisitioning as tolerable as possible, and he began dealing severely with the lawless fringe among his foragers and showing more sympathy for their victims. Consequently, outrages became markedly fewer after the cross-over into North Carolina.

While Sherman was trying out his new psychological weapon of moderation, his opposite number in the Confederate Army was working in a fever of haste to cope with the Federals' far more potent weapon of military might. There was still the possibility (in spite of Sherman's published plan to go straight to Goldsboro) that the blue columns might move on Charlotte after all. Such a move, if successful, would break the Confederacy's last important rail link between the Carolinas and Lee's armies in Virginia. Sherman well might decide to make it. So Johnston left his predecessor, Beauregard, in command of a small force in Charlotte before hastening on to Fayetteville for a meeting with Hardee and Hampton. At the same time he ordered a general troop concentration near Smithfield and a consolidation of Stewart's, Lee's and Hoke's corps into a single unit. This was to move rapidly under General Braxton Bragg against General Schofield. Its purpose would be to break up Schofield's rendezvous with Sherman at Goldsboro. That accomplished, Johnston planned that Bragg's forces would be withdrawn from the Kinston area and combined with other troops preparing to make a stand against Sherman somewhere between Fayetteville and Goldsboro.

After crossing the state line March 8 the XV Corps camped for the night at Laurel Hill, while the XVII Corps, bearing to the south, moved on to the Lumber river before halting for the night. Surgeon and diarist, E. P. Burton, of the 7th Illinois regiment, was not favorably impressed by his first glimpse of North Carolina. He had reached Laurel Hill "in a terrible rain" and found "only a church and two or three buildings." When he was not trying to make headway through swampland, he had had to contend with quicksand. He did not have a chance to eat until 9 o'clock at night. Then he "relished some Hard Tack and bacon roasted on the end of a stick," after which he "lay down on a board and rested a while in the rain."

Nichols noticed, or thought he noticed, a marked difference in the people he saw after crossing into North Carolina. And the difference was in their favor. There, plantation owners worked hard with their hands, not considering physical labor degrading. During that thirteen-mile march from the border he had passed many excellently managed farms. Cotton and corn fields were nicely furrowed. Fences and barns were in excellent repair. Homes were neat and clean, many of them painted white. Everywhere he found a general air of thrift and industry, "which shows that the owner takes a personal interest in the conduct of affairs."

On the whole, Sherman's soldiers reacted quickly to this South Carolina-North Carolina transformation, real or imagined. Their conduct changed markedly, the change often going beyond that called for by Sherman's orders. A feeling of near-friendliness pervaded the whole army. Nichols noted that he had seen "no evidence of plundering." The men "keep their ranks closely." From his overnight resting place there at Laurel Hill, "not a single column of the fire or smoke which a few days ago marked the positions of heads of column, can be seen upon the horizon." The troops, he wrote, "seem to understand that they are entering a state which has suffered for its Union sentiments, and whose inhabitants would gladly embrace the old flag again if they can have the opportunity, which we mean to give them, or I am mistaken as to our future campaigns."

Sherman had had no definite word that Wilmington had fallen to the Federals, but he optimistically gambled on the assumption that it had. He needed certain supplies. He wanted to get word of his progress to his civilian superiors in Washington and to Grant. And he wanted to make arrangements for the junction at Goldsboro with General Schofield, moving inland from the coast. So two highly skillful scouts—a Corporal Pike, who had rejoined the army at Columbia after escaping from a prisoner-of-war camp, and a sergeant chosen by General Howard—were sent on a mission to Wilmington. Traveling separately, they disguised themselves, obtained boats and floated down the Cape Fear. Each carried a copy of the same letter written in code:

> HEADQUARTERS, MILITARY
> DIVISION OF THE MISSISSIPPI,
>
> IN THE FIELD, LAUREL HILL,
> WEDNESDAY, MARCH 8, 1865

COMMANDING OFFICER, WILMINGTON, NORTH CAROLINA:
We are marching on Fayetteville, will be there Saturday, Sunday, and Monday and will then march on Goldsboro'.
If possible, send a boat up Cape Fear River, and have word conveyed to General Schofield that I expect to meet him about Goldsboro'. We are all well and have done finely. The rains make our roads difficult, and may delay us about Fayetteville, in which case I would like to have some bread, sugar, and coffee. We have abundance of all else. I expect to reach Goldsboro' by the 20th instant.

> W. T. SHERMAN, MAJOR-GENERAL

Moving ahead of the main body, troops from the XV Corps [12] made a raid on Laurenburgh (Laurinburg), about five miles southeast of Laurel Hill. Like the other town, it was on the Wilmington-to-Charlotte railroad. After burning the depot and railroad shops, they continued on to the Lumber river at Gilchrist Bridge.

Hearing that the Yankees were headed that way, slaves in and near Laurenburgh held secret meetings to plot a bold bid for freedom. At an agreed-upon signal, they were to gather at a central rendezvous and march to the Federal lines, resisting the efforts of their masters and the local authorities to restrain them. The white people found out about the scheme, and home guardsmen broke into one of their meetings. Twenty-five were convicted and sentenced to be hung.

The furious downpour which began before the XV Corps' main body reached Laurel Hill and kept up during the overnight stop there followed them to tiny Bethel Church, which they reached in the late afternoon of March 9. Sherman called the roads between Laurel Hill and Bethel "awful." Corduroying had to be resorted to practically all the way.

The men made themselves as comfortable as possible that night by pitching their tents in the thickest parts of the forest, where the branches afforded a measure of protection from the pelting rain. Sherman spent the night in the little church building, but refused a soft bed of carpet which a member of his staff had prepared for him on the pulpit platform, preferring to lie on a pew bench.

When the people of the little community went to church the next Sunday, they were surprised and shocked to find in the pulpit Bible crude, irreverent pencil scrawlings, presumably the work of some soldier who fancied himself a wit:

"Mr. McNeill will please preach a sermon on the illusions of pleasure and hope."

"Mr. McNeill will please prove the absurdity of the Universalist doctrine."

"Mr. McNeill will please preach a sermon from the First Epistle of John, 4 Chapter."

"Mr. McNeill will please pray for Old Abe."

"By order of W. T. Sherman, Major Genl. Comd. U. S. Forces."

While the troops of the XV Corps slogged along through the rain and mud, steadily shortening the distance between them and the Cape Fear, their comrades of the XVII Corps maintained their own steady pace along a more southerly route. At Lumberton, where the Wilmington-to-Charlotte railroad crossed the Lumber river, a regiment of mounted infantrymen struck hard. They destroyed the railroad and highway bridges across the river, along with the depot, several freight cars and about a mile of track, making still another break in the Confederacy's dwindling transportation system. They also entered a number of private homes.

House-burning, supposed to have ended at the state line, broke out again in the Antioch section. Bluecoats were in the act of firing the home of Daniel S. Morrison when the Morrison children saw them and started screaming. Sherman happened to be nearby and ordered the men to leave the house alone. He did nothing, however, to save the Morrisons' other property. The soldiers took hens off their nests, seized Mrs. Morrison's jewelry and talked the Morrison Negroes into going off with them. The Negroes soon regretted going, and returned home, sick and disillusioned. Mrs. Morrison nursed them back to health.

On March 10 Sherman was at the home of a Mrs. Nelson in the Rockfish section of Cumberland County. This outspoken North Carolina woman made no effort to conceal from him or anybody else her dislike for all Yankees, especially Yankee soldiers. By a singular coincidence, she told him, March 10 had been an important and significant date in her life. On March 10, 1824, she had received a visit from LaFayette, and the distinguished and gallant Frenchman had kissed her hand. On March 10, 1845, three persons had lain dead in her house, one of them slain by his own brother. "And now, on March 10, 1865, you come with your robbers to rob us."

"Madam," Sherman replied with gallantry, "I assure you that we will not rob you or harm you in any way, and, further, I too shall kiss your hand." Bowing low, he did.

On the night of March 9-10 Federal and Confederate cavalry were encamped close to each other near Solemn Grove, Kilpatrick's men blocking the road to Fayetteville. Kilpatrick himself, General Wade Hampton learned, was with Colonel

George E. Spencer's brigade just a short distance from the Confederate camp. Hampton decided to attack him at daylight the next morning. The scheme was aided by the arrival within the Confederate lines of one of Kilpatrick's officers who had lost his way.

He was taken to General Butler for questioning. From his reluctant answers Butler learned the exact location of Kilpatrick's headquarters, the residence of one Charles Monroe. Subsequent reconnoitering revealed that Kilpatrick had shown his customary carelessness: he had posted no pickets to prevent attack from the rear.

At a post-midnight strategy conference Butler was designated to lead the dawn attack. He was to swing around the head of a swamp with a strong force and approach the enemy from that direction. Wheeler's men were to speed through some nearby woods and strike from there. To a Captain Bostic of Young's brigade went the assignment to capture Kilpatrick. He was ordered to go directly to the Monroe house, surround it and prevent Kilpatrick from escaping until Bostic's troops could be reinforced. They then would enter and make the capture.

During the night reports reached General Thomas J. Jordan of Kilpatrick's First Brigade and General Smith D. Atkins of the Second Brigade of extensive Confederate troop movements nearby. Both men interpreted them to mean that the resourceful Hampton was scheming something spectacular. They tried to communicate their suspicions to Kilpatrick but were stopped by bad roads and skirmishes with Confederate cavalrymen.

Butler's cavalrymen took their positions some time before daybreak waiting for orders to attack. Not a pipe was lighted. Nobody spoke above a whisper. As the first faint gleams of light slanted over the eastern hills, hoarse whispers passed along the order to mount their horses and prepare for the assault. At the order to attack they shot toward the Federal camp, still unprotected by guards or pickets. The surprise was complete. The camp was thrown into confusion, and Kilpatrick's troops, looking most unheroic in their underwear, scurried in all directions like flushed turkeys. Captain Bostic advanced upon the Monroe house and posted his men around it.

Aroused by the piercing rebel yells that signaled the attack, Kilpatrick rushed from the building, leaving his beautiful traveling companion, the notorious Mary Boozer, to fend for herself. Halting momentarily outside while he tried to get his wits together, he was approached by a Confederate cavalryman. The Southerner, unimpressed by a brigadier general in his nightshirt, supposed him to be just another soldier, and asked if he had seen General Kilpatrick. Kilpatrick pointed to a man riding off on a black horse, and the Southerner took off on his trail. As soon as he was out of sight Kilpatrick leapt on a horse and rode off in another direction, a ghostlike figure in the brightening dawn.

The flimsily constructed wooden house was being vigorously peppered with bullets, and some of them were crashing through the thin weatherboarding. Suddenly Mary Boozer appeared in the doorway in helpless despair, a handsome woman in a flimsy nightgown, while Southern men in gray steadily pushed back Northern men, mostly in white. In her ears roared a cacophony of steel striking against steel, gunfire popping everywhere, frightened horses neighing and prancing and jubilant Confederates letting go with the rebel yell. The luxurious carriage Kilpatrick had provided for her stood in the yard, but there were no horses to pull it.

She had been standing there just a few minutes when her striking white figure attracted the attention of a Confederate cavalry captain. Leaping from his horse, he gallantly took her arm and guided her to a nearby ditch. There she reclined in considerable discomfort but relative safety until the fighting subsided and she could climb out and rejoin her paramour.

The battle continued to go badly for the Yankees. After

capturing their artillery the Confederate powerhouse shoved them back until they were in the swamp. They were still disorganized and in no position to reform their lines and counterattack so long as the Confederates kept advancing. But suddenly the advance stopped.

Springing to the offensive, the Federals turned their carbines on them and started moving out of the swamp. The captured artillery was soon back in Yankee hands, and the jubilant victors of just a few minutes before were forced into inglorious retreat.

Kilpatrick's explanation for the sudden halt in the Confederate advance was that they stopped to loot the Federal camp. General Butler claimed that it was not due to looting at all but to one of the mischances of warfare. The swamp Wheeler had to cross had proved more difficult than anticipated. As a result, Wheeler had not been able to carry out his part of the operation as planned. Moreover, Butler contended, there had been a mix-up in orders. Brigadier General E. M. Law's brigade, which had been ordered to follow that first wave of attackers and hold the camp after it had been captured, had been sent by General Hampton to another part of the battle area. That left the first-wave troops with a bigger job than they could do.

In spite of its failure, the Confederate attack was brilliantly planned and gallantly carried out. Even Kilpatrick praised it as "the most formidable cavalry charge I have ever witnessed." Both sides suffered heavily in men and equipment, although there is wide disagreement between the claims of the two contending armies and indeed between different reports by the same side. Kilpatrick reported that only four of his officers and fifteen of his men were killed and seven officers and sixty-one men received major wounds. He admitted that one hundred and three of his troops—officers and men—had been captured. From the Confederate side, General Wheeler claimed his men had taken in excess of three hundred and fifty prisoners. General

Johnston set the prisoner total at some five hundred and claimed the freeing of one hundred and seventy-three captured Confederates. The Federal brigadier general claimed his men found more than eighty Confederate bodies and a great many Confederate wounded. His men, he said, also captured some thirty prisoners, to say nothing of one hundred and fifty horses.

Although the battle at Solemn Grove was indisputably a defeat for the Confederates, it boosted their morale by exposing serious weaknesses of the enemy. The pain of their failure to capture Kilpatrick was lightened by the knowledge that they had made him ridiculous. The Federals had been made to fight when they would have much preferred to continue unimpeded their rapid march to Fayetteville. The battle had upset Kilpatrick's timetable, delaying his entry into the city and thereby relieving the pressure on the hard-pressed Hardee.

XIV

THREE DAYS IN FAYETTEVILLE

As HIS COLUMNS approached Fayetteville from the south in the early morning of March 11, Howard sent seventy-eight horsemen ahead of the infantry to scout. They were commanded by Captain William Duncan, who had led the expedition to make contact with the fleet off Savannah. To their surprise, they met with no resistance. Indeed they saw no signs of enemy troops at all. Even the pickets had been withdrawn. So, instead of returning to their units, they continued on into the city. General Hardee had ordered Hampton to remain behind in Fayetteville with a small force until Federal troops were near and then cross the Cape Fear bridge and burn it.

Hampton was eating breakfast in a Fayetteville hotel when one of his scouts warned him that enemy troops were close at hand. He quickly organized a party and rushed out to meet Duncan. The surprised Federals were unprepared for this sudden show of resistance, and in their confusion they were not able to put up much of a fight. About a dozen were killed and Duncan and several others captured. Those who escaped unharmed returned to Howard's lines.[13]

Major General G. A. Smith, commanding the Fourth Division, which comprised the XVII Corps' advance troops, sent about two hundred cavalrymen into the city to rescue Captain Duncan and his comrades, but they arrived too late. At about the same time another party of Federals made a mad dash through the city to the Cape Fear bridge to prevent its destruction by the enemy. But just two hundred yards ahead of them Hampton's men rode across and fired the rosin with which the span had previously been treated. By the time the Federals reached the river, the bridge was a flaming wreck, and Hampton and his cavalrymen were on their way to overtake Hardee and his troops.

Meanwhile the main body of General Smith's division entered the city from the south. Advance units of Slocum's XIV Corps were already there, having entered earlier from the northwest. Both columns encountered showers of shots, which proved diverting but not a serious impediment.

Mayor Archibald McLean met the XVII Corps in the southern part of the city and formally surrendered it to Lieutenant Colonel William E. Strong, a member of Howard's staff. A similar surrender was made subsequently to Slocum, whose XIV Corps took over the occupation, in accordance with Sherman's orders. Actually, only Baird's division of the XIV Corps remained in Fayetteville. The other units of both wings went into camp outside the city.

When Baird's troops marched in to take control they received a hearty reception from the bummers. Moving ahead of the regulars, as was their wont, they had managed to get possession of a barrel of liquor and ladled it out in gourds as the men marched by. Teetotalers received plugs of tobacco and other purloined luxuries, including books.

Sherman ordered the laying of a pontoon bridge near the destroyed bridge and another about four miles downstream.

The Yankees spent three days—March 11 to 14—in Fayetteville. The primary target was the arsenal, which Sherman regarded as a shining symbol of North Carolina's "treachery": it had been seized from Union forces at the outbreak of the war. A large amount of machinery and other war equipment which had been removed from the United States arsenal at Harper's Ferry, railway equipment, repair shops for locomotives, manufacturing plants, tanneries, grist mills, cotton mills, warehouses and the plants of the Fayetteville *Observer* and the North Carolina *Presbyterian* were destined for destruction.

In Fayetteville the troops found that their impression that Union sentiment was high in North Carolina had to be revised. In spite of a strong dislike which many expressed for Jefferson Davis, Nichols found them "offensively rebellious." Indeed he had encountered "more persons in Columbia who had proven their fealty to the Union cause by their friendliness to our prisoners than [in] all this state put together."

After setting up his headquarters at the arsenal, Sherman received a surprise visit from a friend of his West Point days. Edward Monagan had remained behind when his fellow arsenal employes fled and now had come to see his old friend to ask that his personal property be spared. Sherman recognized him and was on the point of greeting him cordially. But then the realization came that Edward Monagan was now an enemy. His manner chilled. He accused him of betraying not only him but his own country, which had given him a college education for its defense. He lambasted him for asking him "to be again your friend, to protect your property." The conversation was broken off with one of Sherman's most dramatic flourishes: "Turn your back on me forever. I will not punish you. Only go your way."

This was not an empty histrionic gesture. Sherman was completely unnerved. His associates noticed a marked shaking of his hands at lunch after the interview. There were tears in his eyes, and his voice had a ring they had never heard before. "Never," said one who was present, "had I seen him under such emotion."

Sherman's instructions to treat North Carolinians kindly were disregarded in and around Fayetteville. Troops looted many residences and stores while the owners looked on in enraged helplessness, and valuables were seized as roughly as in Columbia.

The son of E. J. Hale, Sr., publisher of the strongly pro-Confederate Fayetteville *Observer,* claimed that the destruction of his father's plant had been ordered by Sherman himself. And, he said, it had been carried out with great satisfaction by General Slocum. In company with several other high-ranking officers, the Left Wing commander had "sat on the verandah of a hotel opposite watching the progress of the flames while they hobnobbed over wines stolen from our cellar."

Troops from Kilpatrick's cavalry ransacked the Duncan Murchinson mansion about twelve miles from town and, angered by their failure to find the carefully hidden valuables, stormed into the bedroom of a young girl gravely ill with typhoid. When relatives and neighbors pleaded with them to show some compassion for a dying child, an officer told his men: "Go ahead, boys. Do all the mischief you can." She died while they were there.

Then they threatened to kill seventy-year-old Mr. Murchinson. While a friend of the old man begged on her knees for his life, the soldiers dragged him half-dressed into the swamps and left him. Inside the house they drove their swords into family portraits, broke up furniture and poured molasses into the piano. The family was left without anything to eat. They managed to stay alive by gathering up corn and other grain that had been scattered about by horses.

At another place the family Bible was spread open, thrown across a mule's back and used as a saddle.

The Negroes suffered along with the white people. Martha Graham, a former slave, told a newspaper writer: "They came from ever'where but outen the ground and down outen the sky. ... They took all the corn outen the crib and the things we'd stored. When they left, we didn't have nothin'." A soldier visited the house while her mother was straining milk. Without saying a word, he picked up one of the two milk pans and drained it. Still uncommunicative, he left. A few seconds later —"as soon as he'd hit the bottom step"—she heard a shot: "They wuz killing our turkey."

Soon after midday on Sunday March 12 there rang out through the town the shrill notes of a boat whistle. By the time the vessel tied up at the dock the river bank was lined with shouting, cheering troops. Sherman called the effect "electric." The arrival of the *Davidson* lifted a great load from his mind. It meant that the scouts he had sent from Laurel Hill had reached Wilmington safely.

Some officers came ashore with dispatches from Major General Alfred Howe Terry, in command at the port city. They had set out at 2 o'clock the afternoon before, gambling on Sherman's getting to Fayetteville about the designated time.

After conferring with the officers regarding the craft's capacity and navigation problems on the river, Sherman ordered them to sail back to Wilmington at 6 o'clock that afternoon, carrying dispatches to Secretary Stanton, General Grant, General Terry and others. They were also told to take aboard as many as possible of the Union sympathizers who had been traveling with the army. Sherman was anxious to get rid of those "useless mouths." They had become a heavy drain upon the army's food supply.

In his letter to Grant, Sherman reported his arrival in Fayetteville the day before. Hardee, "as usual," had retreated ahead of him, he wrote, and the Cape Fear bridge had been destroyed. But "our pontoons will be up today," and as soon as possible "I will be after him toward Goldsboro'." He hoped the *Davidson* would make another trip to Fayetteville before he left. He needed a number of things he had not been able to forage and wanted to get them before his departure. He had a particular need for shoes, hose, sugar, coffee and flour. His men were "in splendid health, condition and spirits," in spite of foul weather and roads "that would have stopped travel to almost any other body of men I ever heard of." Johnston might try to interpose his army between Sherman and Schofield somewhere near New Bern. But he was more likely to concentrate his scattered forces at or near Raleigh. Sherman would try to force him to fight "as soon as I get our men reclothed and our wagons reloaded." He expected to meet Schofield in Goldsboro in ten days.

In his letter to Stanton he said that the campaign had placed General Lee in an extremely precarious position: if he should cling to Richmond, "we will destroy his country." Should Richmond be abandoned both Sherman and Grant must be prepared to cope with its sudden evacuation and Lee's bold dash southward in a desperate effort to escape their trap.

To General Terry, Sherman outlined his more immediate plans. General Howard had seized a Confederate steamboat below the city, and General Slocum was going to try to capture two others known to be anchored a few miles up the river. All three would be loaded with refugees, white and Negro, "who have clung to our skirts, impeded our movements, and consumed our food."

Haste was urgent.

> I want you to send me all the shoes, stockings, drawers, sugar, coffee, and flour you can spare; finish the loads with oats or corn. Have the boats escorted, and let them run at night at any risk. We must not give time for Jos. Johnston to concentrate at Goldsboro'. We cannot prevent his concentration at Raleigh, but he shall have no rest. I want General Schofield to go on with his railroad from New Bern as far as he can, and you should do the same from Wilmington. If we can get the roads to and secure Goldsboro' by April 10, it will be soon enough; but every day now is worth a million dollars. I can whip Jos. Johnston provided he does not catch one of my corps in flank, and I will see that the army marches hence to Goldsboro' in compact form.

Sherman moved most of his army across the Cape Fear March 13. A single division was left behind to serve as a rear guard during the destruction of the arsenal.

The *Davidson* made its second call before the rear-guard division left. On board was Brigadier General George S. Dodge, the Quartermaster General. None of the badly needed clothing was on board any of the boats. There was none to be spared at Wilmington, General Dodge said. But he had brought sugar, coffee and oats.

The army did not head northeast toward its real destination but almost directly north toward Raleigh, in order to deceive enemy scouts. Sixty miles away lay Goldsboro. Not much farther away, Sherman hoped, were Terry and Schofield.

XV

THE BATTLE OF BENTONVILLE

Johnston was certain to strike, and Sherman reasoned that it would be between Fayetteville and Goldsboro. For by the time it reached Goldsboro Sherman's tired and tattered army would be heavily strengthened by Schofield's troops moving in from New Bern and Terry's from Wilmington. His men would get a good rest, they would be re-equipped with new arms, and fresh new uniforms would be issued. The Federal army would be incontestably superior; Johnston's tired, poorly equipped troops would have little chance. It should be as obvious to Johnston as it was to Sherman that to fail to strike west of Goldsboro would be to lose forever the chance to strike at all with any hope of success.

Exactly where along that sixty-mile road Hardee's gray columns would stop retreating and start fighting Sherman had no way of knowing. But, as he carefully studied his maps, he settled upon a narrow strip of land between the Cape Fear and South rivers. Those two streams would greatly strengthen Hardee's defenses. He might hope to hold the Yankees at bay there long enough for Johnston to finish collecting his scattered army farther to the east. Then the Confederates would unite and strike Sherman's men with everything they had.

One thing was certain: Hardee would not challenge Sherman head-on. He would attack his army, or a portion of it, on the left flank. The probability of having to deal with an attack of that kind determined Sherman's choice of routes for his four corps. Howard's XVII Corps was ordered to move on the extreme right. Next to it, using roads that would keep the two Right Wing corps as close together as practicable, would be the XV Corps. To its left would be Slocum's XIV Corps, with his XX Corps on the extreme left. Kilpatrick's cavalry, moving straight toward the town of Averysborough, just east of the Cape Fear river, was to act as the particular guardian of the XX Corps. As an extra precaution against danger from the left, Sherman orderd Slocum to disencumber all but two of his divisions of their vehicles so as to be ready at all times for quick fighting. This was done by attaching all vehicles of the XX and XIV Corps to Geary's and Baird's divisions, respectively, both of which were traveling between the Right and Left Wings. Two divisions of the XX Corps (Jackson's and Hood's) and two from the XIV Corps (Carlin's and Morgan's) joined Kilpatrick's cavalry. Howard was ordered to keep his wagon trains well to his right and to keep four of his divisions unencumbered and ready to fight at once if Slocum's Left Wing should be attacked.

Sherman's worries were increased by the weather. The flooding rains made marching difficult and slow. The mud they created underfoot turned ordinary highways into quagmires and low places into swamps and rivulets. Even when it was not necessary to corduroy, the gummy soil clung to the wagon wheels and animal hooves, made forward movement a struggle and brought fervid streams of profanity from frustrated mule drivers. To Johnston and Hardee these delays were priceless.

Johnston was almost certain Sherman was on his way to Goldsboro. But he could not be sure. Against the possibility that he might continue on to Raleigh, instead of making a sharp turn to the east, the Confederate commander assembled a considerable portion of his troops at Smithfield, almost equidistant from those two places. Hardee, still moving ahead of Sherman's army, was instructed to follow the road from Fayetteville to Raleigh via Smithfield.

Hardee's men had been marching a long time, with little rest or sleep. So he planned to stop for a day at their encampment near Smith's Mill, some six miles south of Averysborough. But, as Slocum's Left Wing continued its pressure on his rear, he decided to fight back. He hoped in that way to find out whether he was being pushed by all or just a portion of Sherman's army and also whether Sherman was headed for Goldsboro or Raleigh. That was March 15, the day after the Federals left the Fayetteville area. Hardee was then near Averysborough, about halfway between Fayetteville and Goldsboro and also about halfway between Fayetteville and Raleigh. The site chosen for his stand was where Sherman had anticipated it would be made, on a narrow strip of swampland between the Cape Fear and South rivers. Just west of it the road Y'd, one branch going to Raleigh, the other to Goldsboro.

Hardee ordered Colonel Alfred Moore Rhett's brigade of Brigadier General William B. Taliaferro's division to take a position to the right of that road from Fayetteville to Raleigh and Goldsboro. There he was to set up a strong skirmish line in front of hastily constructed breastworks. His forces were to absorb the first shock of the Federal advance and hold the enemy at a standstill until the vehicles of Taliaferro's division could be removed to a safer place. Then they were to retreat to a position held by another brigade, commanded by Brigadier General Steven Elliot, Jr.

It was about mid-afternoon when Kilpatrick's advance troops of the 9th Michigan threw themselves against the gray line. General Smith D. Atkins' First Brigade dismounted, deployed and advanced against the skirmishers. As planned, the Confederates fell back to their breastworks, their withdrawal triggering a heavy barrage of artillery fire from the Confederate batteries. Kilpatrick ordered his other troops to take battle positions and construct barricades. When all was ready the 9th Michigan withdrew. During the rest of the afternoon Taliaferro's troops made violent jabs at the Yankee positions. But the thrusts were weakened considerably by Kilpatrick's success in keeping the attackers at some distance from the Federal lines.

Surprised to find the enemy so strong, Kilpatrick asked Slocum, following behind him, for reinforcements. Slocum sent ahead the brigade commanded by Colonel William Hawley. Protected from enemy observation by darkness, these troops took their place in the center of the Federal line. The highway from Fayetteville to Raleigh and Goldsboro was on their left.

That night the commander of the Confederate brigade which had made the initial contact in the afternoon with the 9th Michigan got lost in the woods. Colonel Rhett mistook the Federal cavalry camp for his own and was nonchalantly on his way there, with his aide, when he was challenged by enemy cavalrymen. One of them pushed a pistol against his temple and told him to go along or he would "make a hole" through him. Thinking they were Confederates, Colonel Rhett became indignant and threatened to report him for using disrespectful language. The dumbfounded captive was taken to Kilpatrick and later to Sherman. The one-time commander of Fort Sumter, Sherman said, was "dreadfully mortified" to find himself a prisoner of war and disgusted at having been captured without a fight. His aristocratic bearing and dress caused considerable comment. He was wearing, Sherman observed, "the most approved rebel uniform, with high jack-boots beautifully stitched." To the Yankees the capture of a Southern blueblood like this was indeed a feat to boast about. Their satisfaction was increased by the fact that their captive was a former editor of the strongly anti-Union Charleston *Mercury*.

Rhett received special consideration. He and General Blair shared honors as Sherman's guests at supper, and the South Carolinian spent the night at the commander's headquarters.

After their initial embarrassment and self-consciousness the two men talked freely. Rhett subsequently was furnished a horse.

Confident that Hardee's men were just ahead of Kilpatrick, Sherman ordered Slocum to send additional infantry troops forward to dislodge them. But the weather was bad and the roads worse. Slocum's troops had to edge forward at a snail's pace and did not reach the battle area until about 10 o'clock in the morning of March 16.

Skirmishing had been going on between Kilpatrick's and Taliaferro's cavalry for four hours. At 6 o'clock the 8th Indiana Cavalry, under Lieutenant Colonel F. A. Jones, had forced the Confederate skirmish line back behind their breastworks. Lacking the expected support from Slocum's weather-plagued Left Wing, Jones had found it impracticable to carry on the fight with cavalry alone. The naturally swampy terrain had been made much more so by the heavy rain of the night before, causing his horses to become helplessly embogged in a deep, sticky gumbo. They were then ordered to renew their contact with Hawley's newly arrived brigade.

About the time this change in Federal tactics was taking place Taliaferro sent his cavalry force ahead in a strong attack in which it subjected the Federal line to heavy pressure. A shortage of ammunition was imminent, and the conflict probably would have ended disastrously for the Unionists if the delayed units of Slocum's XX Corps had not arrived just then, preventing the Federal cavalry's right from being turned.

Under the protection of three batteries of artillery from the XX Corps, the reinforced Federals again resumed the advance. Two brigades shoved on beyond Taliaferro's front. A third swung diagonally toward the right of the Confederate breastworks. That third brigade, commanded by Colonel Henry Case, had to move slowly and with great difficulty through a swamp. Beating off a Confederate skirmish line, it reached a position directly on the Confederate right flank, about a fifth of a mile from them. Charging with heavy fire, it drove Colonel

William Butler's brigade (formerly commanded by Colonel Rhett) to the second line of breastworks. Then the First and Third Divisions of the XX Corps marched in, and General Mitchell's brigade from the XIV Corps took a position to the left.

Kilpatrick sent his cavalry forces forward toward the road to Goldsboro to determine enemy strength in that area. Learning from his scouts that a road leading off from the main highway to the right made a loop behind the Confederate position, he ordered the 9th Ohio to follow it. Before it had gone far, it was subjected to a surprise attack by a brigade of General Lafayette McLaws' division, commanded by Colonel G. P. Harrison, which had approached with great secrecy through thick underbrush. The 9th Ohio was forced back but restabilized its lines after yielding some two hundred yards. There, on more easily defended higher ground, it maintained its position in spite of heavy attacks by Harrison's troops. The Confederates withdrew after the 9th Ohio was relieved by infantry.

In danger of being flanked and facing a strong, determined enemy on his front, Taliaferro had to pull back his division to the main defense line. His troops moved quickly into position on both sides of the main road. On his left was McLaws' division and on his right Wheeler's cavalrymen without their mounts. The Butler brigade, having carried the brunt of the fighting, took its position behind the line of Confederate breastworks, to be used as, when and where needed.

The Federal force pounded all afternoon and until after nightfall against that powerful Confederate defense line. Heavy, fitful showers had made the Federals' artillery practically useless in the boggy soil. But at about 8 o'clock Hardee began a general withdrawal toward Smithfield, followed by Wheeler's horseless cavalrymen serving as a rear guard.

General Ward's division of the XX Corps followed them beyond Averysborough. With the way now open the rest of Slocum's troops took the road leading to the South (or Black) river.

The Battle of Bentonville

After bridging the swollen stream they marched on toward Goldsboro.

Federal sources reported that three hundred and twenty-seven Confederates were "buried on the field and paroled wounded." This total was "exclusive of those [Confederates] carried off and the unhurt prisoners we captured." Sherman stated in his official report that one hundred and ten Confederate dead were left behind. As for the Federals, they lost six hundred and eighty-two in killed, wounded and captured. Five hundred and thirty-three of these were wounded according to casualty reports prepared by Kilpatrick and Slocum. Sherman's reports were somewhat different. The Confederates took no prisoners, he said, but twelve Federal officers and sixty-five men were killed and four hundred and twenty-seven men wounded.

Sixty-eight of the Confederate wounded were carried to a temporary hospital set up by the Federals at nearby Smith house. Sherman arrived while the surgeons were carrying on their grisly tasks, walking past piles of arms and legs lying around like cordwood on the porch and in the yard. As he made his way among the pale, frightened men, he stopped to talk to a handsome youngster whose left arm had just been severed at the shoulder. The patient was Captain Macbeth, whose battery had been captured in that day's fighting. This was not the first time the two men had seen each other. Years before, while the young officer's family was living in Charleston, Sherman had been a visitor in the Macbeth home. Sherman asked about his family and told him that, if he would write a letter to his mother, he would take it with him and personally see that it was mailed. A few days later an anxious middle-aged woman learned the details of the tragedy which had befallen her son.

After the surgeons had done all they could, the wounded were left in the care of an officer and four men chosen from among the Confederate prisoners of war, along with a five days' supply of food.

Although the Battle of Averysborough was referred to by

many as just a skirmish, the people in the district did not dismiss it so lightly. In a letter datelined "Where Home Used to Be, April 12, 1865," seventeen-year-old Janie Smith wrote that the battle "beggars description." The blood of the dead and wounded "lay in puddles in the grove," while "the groans of the dying and the complaints of those undergoing amputation was horrible." She called Sherman's troops "fiends incarnate," so different from the "gallant and gentlemanly" Confederates. They "left no living thing in Smithville"—her home town and immediate site of the battle—"but people and an old hen." The hen "played sick and thus saved her neck, but lost all her children." The Yankees "would run all over the yard to catch the little things to squeeze to death." They searched "every nook and corner," and "the things they didn't use were burned or torn to strings." They set the blacksmith shop afire, and "into the flames they threw every tool, plow, etc., that was on the place." As ill-smelling as the battlefield was with its unburied bodies and its puddles of blood, it "does not compare with them [the Yankees] in point of stench." They kicked down fences "like mad cattle" and marched into the house, "breaking open bureau drawers of all kinds, faster than I could unlock" them. They "cursed us for having hid everything and made bold threats if certain things were not brought to light ... all to no effect." They "took Pa's hat and stuck him pretty badly with a bayonet to make him disclose something," but "you know they were fooling with the wrong man." An "impudent dog" came upon her and "Kate"—presumably her sister—in the dining room and wanted to know why they were not in the kitchen cooking breakfast. In the South, she told him, servants usually did the cooking. The intruder muttered something about their not having any servants left to cook for them, intimating that the Negroes would leave to follow Sherman's army. But "not one of the servants went from here."

Everything of value she and her family had was lost, including "all of my stockings and some of our collars and handkerchiefs."

If she ever saw a "Yankeewoman," she intended to "whip her and take the clothes off of her very back." Looking forward optimistically to an invasion of the North, she hoped Johnston's and Lee's armies would "carry the torch in one hand and the sword in the other." She wanted "desolation carried to the very heart of their country . . . the widows and orphans left naked and starving just as ours were left."

During the fighting Sherman, on horseback, saw a man, shoeless and hatless, approaching on foot, his head bandaged with a handkerchief. Saluting, the tattered and limping pedestrian told the general that he was Captain Duncan. After capturing him in that fight at Fayetteville, he said, Hampton's men had taken his coat, hat and shoes, and had cursed him when he protested against such treatment of a Federal officer. He had escaped soon after leaving Fayetteville and made his way to the Federal lines. Sherman, angry as always whenever he considered his men mistreated, sent him to Kilpatrick. Kilpatrick asked for and obtained Rhett's transfer from Slocum's infantry to the cavalry. Then he ordered Rhett to give up the fine horse he had been riding and march afoot. The Confederate colonel was also deprived of his elegant boots. But he got them back, reportedly because none of Kilpatrick's men's campaign-toughened feet were delicate enough to wear them.

The affair at Averysborough had considerable significance from the Confederate point of view. In spite of Hardee's withdrawal, and the opening to the Federals of the road to Goldsboro, it proved to the enemy that the Confederates still had the will and the means to fight hard. It refuted the reports that Confederate morale was desperately low. Nichols, considerably impressed, gave them credit for "more pluck than we have seen in them since Atlanta." It also accomplished much for the Confederates in a military sense. Sherman's advance was delayed long enough for their wagon trains to be ferried across the South river well ahead of the enemy. Even more important, it upset

Sherman's plan to keep all his units in tight formation and close to each other, for mutual aid if attacked. The Averysborough engagement caused the Left Wing to become stretched out to a dangerous degree, and greatly increased the distance between it and the Right Wing, which was one of Hardee's primary objectives in making the attack. He realized as well as Johnston that the only possibility of defeating Sherman was to get his two wings widely separated. With that separation accomplished, Johnston began pushing ahead plans to take advantage of it.

The opportunity came before the Confederate commander was really ready. The task of collecting his troops was far from completed when his cavalry commanders sent him word at his Smithfield headquarters on March 17 that Slocum's Left Wing had made a turn toward the east near Averysborough and was moving away from Raleigh straight toward Goldsboro. The urgency for immediate action was confirmed in the early hours of March 18, when Johnston was awakened by a messenger from General Hampton, in over-all command of Confederate cavalry in that area. Hampton's men, the dispatch said, had had brushes with Sherman's troops, not cavalrymen but infantrymen who had been close behind Hardee since soon after leaving Cheraw. This meant only one thing: the main Yankee army was near. If Johnston was to strike at it, he would have to strike quickly.

Johnston had 8,725 men under his immediate command at Smithfield. They consisted of General Robert F. Hoke's excellent division of 4,775 North Carolinians and 3,950 men of the Army of Tennessee under Lieutenant General A. P. Stewart. Hardee's troops were at Elevation, resting from the battle of the day before.

The Confederate commander ordered his own troops and Hardee's to start marching immediately toward Bentonville, a small town on the southeast side of Mill Creek, a tributary of the Neuse river. They were to bivouac that night between Bentonville and the Averysborough-Goldsboro road. To speed up his own troops' movement, Johnston ordered them to leave their wagons and much of their artillery behind. While awaiting the arrival of these reinforcements, Hampton was ordered to hold the Yankees at bay.

It was of course the Left Wing, supported by Kilpatrick's cavalry, that was now about to meet Hampton's outnumbered troopers. Howard's Right Wing was moving toward Goldsboro on another road south of the one Slocum was following. Thanks to the delay Hardee had inflicted upon Slocum at Averysborough, the Right Wing was also considerably east of the Left Wing. Johnston's maps indicated that the distance between the two wings was so great—more than a full day's march from head of column to head of column—that Howard could not get to Slocum's assistance in time to play a decisive part in the battle. They also indicated that the distance between Elevation and Bentonville was so short—just twelve miles—that Hardee's army could easily get to the Bentonville area by nightfall. The maps were grossly inaccurate. The distance between Sherman's Right and Left wings was actually much less than they indicated. And the distance between Elevation and Bentonville was considerably greater.

In accordance with Johnston's orders, Hampton on March 18 ordered his cavalrymen, without their mounts, to advance against the enemy near Bentonville. The fighting that followed was not decisive, neither side making any important gains after the initial clash, and both withdrew at day's end. While this lively skirmishing was going on, both Johnston and Hardee were driving their forces toward the battle area. The former arrived that evening, and he and Hampton went into conference immediately. But Hardee did not get there that day. Nightfall of March 18 caught him about five or six miles away, considerably farther than Johnston's maps had indicated he would be. There, at Snead's house, he halted his tired men for a few hours of sleep, of which they had had very little the past few days and nights. They resumed the march early the next morning.

The site Johnston chose for the impending battle was on high ground. There was, to the left and at right angles to the road on which Slocum's troops were approaching, an unusually good terrain for artillery. Howard himself, not given to praising an enemy, said it "could not have been better selected." Hampton had added to its natural advantages by ordering light entrenchments to be dug between that site and the Federals.

At dawn Hampton's cavalry, still fighting as infantrymen, advanced as they had done the day before and took up again the position they had held before withdrawing at sunset. Working behind this protective shield, Johnston sent his various but far too few units to their assigned positions. Hoke's division of tough North Carolinians, then under the general command of Braxton Bragg, took its place astride the Goldsboro highway, on the Confederates' extreme left. The position to its right Johnston assigned to Hardee's two divisions, under the immediate command of McLaws and Taliaferro. Stewart's corps, which had arrived during the night, took its assigned place at those two divisions' right. It brought the Confederate line almost parallel to the Goldsboro highway, the entire formation resembling a sickle, Hoke's Tar Heels representing the handle, and Stewart's and Hardee's troops the blade. It was poised ready to swing against Jeff Davis' XIV Corps, then approaching Bentonville on the road to Goldsboro.

Having completed their task of covering the deployment of the main forces, Hampton's dismounted cavalrymen withdrew from their advanced positions and halted on the extreme right. Wheeler's cavalry reinforced them.

So far everything had gone well. But Johnston had been having trouble getting his men deployed. They had to march through closely packed trees and thick underbrush that grabbed at their feet and legs and made every step forward a struggle against weeds and briers.[14]

To facilitate meeting Schofield and Terry near Goldsboro, Sherman, who had been with the Left Wing, started early on the morning of Sunday, March 19, to cross over to Howard's Right Wing. He had not gone more than six miles when he heard the heavy thunder of artillery. Wondering what it might portend and whether he ought to continue, he thought of reining his horse around and going back. But about that time a messenger arrived with reassuring news: Confederate cavalry had been putting up stronger resistance than usual, Slocum's message said, but no serious difficulty was anticipated. The Federal advance was expected to continue with little delay. Sherman, therefore, spurred on his horse toward the Right Wing. However, he took the precaution of ordering Kilpatrick, who had also planned to join the Right Wing, to stay with the Left Wing.

It soon became evident to Brigadier General William P. Carlin and the men of his XIV Corps division that Slocum's message was far too optimistic. Those dismounted Confederate cavalrymen were actually a buffer for Johnston's entire army. Surprised that the Confederates were not being forced back "worth a damn," Carlin deployed his men to drive them off the road, but his troops continued to make only slow progress against that resurgence of enemy power. Then they struck a solid wall of Confederates, not dismounted cavalry this time but battle-trained infantrymen—Hoke's Tar Heel veterans of the Army of Northern Virginia.

The lead troops of Carlin's division, spilling onto an area known as Cole's plantation, ran into a tornado of artillery from Hoke's batteries. Realizing that this was not just another skirmish but a real battle, the like of which they had not known since Atlanta, Carlin's subordinates stopped thinking of advancing and started thinking of defense. General H. C. Hobard's brigade found protection in a wooded ravine on the left. General G. P. Buell took up defensive positions in the same general area, after making an unsuccessful attempt to flank the enemy. Colonel David Miles' brigade moved to the right of the Goldsboro highway and deployed.

Slocum was impressed by this Confederate show of strength, thinking that he was up against only an unusually stubborn cavalry unit, strengthened by a few artillery pieces. The idea of calling for help, if it occurred to him at all, was quickly dismissed.

The XIV Corps' General Jeff Davis was as mistaken as Slocum regarding the enemy strength ahead. After that brief taking to the defensive he ordered Carlin's division ahead once more, led by Buell's brigade.

To move ahead meant moving through a patch of woods, and there the Confederates were waiting. After allowing sufficient time for the Federals to be swallowed up by the trees, the Southerners let loose a storm of shot from the left that broke the advance and sent the enemy reeling backward after they had moved to within a few steps of the Confederate breastworks. The Federals again made a stand, and for a while the fighting was at too close quarters for bullets. Men in blue and men in gray furiously pounded each other with the butts of their guns and ramrods seized off artillery pieces. Finally Buell's brigade could stand it no longer. His men fell back in none too good order, many running, one of them told his parents, "like the deuce."

Slocum and Davis were discussing the surprising Confederate resistance when a staff officer arrived in great excitement. He had found, not just cavalry but infantry "entrenched along our whole front." There were enough of them "to give us all the amusement we shall want for the rest of the day."

Unaware that his and Kilpatrick's combined forces outnumbered Johnston's by more than three to two, Slocum was not willing to risk the outcome of the battle without reinforcements. So another message went out to Sherman, an urgent appeal for help.

The crisis was relieved somewhat by the arrival of a brigade from the XX Corps, commanded by General J. S. Robinson. But Slocum's situation was made more difficult by the exposed position of Hobart's brigade: instead of dropping back, as ordered, one regiment had pushed forward. This left it open to a flank attack. It also dangerously exposed Robinson's brigade. Seeing this danger, Slocum sent an officer to Carlin with the suggestion—it apparently was not a direct order—that he move back in order to close that break in the line. It was not followed, however, and Robinson, who had given up two of his regiments to help fight off a threatened attack on another part of the front, did not have enough men to seal the gap. Barely ten thousand Federals faced the whole of Johnston's army.

For the first time in many months the Confederates were capable of taking the offensive. However, they had lost valuable time in fighting off Carlin's attack. And every minute was used by the Federals to strengthen their breastworks and deploy the newly arrived XX Corps. The Confederates lost much of their advantage, too, when Johnston sent McLaws' division of Hardee's troops to the assistance of the hard-pressed Bragg. McLaws' reinforcements did not reach Bragg in time to help him substantially, and their absence weakened the Confederate right, delaying and reducing the power behind the counter-attack which Stewart and Hardee were preparing.

It was nearly 3 o'clock when Johnston's infantry, strengthened by Hardee's troops, was finally ready to move forward. This it did in two columns, plunging at the enemy across the six hundred yards separating the armies. A Confederate watching from a distance called the advance "truly beautiful." But he also saw how small the Confederate units were, "regiments being scarcely larger than companies and a division not much larger than a regiment should be." The going got tougher as they passed the halfway mark. The break in the Federal line had not been closed, and the excited graycoats poured through it, outflanked Buell's exposed brigade and pushed on three hundred yards to overwhelm Robinson's men. Carlin's troops were completely routed.[15] Federal Lieutenant Charles S. Brown admitted he and his comrades showed "some of the best running ever did." The coup was so successful that Slocum's entire left was smashed. The units upon which he had been depending to deal the Confederates a sharp defeat—Hobart's, Buell's and Robinson's—were forced back in disorder to the protective bosom of the XX Corps, just getting ready to enter the battle. A Federal saw "masses of men slowly and doggedly falling back along the [Goldsboro] road and through the fields and open woods on the left of the road." Minnie balls were "whizzing in every direction." Confederate troops, "stretching through the fields to the left as far as the eye could reach," were "advancing rapidly, and firing as they came." They reminded him of "the waves of the ocean, resistless."

To fill the vacuum created by Carlin's retreat, General Jeff Davis ordered Morgan to send Fearing's brigade, which he had been holding in reserve, to the left. "Strike them wherever you find them!" he shouted to the departing warriors. "Give them the best you've got, and we'll whip them yet!"

Confusion developed when Fearing's men reached the Goldsboro road. Making a flank attack upon the troops pursuing Carlin's men, they forced the Confederates back. But Fearing's troops themselves were attacked on the flank by a second group of Confederates rushing down the road on their right. Yielding to this new pressure, they fell back and formed a new line just to the right of the Goldsboro road. The fighting gradually diminished and eventually ended as only a skirmish.

Fearing's departure created a gap between his brigade and the rest of Morgan's division, and the Confederates rushed in to make the most of it. Three brigades from D. H. Hill's corps began battering at the rear of Morgan's breastworks. Had this advantage been followed up vigorously, as Hoke wanted done, by sending his own division into that gap, the outcome probably would have been disastrous for the Federals. Instead Bragg ordered a frontal attack.

Their feet gripped by gooey swampland and their limbs harassed by undergrowth, the Federals and Confederates engaged in desperate hand-to-hand combat. Veterans of the long, bitter fighting in Virginia said this segment of the battle was worse than anything they had seen there except Cold Harbor. Morgan's men were in a desperate situation. They were forced for a while to fight Southerners in front of them and Southerners behind them at the same time. Nearly six hundred men from Hoke's division alone were killed and wounded. More than half of them belonged to a single regiment, the 36th North Carolina.

While this frenzied slugging was going on General Jeff Davis, watching it from the eminence of his saddle some distance from the carnage, was assailed by stabbing doubts. It seemed most unlikely that his men would be able to "whip them yet." The XIV Corps' commander had thrown everything he had into the struggle. His last reserves had been used up. Even his personal protectors and the men assigned to guard his headquarters were now out there fighting and clubbing and sweating and dying like the others. But all was not yet lost. "If Morgan's troops can stand this," he said anxiously to an aide, "all is right; if not, the day is lost."

Morgan's men did not have to stand much more. Cogwell's brigade of the XX Corps arrived with potent help. Tired though these veterans were from their fast march, Davis sent them forward immediately, hoping they had come in time to turn the balance in his favor. Shoving through a troublesome wilderness of swampland and undergrowth, they encountered Hill's troops just as the Southerners began pounding Morgan's breastworks from the rear. In the ensuing struggle Cogwell's troops overpowerd Hill's and shoved them back to the Goldsboro highway. This action proved decisive. The battle of movement was succeeded by a battle of position. Lines were strengthened during the night. New breastworks went up.

Meanwhile, the main body of the newly arrived XX Corps, under General Williams, had been preparing to meet the next thrust—Johnston's third advance—which Williams had good reason to think would be directed at him. He sent Hawley's brigade to the left to help fight off an attack that appeared imminent in that sector. Robinson withdrew two of his regiments from the area where they had fought with Carlin's ill-fated division and sent them to the new danger point to reinforce Hawley. They took up their position about a mile behind Carlin's breastworks. When Hardee and Stewart plunged forward, driving Carlin's division ahead of them in confusion, Robinson's three regiments still with Carlin dropped back across the open fields. That placed their line parallel to the original line, and their right then rested on the Goldsboro road. Between Hawley's and Robinson's forces was a four-hundred-yard gap. On a small hill slightly behind it stood a powerhouse of Federal artillery ready to make that gap a death trap for advancing Confederates. The Federal position was strengthened by the arrival of Ward's division. It was used to extend Hawley's lines to the left. Kilpatrick's cavalry, brought to the area by the noise of battle, took up its usual task of guarding the Federal left flank. Selfridge's brigade was held as a reserve force, to be sent where needed.

The Federals' preparations to meet the assault were unwittingly aided by the enemy. In their headlong pursuit of Carlin's troops the Confederates became careless and confused and failed to follow up their victory as expeditiously as they should have. They were distracted, too, by Fearing's attack on their flank. This gave the Federals valuable time, which they turned to excellent use. They used fence rails and everything else they could find to build breastworks. Carlin's troops were reorganized into a reserve unit. They and others received fresh ammunition. Gunners were told to double the number of shots in their guns. Other improvisations, such as the use of bullet-filled bags and whole boxes of cartridges, were tried out. By the time Johnston struck, a rejuvenated XX Corps was waiting and confident.

The Battle of Bentonville

The Confederates struck at about 5 o'clock, erupting from a patch of pine forest and moving steadily toward the XX Corps directly ahead. Soon after reaching the open field they ran into concentrated Hell. From its hilltop position to the rear of the Federal lines the mobilization of artillery exploded with murderous effectiveness, aided by rifle fire from the waiting infantrymen. The Confederates first slowed, then halted and finally, seeing their comrades die all around them, withdrew. Again they moved in, trying to reach and exploit the wide-open gap between Hawley and Robinson. But again their line crumbled and fell back. In all, they made five tries. Casualties were fearful. Some units lost a quarter of those engaged. A single regiment lost a hundred and ninety men in dead and wounded. A Confederate sergeant said that final lunge was as tough as anything he had seen at Gettysburg. Gathering darkness mercifully brought the blood-letting to an end. Leaving skirmishers at the line originally held by Carlin's men, the Confederates dropped back to where they had stood in the morning.

While that battle was raging at Bentonville Howard's Right Wing was continuing on toward Goldsboro, unaware that the Left Wing was in trouble. It is true, Howard became disturbed over that distant roar of guns, but, like Sherman, he assumed that Slocum and Kilpatrick were merely finding enemy cavalry more stubborn than usual. Later in the day when the rumble not only continued but steadily increased in volume, he became more concerned. He ordered Hazen's division, bringing up the rear, to leave the Right Wing and march toward the source; however, Sherman countermanded the order.

Later Sherman began to have doubts. But until Slocum's courier arrived during the night of March 19-20 with the urgent appeal for help he had no idea his Left Wing was having serious trouble. Stirred to action and oblivious to his red-flannel nightshirt and drawers, he snapped out orders like an excited sergeant, orders sending the entire Right Wing to Bentonville.

"Fighting Joe" Wheeler's cavalry harassed and delayed it by attacks from behind hastily constructed breastworks. But he was not able to prevent the most advanced units—four brigades which had been on wagon-guard duty—from reaching the Bentonville area at about dawn, using a short cut which carried them to the rear of Johnston's forces. Hazen's division, also using that short cut, arrived soon afterward. It was followed along that same route by others. By noon units of the two wings had coalesced and Hoke's breastworks began to feel from the rear the strong pressure of Woods' division, leading the Right Wing advance. At first the attacks were beaten back. But finally, finding this pressure too strong to stand, Hoke was forced to drop back to another position running parallel to the Goldsboro road and close enough to prevent its use by the enemy.

Hoke's men hastily prepared entrenchments in this new position. The line was extended to the left to Mill Creek by the arrival of Butler's and Wheeler's cavalry. Howard called the V-shaped stronghold "an enlarged bridgehead." Johnston was now so situated that he could face both the Left Wing on the west and the rest of the Right Wing approaching from the east. It provided probably the best possible defense of Bentonville (which it embraced).

The last of Howard's troops reached Bentonville about 4 o'clock in the afternoon and took their places facing Hoke's new line. Howard complained later that the nature of the terrain added to his difficulties. On the surface it seemed dry and solid. But it was watery and swamplike underneath. So "we could not draw artillery over it," and "the battle was fought mostly by infantry."

Howard's arrival brought overwhelming strength to the Federals. The Confederates now faced the enemy in three directions. Johnston's only escape route would be across Mill Creek, at his rear, difficult to cross because of heavy rains. He was now clearly on the defensive.

The Battle of Bentonville

There was no serious fighting on March 20, certainly not by the standards of the previous day. Johnston was in no position to attack, and Sherman did not choose to do so. He preferred to give the Confederates a chance to escape while he resumed his march toward Goldsboro and his rendezvous with Terry and Schofield. It was more important than risking heavy losses in a test of strength at Bentonville. The Southerners themselves expected to be marched out of the battle area during the night and on to Smithfield. In expectation of such an order, a few took advantage of the darkness and the end of the skirmishing to drop off to sleep. The weather was on Johnston's side, making escape easier. A drenching rain started about sundown and was still falling at daybreak and thereafter.

But Johnston and his men were still there the next morning. The Federals opened up by applying heavy pressure against them on the Federal right and center. Expert marksmen fired at Hill's troops from the relative safety of farm buildings. An attack on the right by Logan's XV Corps drove skirmishers of McLaws' and Hoke's outfits out of their advanced rifle pits. They never were in Confederate hands again.

In the early afternoon General J. A. Mower, on the Federals' extreme right, sent two brigades of the XVII Corps around the enemy's left flank. After about four hours of fighting they overwhelmed and captured two lines of Confederate rifle pits guarding that single bridge across Mill Creek. They followed up this victory by plunging foward to within fifty yards of Johnston's headquarters. Had they been able to continue the advance and seize the bridge, Johnston would have been completely sealed in. He would then have had no choice except surrender of his whole army or a desperate, virtually doomed fight to break out of the ring. But Mower had moved faster and farther than anticipated, considerably ahead of General Blair's XVII Corps. That had left a gap of some three quarters of a mile between those brigades and the supporting forces. "With fifteen thousand such veterans as those of the glorious 17th Corps entrenched on Johnston's line of retreat," Nichols wrote somewhat lyrically, "an attack along the entire line would have insured the total destruction of the Rebel army."

The Confederates commenced a counterattack. In his exposed advanced position Mower felt almost simultaneously a head-on attack from Cumming's Georgia Brigade near the Smithfield road and one on the left flank from the 8th Texas Cavalry, led personally by General Hardee. Wheeler's cavalry also made a powerful thrust to the right of the Texas cavalrymen, and forced a wedge in the gap between Mower's troops and the rest of the XVII Corps. At about the same time Wade Hampton, leading Young's cavalry brigade, struck powerfully at Mower's right flank.

The desperate Confederate counterstroke was successful. The two Yankee brigades stopped short of their goal and withdrew to the relative safety of a ravine.[16] Later, when that part of the battlefield became less violent, Mower made another move, this time to the position he had held before beginning his advance. This was in preparation for another drive toward that coveted prize, the Mill Creek bridge. Howard ordered Blair to support him with his entire XVII Corps, if needed. However, before Blair could move effectively to Mower's assistance or Mower could resume the advance toward Mill Creek bridge, Sherman canceled both orders.[17]

Sherman's forbidding of Mower's second drive virtually ended the Battle of Bentonville, except for occasional lobbing of shells into opposing lines. That night—as rainy and miserable as the one before—Johnston ordered an evacuation. First the wounded were taken across Mill Creek bridge, then, soon after 2 o'clock, their able-bodied comrades began moving out of their positions in the direction of the bridge and Smithfield. Federal skirmishers, making inquisitorial stabs across the intervening fields and woods, found only empty breastworks.

Sherman sent his army in pursuit. Johnston wrote in his

memoirs that the first Federals to reach the stream "made re-peated efforts" to get across the bridge but "failed in all." He gave them credit, however, for "brave efforts." Three Federal color-bearers "fell within fifty feet of the Confederate rear guard."[18]

Actually, Sherman's attempt to overtake and capture John-ston's army was not very spirited. He had no particular desire to take it on at that time. Schofield was already in Goldsboro. Terry would be there soon. Sherman's main desire was to give his troops a rest, exchange their worn and tattered clothing for fresh uniforms, shoes and underwear and obtain fresh supplies and equipment.[19] Johnston's troops bivouacked that night near Smithfield.

When the casualty lists were made up it was found that the indecisive Battle of Bentonville had cost the two armies 4,133 in killed, wounded and captured. Sherman, with about three times as many engaged as his antagonist, lost 1,527, including General Fearing. Fearing was seriously wounded in his charge against the Confederate center. Johnston, notwithstanding his comparatively small force, lost many more—2,606.

One of those 2,606 Confederate casualties brought personal grief to high-ranking officers in both armies. Sixteen-year-old Willie Hardee, General Hardee's only son, joined the 8th Texas Cavalry on the eve of the battle, kissed his father good-bye and, with the gallant buoyancy of youth, advanced into that flaming inferno alongside his new comrades. He had been there only a few minutes when a bullet struck him down with a wound that was plainly mortal. After the battle Confederate General Stephen D. Lee passed a note through the lines to the Right Wing commander. He knew Howard would want to know. For Howard had been Willie's Sunday School teacher at West Point while Hardee was commandant of cadets there and had admired the lad immensely. Willie was taken to Raleigh with other battle wounded and died there.

Howard's Right Wing and Kilpatrick's cavalry were ordered

to remain in Bentonville March 22 to bury the dead and remove the wounded to hospitals. That day Sherman rode on to Cox's Bridge, ten miles west of Goldsboro, where General Terry, with his two divisions from the X Corps, had just thrown a pontoon bridge across the Neuse river and was ready to march into the city. There he would link up with Schofield, whose XXIII Corps had arrived the day before.

XVI

RALEIGH

SHERMAN AND TERRY rode into Goldsboro March 23. Part of Slocum's Left Wing arrived the same day. The Right Wing, after completing its post-battle duties at Bentonville, and the rest of the Left Wing reached the Goldsboro area the next day.

The following day the men were stirred by a sound they had not heard in months, a locomotive whistle. Repairs to the Morehead City railroad had been completed, and the first train, bringing supplies from warehouses on the coast, was blowing for the station.

Sherman was angry and chagrined to have had to wait two days before the train came. He had expected the two railroads —to Morehead City and Wilmington—to be in full operation when he arrived. Mountains of new uniforms, shoes and other equipment his troops needed so badly should have been waiting for him, he thought, and he was not a man to accept such disappointments philosophically.

His chief complaint was to Quartermaster General L. C. Easton. In spite of his having reached Goldsboro later than expected, he wrote, both railroads were idle and useless when he arrived. He had found neither the "vast store of supplies I hoped to meet here" nor any statement from anybody in authority as to when they might be expected. He had sent wagons to Kinston to get whatever he could, but that was only a makeshift arrangement. A military commander at a base served by railroads running to two deep-water ports should not have to do that. And Goldsboro's bare-shelved warehouses had made him break faith with his men. He had been importuning them all along to "bear patiently" the lack of suitable clothing and other supplies. At Goldsboro, he had been promising, there would be enough of everything. Now, he told the Quartermaster General, he was under the embarrassing necessity of telling them they would have to wear their rags and soleless shoes a while longer.[20]

The letter urged Easton to "expedite the movement of stores from the sea to the army," and "don't stand on expense."

He ordered Colonel W. W. Wright of his army's Railroad Department to "use extraordinary means, night and day," to get those railroads ready to handle three hundred tons of freight a day. He told Wright to "pay any price for labor." Soldiers were to be used for work they could do. Rolling stock was to be requisitioned anywhere in Sherman's command area, even as far away as Charleston and Savannah. Commanding officers and quartermasters were to give railroad equipment priority over all.

While waiting for the trains to start running Sherman ordered a review. But it emphasized the men's ragged and bedraggled state far more than their military prowess. One of them doubted, out loud, whether even the Confederates were "more ragged than we." Only a small minority—somebody estimated it at about one in a dozen—were wearing uniforms that did not lack essential components, and it was a rare outfit that was not a ridiculous patchwork of holes. Men who had lost their hats were wearing handkerchiefs around their heads. Others were sporting miscellaneous headgear picked up in attics and bedrooms from Atlanta to Goldsboro. Conspicuous in these bizarre get-ups were stovepipe hats, hats of the Revolutionary era, topless hats, ragged caps, through which unruly hair burst out like underbrush, caps without sun visors and caps that were nothing but sun visors. Hairy, sweaty chests were left bare by shirts that could not be buttoned and flapped gaily in the breeze. Sleeves were missing because the material had been used to patch holes in pants. Few trousers reached below the knees, the legs having been snagged by branches or cut off when they became more rags than breeches. Some of the troops without shoes or socks had wrapped blanketing about their feet. But, Howard observed with satisfaction, the men "were evidently in the best of health and full of vigor."

General Blair, in the reviewing stand, commented pityingly on "those poor fellows with bare legs." Sherman, hearing him, called them "splendid legs." He would, he said, "give both of mine for any one of them."

Sherman, who had never liked reviews, found no pleasure in this one. As proud as he was of his men's fighting capabilities, he could take no pride in their marching and parading. And since Schofield and Terry agreed that it was "a sorry sight," the ceremony was called off after two regiments had passed the reviewing stand.

Colonel Wright's job was nearer completion than Sherman realized when he wrote his impatient letters, and it was not long after that first locomotive whistle aroused the neighborhood that the second line was open. But transportation and supply troubles were not over. The locomotives, cars and other rolling stock were scanty, ancient and undependable. For some time trains on the Morehead City line ran only as far as Kinston. That made it necessary to unload supplies from ships and reload them onto smaller craft at Morehead City, Newbern and Beaufort. Then they had to be ferried up the Neuse river to Kinston and transshipped by train to Goldsboro. Washington, anxious to help, sent rolling stock which only added to the confusion and frustration because it was of the wrong gauges.

Sherman got along handsomely with Schofield, and on March 25 he turned his command over to his new comrade-in-arms and left Goldsboro for Grant's headquarters at City Point, Virginia, arriving on the evening of March 27. He was surprised to find that Abraham Lincoln was there too. Accompanied by Grant, Sherman paid his first call upon the President on the evening of his arrival and returned for a second visit the next day. In both conversations the President expressed anxiety lest Lee, forced to evacuate Petersburg and Richmond by Grant's steady pounding, would move rapidly south and combine forces with Johnston. Both generals were confident such a move could be checkmated. Sherman told Lincoln flatly that he had Johnston in such a position that the Confederate general could not make any significant move without causing his army to fall to pieces. And, if that should happen, he went on, it could never be brought together again as an organized fighting force.

Lincoln gave Sherman the impression that he was anxious to get the war over with as quickly as possible, even to the extent of granting generous terms to the enemy. "My God, my God!" the President moaned during one of those talks. "Can't you spare more effusion of blood? We have had so much of it."[21]

At City Point Sherman obtained Grant's permission to carry out a reorganization of his army. Its purpose was to increase the troops' effectiveness, making the best possible use of those added to his forces by Terry and Schofield and relieving him of administrative details through a better distribution of authority. His men now numbered some eighty-nine thousand.

The two-wing system which had worked so well since leaving Atlanta was replaced by a three-wing system. Howard's Right Wing became known as the Army of the Tennessee, while Slocum's Left Wing was designated the Army of Georgia. To Schofield went the command of the newly created Army of the Ohio, consisting of the XXIII Corps, under General Cox, and portions of the XXIV Corps, commanded by General Terry. Kilpatrick's cavalry, strengthened by a regiment of Pennsylvania cavalrymen, remained an independent unit. As before, it was answerable only to Sherman. General Mower succeeded

General Williams as commander of the XX Corps. All the other corps commanders retained their posts.

On April 5, the outfitting and equipping practically accomplished, Special Field Orders, No. 48, were issued for the beginning of a new campaign seven days later. The plans called for a feint on Raleigh. Then there would be a rapid march across the Virginia line to Burkeville, forty-five miles west of Petersburg, where Sherman's powerful force would plant itself between Lee and Johnston, making a junction of their armies impossible. Sherman would have a base of supplies at Norfolk and another at either Winton or Murfreesboro on the Chowan river and would be in full communication with Grant's Army of the Potomac in the Petersburg area. In its new position north of the Roanoke his troops would be capable of striking mightily in whatever direction military contingencies might call for.

But momentous happenings on the Virginia battlefields brought a drastic change in the outlook. Sherman learned April 6 that Petersburg and Richmond had been captured and the Confederates were in precipitate flight southward.

"We have Lee's army pressed very hard, his men scattering and going to their homes by the thousands," Grant's message said. "He is endeavouring to reach Danville, where Davis and his cabinet have gone. I shall press the pursuit to the end; push Johnston at the same time, and let us finish up this job all at once."

This development called for a new plan of action. Special Field Orders, No. 48, were rescinded and new ones issued. The army would leave Goldsboro on April 10, two days earlier than planned, and move against Johnston. The Confederate Army, then at Smithfield, was believed to consist of some thirty-five thousand men. After defeating it Sherman's troops would continue on to Greensboro and Charlotte.

Two days later Sherman received another dispatch from Grant, dated April 5:

All indications now are that Lee will attempt to reach Danville with the remnant of his force. Sheridan, who was up with him last night, reports all that is left with him—horse, foot, and dragoons—at twenty thousand, much demoralized. We hope to reduce this number one-half. I will push on to Burkeville, and, if a stand is made at Danville, will, in a very few days, go there. If you can possibly do so, push on from where you are, and let us see if we cannot finish the job with Lee's and Johnston's armies. Whether it will be better for you to strike for Greensboro or nearer to Danville, you will be better able to judge when you receive this. Rebel armies now are the only strategic points to strike at.

Sherman shot back his reply. He would move at daybreak April 10, "prepared to follow Johnston wherever he might go."

Sherman's columns entered Smithfield at 10 o'clock on the morning of April 11, after encountering Confederate cavalry and hastily erected barricades much of the way. They found that Johnston had retreated across the Neuse river and burned the bridge two days earlier. Thanks to one of the Confederacy's few remaining railroads, which relieved his troops of much of their equipment and supplies, he had moved along rapidly and was now encamped near Raleigh. The burning of the bridge did not delay the Federals much. Slocum's engineers had pontoons ready quickly, and they soon started across.

About 4 o'clock on the morning of April 12, while Sherman's troops were still in the Smithfield area, two officers rode into the town in great excitement: Lee had surrendered. Along with Grant's dispatch they brought copies of the Lee-Grant correspondence leading up to the surrender and the surrender terms.

The news spread rapidly. The first troops to hear it were the veterans of Slocum's Left Wing, now the Army of Georgia. They were marching through Smithfield en route to the Neuse when it was announced at the head of column. Hitchcock tells about the "billows of tumultuous cheering" that rolled down the line like a tidal wave. Regimental bands "made the old town echo with music as beautiful as it was patriotic."

Major General J. D. Cox's outfit was a few miles outside Smithfield when the news came. The weather was warm and springlike. The men were lounging about on the grass enjoying the customary rest that came at the end of each hour's marching. Then, Cox recalled:

> . . . a staff officer was seen riding from the front, galloping and gesticulating in great excitement, the men cheering and cutting strange antics as he passed. When he came nearer, he was heard to shout, "Lee has surrendered!" The soldiers screamed out their delight; they flung their hats at him as he rode; they shouted, "You're the man we've been looking for these three years." They turned somersaults like over-excited children. . . .

A country woman was standing at the gate of her ramshackle home, her children tugging at her frayed skirt. Tears began pouring from her tired eyes. "Now," she said to her brood, "Father will come home."

Sherman made the news official in Special Field Orders, No. 54:

> HEADQUARTERS, MILITARY DIVISION
> OF THE MISSISSIPPI
> IN THE FIELD, SMITHFIELD, NORTH
> CAROLINA,
> APRIL 12, 1865

The general commanding announces to the army that he has official notice from General Grant that General Lee surrendered to him his entire army, on the 9th instant, at Appomattox Court-House, Virginia.

Glory to God and our country, and all honor to our comrades in arms, toward whom we are marching!

A little more labor, a little more toil on our part, the great race is won, and our government stands regenerated, after four long years of war.

W. T. SHERMAN, MAJOR-GENERAL COMMANDING

When Sergeant Upson went to General Woods' headquarters to take command of the headquarters guard, Woods ordered him to dismiss the guard and "come into my tent." Upson thought he was "crazy or something" to give such an order. He asked him why.

"Don't you know Lee has surrendered?" Woods replied. "No man shall stand guard at my quarters tonight. Bring all the guard here."

There was a giant bowl of potent beverage in the general's tent. Everybody drank. Brimming cups and glasses were carried to those unable to get inside. Lee's surrender, the jubilant Woods proclaimed, meant the end of the war, and that meant "we should celebrate as we have never done before." A band appeared and started playing and drinking, stopping the former to do the latter. "Some of them could not wait till they got through with a tune till they had to pledge Grant and his gallant army, also Lee and his gallant fighters," Sergeant Upson wrote in his diary. "Some of them seemed to think perhaps that was going a little too far but it passed. The band finally got so they were trying to play two or three tunes at once."

Officers from other outfits, attracted by the singing and joviality, drifted over to the Woods headquarters tent. A Colonel Johnson of Upson's own regiment took the sergeant by the arm, guided him to General Woods and "introduced me in a flattering speech." Then:

> ... General Woods shook my hand and said he would promote me, that I could consider myself a Lieut. After a little more talk from Colonel Johnson he made me a captain, and I might have gone higher if the General had not noticed that the band was not playing. Going out to see about it, he found the members seated on the ground or anything they could find, several on the big bass drum. Then he realized that they were tired, very tired, and he would relieve them. He got the big drum, other officers took the various horns and started on a tour through the camps—every fellow blowing his horn to suit himself and the

jolly old General pounding the bass drum for all it was worth. Of course we all followed and some sang, or tried to sing, but when "Johnny Comes Home Again" and "John Brown's Body" or "Hail Columbia" and "The Star Spangled Banner" are all sung together they get mixed so I don't really think the singing was a grand success from an artistic standpoint at least. But it answered the purpose and let out a lot of pent up exhuberant feeling that had to have an outlet.

The parade kept on and on, but along toward daylight the tired marchers began drifting back to their tents. A day or two later General Woods recognized Sergeant Upson and spoke, but the sergeant's rapid promotion had apparently vanished with the festivities.

The tidings from Virginia, as welcome as they were, nevertheless brought a fresh crop of problems for the Yankee commander. He no longer had the relatively simple duty of preventing Lee's army fom joining Johnston's or of assisting Grant to defeat those two armies if they should unite. It would now be necessary not only to win a clear-cut victory over Johnston, but also to prevent chaos among the civilian population of the South. That, he was sure, would follow if Johnston's army degenerated into guerilla bands, attacking the Federal forces in small units and committing crimes against the people. Unless it could be prevented, Sherman was convinced, it would be necessary to keep an army of occupation in the South indefinitely. This would add heavily to the country's financial burdens and keep the South in a condition of servility that would increase the bitterness already existing.

Sherman was sure he could readily defeat Johnston, if the Southerner would turn and fight. But he doubted whether he could overtake him if Johnston should choose to avoid a battle by retreat. By discarding their wagon trains, the Confederates could keep well ahead of their enemies, disperse and assemble later at agreed-upon places, to molest and harass Sherman's men. In that way, the war might be dragged on for months or even years. Such a prospect did not appeal to Sherman, who wanted battlefield victories and the routing of the enemy.

Such consequences could be prevented, he hoped, by convincing Johnston that the Confederate cause was hopeless and obtaining his surrender and cooperation. Sherman thought this could be done by offering generous terms, following Grant's example at Appomattox. "The terms you have given Lee are magnanimous and liberal," he wired Grant. "Should Johnston follow Lee's example, I shall of course grant the same."

Soon after Sherman's men left the Smithfield area they found the weather favoring the enemy again. Heavy rains set in, and quagmires and treacherous torrents loomed ahead. Corduroying was needed not only for the wagons and other heavy wheeled equipment but for the ambulances as well.

Raleigh awaited the coming of the bluecoats with mounting anxiety, unallayed by the arrival of the Confederate army April 11.

Johnston's columns stirred much pride but no joy in those watching from the curbs. Bands played "Dixie" and other patriotic and popular songs. There were jestful exchanges between spectators and men. Everybody made a brave pretense of being cheerful, and everybody made a failure of it. The men showed plainly how tired, hungry and discouraged they were. The Yankees, they said, were not far behind. No attempt was to be made to defend the city: they would soon be heading west again, exactly where nobody but the highest officers knew.

Shortly after arriving Johnston received a telegram from Jefferson Davis telling him of Lee's surrender and ordering him to turn over his command to Hardee and join him in Greensboro as quickly as possible.

In anticipation of such a contingency, Governor Zebulon B. Vance had already set in motion a series of events which he hoped would take North Carolina, if not the whole Confederacy, out of the war. The day before Johnston entered the city, the Governor had conferred with one of his predecessors, President David L. Swain of the University of North Carolina, still carrying on with a handful of students after four hard years of war. The plan under discussion had been conceived by Swain and another ex-governor, W. A. Graham. It consisted of the calling of a special session of the North Carolina Legislature at which resolutions would be adopted expressing a desire to end the war. Like-minded Southern states would be invited to take similar action. The Legislature would choose commissioners to make peace overtures to Washington, and the outcome would be reported to a convention to be called for that purpose. Meanwhile—with the enemy less than fifty miles away—the Governor would send a delegation to meet Sherman and ask him to suspend hostilities until the peace commissioners had accomplished their mission. Governor Vance had considered the hour too late for any good to be expected from the proposed convention, but he had agreed to send a delegation to meet Sherman, provided that Johnston approved. Wanting the matter settled as quickly as possible, he had ridden out of the city on the Smithfield highway to confer with Johnston. Johnston had advised him to stay in Raleigh, communicate with Sherman, and cooperate with him after the occupation, provided Sherman showed him the proper respect.

In response to a telegram from Governor Vance, Graham reached Raleigh from his home in Hillsboro at about 3 o'clock on the morning of April 12. He, Vance and Swain talked over the plan at breakfast a few hours later. Then they went to Vance's office in the Capitol to frame a letter to Sherman, which Vance signed:

> Understanding that your army is advancing on this capital, I have to request, under proper safe-conduct, a personal interview, at such time as may be agreeable to you, for the purpose of conferring upon the subject of a suspension of hostili-

ties, with view to further communications with the authorities
of the United States, touching the final termination of the existing war. If you concur in the propriety of such a proceeding I
shall be obliged by an early reply.

Carrying a safe-conduct permit from General Hardee, in
temporary command in Raleigh during Johnston's absence from
the city, Swain and Graham left at 10:30 that same morning on
their adventure. Accompanying them were Colonel James G.
Burr of the North Carolina State Guard, Major John Deve-
reux, of the governor's staff, and Dr. Edward Warren, North
Carolina Surgeon General. As the special train consisting of
the locomotive and one coach puffed out of the station a
seventeen-year-old youth stood on the cowcatcher. He was
holding a white flag.

Just beyond the city limits the train was stopped by Wade
Hampton's cavalry, and the delegation was taken to him. He was
not at all enthusiastic about its mission but agreed to send a
message to Sherman requesting safe passage through the Federal
lines.

The train had not gone far when it was stopped again, this
time by a courier from Hampton. The Confederate cavalry
leader, the courier told them, had received a message from
Johnston canceling their safe conduct permit and ordering
them back to Raleigh.[22] Angry at this threat to their enterprise,
they demanded that Hampton's orders be given to them by
Hampton personally or in writing. While they were still talking
Hampton himself rode up and repeated the message he had
given the courier. He also wrote out a second note to Sherman
rescinding that earlier request for safe conduct. This apparently
left the crestfallen commissioners no choice but to return to
Raleigh and report the complete failure of their mission. But,
before they could do so, Confederate cavalrymen rode out of
some nearby woods hotly pursued by carbine-shooting Federals.
In a few exciting minutes Hampton and his men were well out

of sight. The train, without moving an inch, was now in Federal territory.

The two ex-governors explained their situation to the inquisitive enemy cavalrymen, who could not understand what a couple of elderly gentlemen in high hats and frock coats were doing in a war theatre. They asked that they be permitted to return to Raleigh, but this was not to be accomplished so simply. They were not innocent noncombatants, for all their civilian attire, they were told. They were prisoners. The only way they could get back to Raleigh was to obtain permission from Sherman himself.

This was entirely agreeable to them, but they would first have to see Kilpatrick and get his permission to see Sherman. He gave it after a stern lecture on the folly of allowing themselves to be caught in a skirmish area.

When the fighting subsided and they returned to their train they found that the fire in the locomotive had gone out. Some of Kilpatrick's men, attracted to the scene like curious schoolboys, helped the engineer get it started up again, and then piled on top of the coach for a ride. At Sherman's headquarters some fourteen miles from Raleigh the wandering and bewildered envoys were met by Sherman himself, who invited them to his tent.

Sherman treated his guests with great consideration and courtesy and told them he was quite willing to come to terms with Governor Vance. He did not wish, he said, to subject him or the people of North Carolina to undue hardships or embarrassment. He hoped Vance and the other officials would stay in Raleigh: they would be needed to keep the governmental machinery in operation. Sherman showed a particularly conciliatory attitude in his note to the governor which he asked the commissioners to take back with them:

> I have the honor to acknowledge the receipt of your communication of this date, and enclose you a safeguard for your-

self and any members of the state government that choose to remain in Raleigh. I would gladly have enabled you to meet me here, but some interruption occurred to the train by orders of General Johnston, after it had passed within the lines of my cavalry advance, but as it came out of Raleigh in good faith, it shall return in good faith, and shall in no measure be claimed by us. I doubt if hostilities can be suspended as between the army of the Confederate Government and the one I command, but I will aid you all in my power to contribute to the end you aim to reach, the termination of the existing war.

It was quite late. It would be dangerous for the gentlemen to start back until the next day. They were glad to accept Sherman's invitation to spend the night at his headquarters. He treated them royally, feeding them choice viands and serenading them with music by a regimental band.

Meanwhile, Governor Vance had been spending worried hours in Raleigh. It was expected that the commissioners would be back in the early afternoon, not later than 4 o'clock in any case. When 4 o'clock came the governor was sure some serious misadventure had befallen them. When General Wheeler advised him they had been taken prisoners, he sorrowfully dismissed the Graham-Swain enterprise as a gallant failure, and took other steps to protect the city. He wrote a letter to Sherman stating that he had authorized Raleigh's Mayor William H. Harrison to surrender it and requesting that public buildings be spared. Then, at midnight, he rode to the camp of General Hoke, about eight miles west of Raleigh.

Sherman, still at his gracious best, went with Graham and Swain to their train at daylight the next morning (April 13) and bade them a cordial farewell. About five miles from Raleigh the train was stopped briefly by General Kilpatrick, who gave them a stern warning: if Federal troops encountered any resistance when entering the city, the Yankees would "give you hell."

Back in Raleigh Mayor Harrison had been up all night

bracing himself for the rendezvous. About daylight, weary and heartsick, he rented a carriage and driver, picked up others in the delegation and started out to the city limits. Rain was falling in a steady, depressing downpour. In his pocket he carried Governor Vance's letter to Sherman requesting "the extension of your favor" to the city and its people. It bespoke special care to safeguarding the State Capitol, museums, libraries, archives and other public buildings soon to be "left in your power." One of the mayor's companions, riding with the driver, carried a stick to which he had attached a white handkerchief. Reaching the fortifications that had been built to defend the city in more optimistic days, they stopped their horses. Then they waited, in that dreary, downpour, for the Yankees. At about 8 o'clock they sighted in the hazy distance a cluster of horsemen.

The blue-uniformed cavalrymen halted, and one of them leveled a spyglass upon the nervous delegation. Someone attached his handkerchief to the topmost part of the fortifications. The troops rode up.

"What does this mean?" one of them demanded.

Someone explained. Lacking any kind of military organization, he said, the delegation wished to surrender the city and request protection of civilian and public property. The officer in charge of the troops replied that only General Kilpatrick had authority to discuss surrender or arrange surrender terms.

The officer and his escort rode back to the main cavalry force. Soon General Kilpatrick rode up.

"This is General Kilpatrick, I presume?" queried the delegation's spokesman.

"That is my name. Whom do I address?"

"My name, sir, is Rayner—Kenneth Rayner—and I have been selected to formally surrender the city of Raleigh to General Sherman's army."

Rayner's emotion got the better of him. Tears began running down his cheeks. Kilpatrick, on the other hand, appeared to be chillingly indifferent, even to the point of discourtesy. But he agreed to protect the lives and property of those who caused the army no trouble, threatening at the same time to pursue "with relentless fury" all "traitors in armed opposition to the integrity of the Union." Rayner, Mayor Harrison and the other discouraged and humiliated committee members, having done all they could, climbed into their carriage and drove back to the city.

Meanwhile, Graham and Swain had returned. Much had happened in Raleigh since their departure less than twenty-four hours earlier. Hardee's troops were gone. Wheeler's cavalrymen, left behind to protect the city until the Federals approached, had also left, except for some stragglers. But, before riding off to the west, they had looted the railroad station and set it afire. Fayetteville Street, the city's main thoroughfare, was a vale of emptiness and silence, stores and offices closed and shuttered.

Swain walked through the eerie quiet to the Capitol, tried the doors to room after room. He could not get in, all had been locked. All the windows had been closed and bolted.

Going from corridor to corridor in that tomblike structure that made every footstep resound hollowly, he at last found another person, a faithful Negro servant who for many years had been running errands for the governor's office—"the only human being," Swain said, "who had dared to venture beyond his doors." Just before leaving the night before Governor Vance had turned the building's keys over to him. He gave them to Swain, and the two men went through the building unlocking doors and throwing open windows. Everything was in chaos. The floor of the State library was littered with bound documents. Somebody evidently had jerked them off the shelves and thrown them helter-skelter. Glass cases in the State Museum had been shattered and robbed of their specimens, some of them quite rare and valuable. The prized rock collection, painstakingly assembled from all over the state, was in chaotic disarray. Inkwells and scraps of paper all but covered the floors of the houses of the General Assembly, where nearly four years earlier, Secession had been voted in a mood of noisy jubilation. There was a bust of John C. Calhoun on which someone had emptied a bottle of ink.

The Yankees would be there any time now. Swain wanted to be ready for them with a reminder of their promise. Clasping the safe conduct permit Sherman had given him, he took his position at the entrance to the Capitol to await the on-coming horde. What he saw, however, as he peered through the morning air, was not Sherman's army or any portion of it but a band of stragglers from Wheeler's cavalry, bent on loot. Dismounting from their horses, they began the systematic sacking of the stores just across the street from Capitol Square. He called to them to desist and get out of the city at once. Resistance on their part, he warned, might result in devastation and bloodshed. They paid no attention until Swain shouted that he had just seen the head of Kilpatrick's cavalry. Then they ran to their horses, leapt into the saddles and raced away—except for a Texan named Walsh, who seemed to be their leader.

While Swain stood nervously and self-consciously at the Capitol's entrance, Kilpatrick's advance units moved smartly up the wide thoroughfare toward him. The air was alive with flags, and regimental bands were playing victory marches. The parade ground atmosphere subsided quickly, however. That lone Confederate cavalryman rode his black horse down the middle of the street in front of the Federals, shouting "God damn 'em!" and "Hurrah for the Southern Confederacy!" He fired five pistol shots at the approaching columns, then reeled his horse about and galloped away. The Federals started in pursuit, but he had a good start and probably would have escaped if his horse had not stumbled and fallen. He was carried to Kilpatrick, who by this time had reached Capitol Square.

Kilpatrick gave him a stern, cold look.

"Don't you know," he asked, "what the penalty is for resisting after terms of surrender have been agreed upon?"

"I knew nothing about the surrender," the Texan replied, "and I didn't shoot at anybody."

"I understand you are one of those fellows who have been breaking open stores and committing robbery last night and early this morning. Your action today has endangered the lives of many citizens of this town."

Kilpatrick turned to one of his aides.

"Orderly," he commanded, "take this man out where no ladies can see him, and hang him."

Walsh pleaded for permission to write to his wife, but Kilpatrick ordered the hanging to take place at once. It was carried out at what was then known as Rayner Grove, not far from the Governor's Mansion. Walsh was buried under the tree from which he had been hung.

Kilpatrick paused only briefly in Raleigh. As soon as the Star Spangled Banner reached the top of the flagpole on the Capitol dome, his men continued on in pursuit of Wheeler's men, now on their way to Chapel Hill. Only a single regiment remained behind to keep order until Sherman and his infantry arrived.

Sherman set up his headquarters in the Governor's Mansion. At about 3 p.m. Graham and Swain called to deliver the keys to the Capitol. Sherman was surprised to find that Vance had left the city. It had been his understanding, he said, that the Governor would remain there and cooperate with him in keeping state functions in efficient operation. He would like him to return. To that end, he wrote out another safe conduct order which he asked Graham to deliver to the Governor, then in Graham's home town of Hillsboro.

When Graham delivered the document, the Governor decided not to return to Raleigh. Instead, he went to Greensboro to confer with Jefferson Davis, but Davis had left for Charlotte. He decided then to go back to the capital. But en route he was stopped by Confederate troops, so he went on to Charlotte and had an interview with Davis. On a second attempt to return to Raleigh, he was again stopped by Confederate troops.[23]

Raleigh

Sherman reported his latest conquest to Grant by telegraph. He would be there only a short time, he said, then he would continue westward toward Ashboro and from there move on to either Charlotte or Salisbury, depending upon the military situation. He hoped to overtake Johnston before the latter could get across the Yadkin river. But that would be difficult in the face of Johnston's two-day start.

Later, instead of moving after Johnston, Sherman decided to remain in Raleigh awhile. News had reached him that Major General George Stoneman's cavalry division had crossed the mountains from east Tennessee and torn up the railroad at Salisbury, thereby destroying the Confederates' final supply line and last rail escape route. Stoneman was now reported to be moving steadily on Greensboro. A delay in Raleigh, Sherman decided, would enable Phil Sheridan's cavalry to move down from Virginia in front of Johnston and, with Kilpatrick's help, block his retreat. Then Sherman could advance against Johnston's rear with his slower-moving infantry and crush the Confederate army between these two forces.

"I am very anxious to prevent his escape into Georgia," Sherman wrote Kilpatrick April 14. "If he does go to Georgia, we can capture all rolling stock and vast amounts of property on the road south of Saulbury to Greensboro. The governor asks me to suspend hostilities. I will not suspend hostilities until Johnston's army is captured or scattered. . . . My army is very large and cannot run as fast as Johnston's who has the assistance of the Railroad. I am in hopes that Sheridan will come down, when he, with your Cavalry, can get ahead of him and hold him till we get up when we can make short work of him."

The people in and around Raleigh "manifest more signs of subjugation than I have yet seen," the letter went on. But "Jeff Davis has more lives than a cat and we must not trust him."

Another reason for not moving on immediately was that time was needed to complete rebuilding of the railroad from

Goldsboro. With it in operation, Sherman could use Raleigh as a base for extended movements into central and western North Carolina.

In spite of promises of leniency, the citizens of Raleigh, not knowing what to expect, were anxious that first day. Most of them did not venture outside, keeping their houses locked, and shuttered to prevent the lights from being seen from the streets.

Some women braved the real and fancied dangers of the streets to go to neighbors' houses and various public buildings that had been set up as hospitals, as they had been doing for three weeks or more, to care for the wounded men who had been brought to Raleigh after the battles of Averysborough and Bentonville. One, helping out at Christ Episcopal Church, wrote later of her distress because her best "seemed nothing" against the overwhelming need. She was distressed because the shortage of beds made it necessary for many of the wounded to lie on benches, designed for the happier service of worshipping God. Some were "in high delirium," some "in the agony of death." One youngster had lost his identification papers. Nobody knew who he was or where he had lived before he heard the call of war. As the coffin lid was about to be screwed tight a "dear old lady" could not see him carried away and buried without some show of tenderness. She leaned over and pressed her lips against his brow. "Let me," she said, "kiss him for his mother."

In general, Sherman made good his promise to spare Raleigh and its people the depredations suffered in other places. With the inevitable exceptions, the men's conduct was exemplary. Confident that the war was all but over, he tried to make this final phase of the conflict as painless as possible. To curb the disorderly element among his men, he stationed guards at every place where trouble was likely to break out. As a consequence, very little trouble did occur. The men, Hitchcock wrote, behaved "as well as in Savannah." Everywhere, he said, "we hear mingled admiration and astonishment at the good conduct, the fine appearance and condition and the soldierly bearing of our army." Discipline was so good, another Yankee visitor wrote, that "the men didn't know themselves." They "took out their mischief in frightening Negroes." Foraging was curtailed, each brigade or regiment being allowed to do only as much as was necessary to keep itself supplied. Men caught seizing private property, except as specified, were punished.

The rural area did not fare so well. Outrages were perpetrated by both the Federals and Confederate cavalrymen.

Mrs. Mary Northcutt Bryan had to give up a fine cow to Sherman's men, which was butchered on the spot and "only a steak cut from her side." They also killed a mare with complete indifference to the fate of her colt. Mrs. Bryan and some neighbors kept it alive with bottle feeding.

Rural homes were stripped of their flooring, weather boards and windows, and farm equipment battered to pieces. Men tore down fences to build fires, allowing valuable farm animals to wander far from home.

Negroes also suffered. Seven on one plantation had to give up everything they had. One lost his prized timepiece to a soldier who shouted to him: "Darn your black skin, give me the watch in your pocket!" A blind colored woman lost her brand new dress.

Sherman's policy of conciliation toward North Carolinians took strange forms and brought strange relationships. Among his Raleigh intimates was the family of former Secretary of the Navy George E. Badger, whom he had known in Washington before the war. He invited Mrs. Badger and her two daughters to watch a corps review as his guests. And they accepted, although one of the daugthers was the wife of a Confederate army officer then somewhere in Virginia. After the review the group returned to the Badger residence. There, Hitchcock tells us, they "had an extremely pleasant visit."

Sherman also tried to melt animosities by visiting various

institutions in Raleigh. One of them was the insane asylum. His arrival created great excitement among the inmates, who had their own ideas of what a military conqueror would be like. He admonished one fellow, a Northerner caught in enemy territory by the war, to "put your faith in God" and "His power to take care of all of us." The man replied that he had faith of that kind. But "when it comes to the question of power, it strikes me that a man who has been walking about the country whipping those accursed rebels has a damned sight more power than anybody I know of."

XVII

THE BENNETT HOUSE

IN RESPONSE TO Jefferson Davis' telegram, Johnston had arrived
by train in Greensboro at 8 o'clock the morning of April 12.
He was welcomed by General Beauregard. Two hours later they
were summoned to Davis' office where they found not only
Davis but three members of his cabinet, Secretary of State Judah
P. Benjamin, Postmaster General John H. Reagan and Secretary
of the Navy Stephen R. Mallory.

Johnston had been under the impression that Davis wished
to question him about the military situation and ask his advice
about continuing the war. Instead Davis wanted "to give, not
to obtain, information." In two or three weeks, Davis informed
them, he would have a large army in the field by somehow—
he did not say how—bringing back into uniform thousands who
had deserted and by enlisting—again he did not say how—
other thousands who had succeeded in slipping through the
fingers of the conscription authorities. The two generals were
full of doubts. How could men who had deserted when the
outlook was far less grave be induced to take up arms again
under the prevailing conditions? How could those who had
escaped military service when it was far more popular be persuaded to come out of the woods and swamps and offer

themselves for duty? But the President asked for "neither opinions nor information," and "the conference terminated."

Back at Beauregard's headquarters Beauregard and Johnston went into a thorough examination of the grim situation. They were subsequently joined by Secretary of War John C. Breckinridge, who brought them details of the latest Confederate reverses in Virginia, including of course Lee's surrender. Resuming their discussion after Breckinridge left, both men were certain, notwithstanding Davis' stubborn optimism, that the Confederacy was experiencing its dying gasps.

Johnston expressed his pessimism in a later conversation with Breckinridge. Jefferson Davis had lost every power of government he had ever held except one, the power to end the war —Johnston said. And that power Davis ought to exercise without further delay.

Johnston talked later to Mallory, who expressed "great anxiety" that peace negotiations be started as soon as possible and told Johnston he considered him the most suitable person to urge such a step upon the President. After thinking it over, however, Johnston objected to assuming that role. He was a military man, he said, not a civilian official. Such a suggestion should come from one of Davis' "constitutional advisers." Mallory agreed to broach it to Davis himself.

The next morning Johnston and Beauregard were again summoned to Davis' office and asked to describe the military situation. The Confederacy, they told him, had an army of about twenty thousand infantrymen and artillerymen and five thousand cavalry. Against this puny force the United States Government had in the field no fewer than three armies, every one of them vastly superior in numbers and equipment. Grant, they said, had a hundred and eighty thousand men. Sherman had a hundred and ten thousand at least and Edward R. S. Canby, in west Mississippi, some sixty thousand. If these three armies united, they would outnumber the Confederates by seventeen or eighteen to one. Moreover, with increasing enlistments in the North, those odds could be doubled in a few weeks. The Confederate cause was absolutely and irrevocably hopeless.

With the situation as it was, Johnston told the President, it would be "the greatest of human crimes" to prolong the war. He and his men, he emphasized, had "neither money nor credit, nor arms but those in the hands of our soldiers." [24] They had "no ammunition but that in the cartridge boxes, nor shops for repairing arms or fixing ammunition." Under such desperate conditions, the result of the war's continuation would be "not to harm the enemy, but to complete the devastation of our country and ruin of its people." It was the President's imperative duty, he told him, to exercise immediately the sole governmental prerogative still within his power: peace negotiations should be started at once.

Davis turned to the four cabinet members present—Breckinridge, Mallory, Reagan and Benjamin—and asked for their opinions. Only Benjamin took the opposite position. His "speech of war" reminded Johnston of Joseph Addison's Sempronius. It was obvious that the "Sphinx of the Confederacy" was speaking the President's mind as well as his own. Davis argued that it would be futile for him to try to open negotiations with the enemy for two reasons: first, the United States Government had shown by its reaction to a previous overture of this kind that it did not recognize his authority to negotiate, and there was no reason to think it would negotiate with him now; second, the United States Government was almost certain to flatly reject any peace terms he was willing to offer.

Johnston stepped in. Why not let him initiate peace negotiations with Sherman, soldier to soldier? Such procedures, he pointed out, were not at all unusual between military commanders.

After some discussion Davis outlined the subject matter of a letter that Johnston would send to Sherman, aimed at bringing the two enemy military commanders together to arrange an armistice. Their meeting would be followed by a meeting of the two governments' civil authorities to agree upon peace terms. That was not exactly what Johnston wanted, but he accepted it and proposed that Davis dictate the letter to Mallory at once. Johnston signed and sent the letter by courier to General Wade Hampton, near Hillsboro, for transmission to Sherman, and then rejoined his troops. Sherman received it the next day (April 14).

"The results of the recent campaign in Virginia," the message said, "have changed the relative military condition of the belligerents. I am therefore induced to address you, in this form, the inquiry whether to stop the further effusion of blood and the devastation of property, you are willing to make a temporary suspension of active operations . . . the object being to permit the civil authorities to enter into the needful arrangements for terminating the existing war."

Sherman answered at once:

> HEADQUARTERS, DIVISION OF THE
> MISSISSIPPI, IN THE FIELD,
> RALEIGH, N.C., APRIL 14, 1865

GENERAL J. E. JOHNSTON, COMMANDING CONFEDERATE ARMY: *General,*—I have this moment received your communication of this date. I am fully empowered to arrange with you any time for the suspension of farther hostilities as between the armies commanded by you and those commanded by myself, and will be willing to confer with you to that end. I will limit the advance of my main column tomorrow to Morristown and the cavalry to the University, and I expect you will maintain the present position of your forces until each has notice of a failure to agree.

Thus a basis of action may be had. I undertake to abide by the same terms and conditions as were made by Generals Grant and Lee at Appomattox Court House of the 9th instant, relative to the two armies, and furthermore, to obtain from General Grant an order to suspend the movement of any troops from the direction of Virginia. General Stoneman is under my com-

mand, and my orders will suspend any devastation or destruction contemplated by him. I will add, that I really desire to
save the people of North Carolina the damage they would
sustain by the march of this army through the central or western
parts of the state.

I am, with respect, your obedient servant,
W. T. SHERMAN, MAJOR GENERAL

Sherman's message (unaccountably delayed in transmission
—by Federal officers, Johnston charged, "not ours") reached
the Confederate commander on the morning of April 16. By
that time Johnston and his fast-moving troops were just a few
miles from Greensboro, where he supposed President Davis was
awaiting him. But, when he arrived he found that Davis had
left for Charlotte.

General Hampton had been instructed to make arrangements
for the meeting with Sherman. So Johnston rode to his headquarters near Hillsboro to find out what had been done.
Hampton told him the meeting had been set for noon the next
day. The place chosen was on the Raleigh road halfway between
the pickets of the two armies.

At 8 o'clock on the morning of April 17 an engine pouring
black smoke from its massive stack was standing in the Raleigh
station, on orders from the military. Behind it were two
passenger coaches. Several men in Federal blue stood nearby.
Sherman was about to climb aboard when he was halted by the
excited voice of the telegraph operator, racing down the stairs
from the telegraph office above the station. At that very moment,
he stammered, the ticker was spelling out a message of the
greatest importance. Sherman, he said, would certainly want
to see it before leaving.

The train idled while Sherman and his companions waited
for the message to be decoded. At 8:30 the telegraph operator
returned with it. It was from Secretary of War Stanton, sent
via Morehead City. Abraham Lincoln, it said, had been shot

at Ford's Theatre on the night of April 14. He had died at 7:22 the next morning. General Grant, who had expected to accompany the President and Mrs. Lincoln to the theatre, had changed his mind and remained away. Another assassin had stabbed Secretary of State Seward and his son Frederick at the Seward home at about the time of Lincoln's assassination. The Secretary's injuries did not appear to be serious, but the young man would almost certainly die. A third member of the assassin gang was believed to be on his way to Raleigh to kill Sherman. Andrew Johnson would take the oath of office immediately.

That was just about the worst possible time for such news. It might turn the Federal troops in and near Raleigh into a wild, uncontrollable mob, and destroy any chance for an imminent ending of the war. Indeed, if the men heard it while Sherman was away, almost anything might happen.

But possibly the news could be suppressed until his return that afternoon. Then, when he announced it, he could make a plea to the troops for self-control and consideration for the civilian population and take other measures to restrain them. He asked the operator if anybody else knew about the message. No, the operator replied. Sherman admonished him not to reveal or even hint at its contents "by word or look."

Troubled by this new and complicating development, Sherman rejoined the staff officers who were to accompany him and climbed aboard. At Durham's Station, Sherman and his party were met by Kilpatrick and a squadron of cavalry. After a short wait they mounted horses and rode off toward Hillsboro, preceded by a man carrying a white flag. Behind him was a small platoon of guards. A second platoon brought up the rear.

After riding about five miles the flag-bearer reported that another flag-bearer was approaching from the opposite direction, followed by General Johnston. All the members of Sherman's party except Sherman and his aides halted, while they rode forward. The two generals dismounted, shook hands and introduced the members of their parties. Sherman asked if there was not a place close by where they might talk in privacy. Johnston had passed a small farmhouse and suggested that they go there. The two men, who, Sherman wryly commented, "had been interchanging shots constantly since May, 1863" but had never met before, rode along side by side. Their staff officers and escorts followed. They "knew enough of each other," Sherman commented later, "to be well acquainted at once."

Major Nichols, like his chief, was getting his first look at Johnston. The Confederate general made an excellent impression. Nichols found his appearance "striking." His neat gray uniform harmonized gracefully with his full beard and silver-white mustache, "partly concealing a genial and generous mouth, that must have been habituated to a kindly smile." Johnston's eyes, he noted, were dark brown, varying in expression—"now intense and sparkling, and then soft with tenderness, or twinkling with humor." Jutting out from the rugged face like a bold crag from his native Virginia coastline was a Roman nose. The forehead was "full and prominent." His visage as a whole left an impression of "goodliness and manliness, mingling a fine nature with the decision and energy of the capable soldier." Nichols did not wonder that his chief had long had an ungrudging respect and admiration for his brilliant adversary.

Captain Conyngham, also a member of Sherman's party, wrote that while Sherman looked at ease, and "perfectly master of the situation," as befitted the conqueror, Johnston was "taciturn." He looked "haggard and careworn," but through it all he "still maintained the dignity of the soldier and the gentleman, as he certainly is."

The group reached the little farmhouse Johnston had mentioned, an insignificant frame structure with a shingle roof and huge chimney. All dismounted. Orderlies stepped forward to take the reins of the two conferees' horses. The other officers drifted from the road to the yard and began talking in friendly, informal fashion. At the door Sherman and Johnston were greeted by Mrs. Daniel Bennett, who looked wonderingly at them, at the men in the yard and at the horses in the road. Could they, Sherman asked, use her house for a conference? She told them it would be all right, gathered up her four wide-eyed youngsters and left with them, going to a small log outbuilding nearby.

As soon as the two men were alone in the large, sparsely furnished room that comprised the ground floor, Sherman reached into his pocket and pulled out Stanton's dispatch. His keen eyes focused upon Johnston's face.

Beads of perspiration formed on Johnston's forehead and cheeks as his mind grasped the significance of the message. He "did not attempt to conceal his distress," Sherman said. He denounced Lincoln's assassination as "a disgrace to the age." He was afraid, he said, that it would cause Sherman to take a harsher attitude toward the South and make the task of peacemaking much more difficult. Sherman tried to relieve his distress. He did not blame him in any way, he said. He was sure neither Johnston nor Lee nor any other Confederate military man had had any part in, or knowledge of, the crime. But he "would not say as much for Jeff. Davis, George Sanders, and men of that stripe." [25] Sherman told him nobody in his army except himself knew about it and he was fearful of his men's reaction when it was announced. Some irresponsible civilian in Raleigh might say something like "I'm glad of it" or "It's just what he deserved," bringing to the city "a fate worse than that of Columbia." Johnston called the assassination "the worst possible calamity to the South."

They got down to the business at hand. It certainly must be evident to Johnston, Sherman said, that the Confederate position was hopeless. Any further fighting would mean only more bloodshed without any gain. Now that Lee had surrendered, Johnston could do so with honor and dignity. Johnston did not pretend otherwise.

The Bennett House

But he differed from Sherman regarding the purpose of the meeting. For one thing, his thought in asking for the conference was not to discuss peace terms—which he considered outside his province as a military commander—but to arrange an armistice which would enable the civil officials of the two governments to meet and agree upon terms for ending the war. He reminded Sherman of his emphasis upon that kind of meeting in his note. Sherman replied that it was impossible for agreement of that kind to be made. The Government of the United States, he pointed out, did not recognize the Confederate Government as such. Its officials, therefore, could not deal with Confederate civil officials. He could not receive for transmission to Washington any proposals from them. But he was both able and willing to deal with Johnston as one military commander with another. And he was prepared to offer him the same terms that Grant, also dealing with Lee purely as a military commander, had offered at Appomattox.

Johnston objected. His position, he said, while admittedly serious, did not approach the seriousness of Lee's. He now had a four-day start on Sherman and could probably keep ahead of him indefinitely, if he should choose flight rather than capitulation. His troops could do what Jefferson Davis had suggested they do, break up into small guerilla bands and plague the Federals for years. But Johnston made it plain that he preferred honorable surrender. What, he asked, could Sherman offer him as conditions to an armistice?

More specifically, what he wanted was something in the nature of "general concessions"—the phrase is Sherman's—"that would enable him to allay the natural fears and anxieties of his followers, and enable him to maintain control over them until they could get back in the neighborhood of their homes," thereby "saving the State of North Carolina the devastation inevitably to result from turning his men loose and unprovided [for] on the spot, and our pursuit across the State."

Sherman replied that, on the basis of Congressional resolutions and statements by Lincoln, he thought the United States Government was interested primarily in restoring the Union. He did not think it wished to inflict undue harshness upon those who had taken part in the war. Federal soldiers and officials alike, he emphasized, were eager to end the bloodshed and, to that end, were willing to make reasonable concessions.

A thorny point of disagreement concerned Jefferson Davis. Sherman flatly refused to promise amnesty for him or any of his high civilian officials. Johnston, in spite of his loss of confidence in his chief and the coldness that had grown up between them, was not willing to leave Davis and his cabinet to the mercy of his enemies.[26]

Johnston approached the whole problem of peace-making from another direction. Instead of surrendering his army only, why not engineer terms under which all Confederate armies in the field—Dick Taylor's in Louisiana and Texas and others in Alabama and Georgia—would lay down their arms? Then the war would really be over. People everywhere could turn to the tasks of peace and reconstruction.

Sherman, not expecting a capitulation of this dimension, was surprised. The suggestion appealed to him. There was a big question in his mind, however. How could Johnston, commanding a single army, bring about the surrender of those other armies in distant states? Johnston's reply was that Secretary of War Breckinridge would order those armies' commanders to surrender, if satisfactory peace terms could be worked out.

The discussion dragged on for hours. Late afternoon caught them far from agreement, especially regarding the fate of Jefferson Davis and his cabinet, although both men felt sure they were well on their way to some kind of understanding. At sunset they agreed to quit for the day and to meet at the same time the next day. The "extremely cordial" nature of their conversations made Sherman virtually certain the discussions would end successfully.

Back in Raleigh Sherman ordered troops in the city to return to their camps, causing them to wonder what it was all about without guessing the truth. Guards were strengthened. Strong forces were posted along the roads leading to the various encampments. Then he issued Special Field Orders, No. 56, announcing "with pain and sorrow" the tragic happening of some seventy-two hours before.

"Thus it seems," the message went on, "that our enemy, despairing of meeting us in open, manly warfare, begins to resort to the assassin's tools." However:

> Your general does not wish [you] to infer that this is universal, for he knows that the great mass of the Confederate army would scorn to sanction such acts, but he believes it the legitimate consequence of rebellion against rightful authority.

That same view—that the people of the South, and even their officials, should not be blamed or punished for the crimes of a small band of assassins—was expressed in Sherman's letter to Halleck reporting on his meeting with Johnston. He could not, he said, "believe that even Mr. Davis was privy to the diabolical plot." The murder, he thought, was "the emanation of a lot of young men of the South who are the very devils."

In spite of the elaborate precautions against violence, Sherman, Howard and the others in command spent some anxious hours that Monday night. Men who had consistently condemned outrages in Georgia and South Carolina swore bitterly that, if the army started moving again, they would joyfully go along with those bent on house-burning and general devastation. Hitchcock wrote about stunned men standing in little knots "silent or talking in subdued but bitter tones." Many were "weeping like children." Sergeant Upson told about a mob of some two thousand fanatical troops who started marching toward the city, vowing to destroy it. General Logan ordered them back, but "they still went on." Not until he threatened to fire into their ranks with artillery did they listen to him and return to their tents. In other camps troops demanded that the armistice talks be called off and the advance resumed.

Few in Raleigh slept that night. Rumors of impending violence and wholesale devastation swept through the city. The Capitol, many heard, would be burned. But, when the sun rose flaming over Capitol Square, it lighted a city that was serene and undisturbed. Some attributed the men's good conduct to their grief, which was as personal to many as if a kinsman had been killed. General Howard observed that it "seemed to overwhelm them for a time," and "there was little thought of revenge." Others were less charitable. They had seen angry men bent on devastating retaliation. And they gave credit to the stern restrictive measures.

In spite of his preoccupation with the danger of mob violence, Sherman sounded out some of his chief officers regarding Johnston's proposals. Schofield, Howard, Slocum, Logan and Blair were in complete agreement. Every one of them "dreaded the long and harassing march in pursuit of a dissolving and fleeing army"—the words are Sherman's—"a march that might carry us back again over the thousand miles we had just accomplished." There was of course no question regarding the outcome of a battle if Johnston could be brought to battle: the Federals' preponderance in manpower, morale and equipment was so overwhelming that "we could destroy it in an hour." But they all knew, as Johnston did, that they probably could not make him fight. Some of Sherman's advisers even went so far as to urge him to agree, if necessary, to let Jefferson Davis and his cabinet get out of the country. Johnston was welcome to that concession, as far as they were concerned. Either Logan or Blair—Sherman could not remember which—"insisted that, if asked for, we should even provide a vessel to carry them to Nassau from Charleston."

After returning to his Hillsboro headquarters Johnston had wired Breckinridge to join him there as soon as possible. The

Secretary of War, accompanied by Postmaster General Reagan, traveled most of the night and reached Hillsboro about an hour or two before daylight (April 18). Going into conference immediately, they were briefed on the previous day's meeting. At Reagan's suggestion, it was decided to put into writing the terms that had been agreed upon. It would give Johnston and Sherman something concrete to work on. Johnston had to leave before the draft was completed, so he told Reagan to rush it to the Bennett house by courier as soon as it was ready.

Confident as he was that he was in a strong bargaining position vis a vis Sherman, Johnston nevertheless felt he needed help in dealing with the legal aspects of an agreement. He had, therefore, asked Breckinridge to come along with him, hoping Sherman would consent to his being admitted to the meeting, for the Secretary of War was one of the South's most brilliant men and something of a genius in legal matters. He asked Breckinridge to wait down the road a piece, where he would be quickly available if sent for but unembarrassed if ignored.

Sherman reacted as Johnston had expected when Breckinridge was mentioned. He stiffened rigidly at the suggestion. His answer was a positive "No." As far as he was concerned, he reiterated, there were no civilian officials of the Confederate States of America. Since he refused to recognize them, he could hardly discuss armistice terms or anything else with one of them. At that moment, however, Johnston had a thought: Breckinridge was not only Secretary of War but also a major general in the Confederate Army. Sherman's objections melted. He agreed to admit Breckinridge to the discussions, but with the clear understanding that he was dealing with Major General Breckinridge, not Secretary of War Breckinridge. Johnston stepped to the door and ordered one of his aides to fetch him. The tall, soldierly-looking Kentuckian dashed up a few minutes later, lept from his horse, tied the animal himself and made his way through small knots of Federal and Confederate officers into the house.

As Johnston had expected, Breckinridge's presence was of great assistance. For one thing, it gave substance to Johnston's claim that generals in command of other Confederate armies would be ordered to carry out the surrender terms agreed upon. Sherman seemed satisfied on that point.

But there were others on which agreement did not come so easily.

His men, Johnston said, were worried about their postwar status, particularly their political rights. Sherman tried to reassure him by reminding him of Lincoln's proclamation of December 8, 1863, which promised complete pardon for all Confederate soldiers below the rank of colonel who would surrender their arms and take the oath of allegiance. He also called attention to Grant's extension of amnesty to Confederate officers of all ranks, including Lee. It was true, Lincoln was no longer President, but Sherman was fully confident that soldiers of all ranks would be restored to full citizenship after taking the oath of allegiance.

This, however, was not what Johnston wanted. Broad assumptions, he argued, would not satisfy his men. They wanted something specific and binding.

He also brought up some other matters that were troubling him, as well as many other Southerners. What form of government was the South to have? Were its people to be denied representation in Congress? Would Virginia, North Carolina, Georgia and the others have no separate political existence? Would the South, in brief, become a puppet of the North?

And what about the proposal to disarm Confederate soldiers? Would the South be left powerless against depredations by wandering bandits and killers? Would law-enforcement officers be stripped of the means of enforcing the law?

Sherman pooh-poohed these fears. He again mentioned Lincoln's amnesty proclamation, Grant's generous terms to Lee, including the extension of amnesty to Lee himself and all other officers of the Confederate Army, and other official and private expressions which, he said, left no doubt in his mind that Southerners would be treated with consideration after submitting to the legal authority of the United States. They would, the Federal general insisted, have essentially the same status and protection against the outlaw element that other citizens would have.

Johnston and Breckinridge were both impressed by the Sherman reasoning. But their doubts were not altogether dissipated. They insisted that the armistice terms contain specific provisions for the personal safety of former Confederate soldiers and guaranties of their civil rights.

The discussions ended temporarily when Sherman became thirsty. Stepping to the door, he called to his orderly and asked him to fetch his saddlebag. From it he removed a whisky bottle and passed it around, inviting the others to pour themselves a drink. Breckinridge's eyes widened happily when he saw the bottle coming toward him. He poured himself a jumbo-sized swig and swilled it with enthusiasm. Forthwith was unloosed a stream of eloquence in which rambling tributes were made to Southern and Northern leaders in many fields, and war heroes of both sides were fulsomely praised. During this interlude, in which the main business of the conference stood stock still, Sherman, who had grown somewhat friendly toward Breckinridge the soldier, let him run on and on. But at last he decided it was time to call a halt. "See here, gentlemen," he protested. "Who is doing this surrendering? If this thing goes on, you'll have me sending a letter of apology to Jeff Davis." [27]

The meeting returned to a serious vein. His fling at an end, Breckinridge became once more the brilliant and able counselor. The discussions were in full swing when a courier arrived with the papers on which Reagan had been working. Johnston and Breckinridge looked them over and discussed them between themselves. Then Johnston handed them to Sherman.

The document began with a rambling preamble leading up to the surrender terms. Sherman took a quick look and found it "general and verbose." He did not like it and told the others so.

Sherman sat down at the table and, with the Reagan document before him, started writing rapidly. When he was finished he handed the paper to the others and told them these terms were the best he could offer: [28]

Memorandum, or basis of agreement, made this 18th day of April, A.D., 1865, near Durham Station, and in the State of North Carolina, by and between General Joseph E. Johnston, commanding the Confederate Army, and Major-General W. T. Sherman, commanding the army of the United States in North Carolina, both present:

1. The contending armies now in the field to maintain their *status quo,* until notice is given by the commanding general of either one to its opponents, and reasonable time, say forty-eight hours, allowed.

2. The Confederate armies now in existence to be disbanded and conducted to the several state capitals, there to deposit their arms and public property in the State Arsenal, each officer and man to execute and file an agreement to cease from acts of war, and abide the action of both Federal and State authorities. The number of arms and munitions of war to be reported to the chief of ordnance at Washington City, subject to future action of the Congress of the United States, and in the mean time to be used solely to maintain peace and order within the borders of the States respectively.

3. The recognition by the Executive of the United States of the several State governments, on their officers and legislatures taking the oath prescribed by the Constitution of the United States; and, where conflicting State governments have resulted from the war, the legitimacy of all shall be submitted to the Supreme Court of the United States.

4. The re-establishment of all Federal courts in the several States, with powers as defined by the Constitution and laws of Congress.

5. The people and inhabitants of all States to be guaranteed, so far as the Executive can, their political rights and franchises,

as well as their rights of person and property, as defined by the Constitution of the United States and of the State respectively.

6. The executive authority of the Government of the United States not to disturb any of the people by reason of the late war, so long as they live in peace and quiet, abstain from acts of armed hostility, and obey laws in existence at any place of their residence.

7. In general terms, war to cease, a general amnesty, so far as the Executive power of the United States can command, or on condition of the disbandment of the Confederate armies, the distribution of arms, and resumption of peaceful pursuits by officers and men, as hitherto composing said armies. Not being fully empowered by our respective principals to fulfill these terms, we individually and officially pledge ourselves to promptly obtain necessary authority, and to carry out the above programme.

Outside the attendant officers mingled freely and in a spirit of gay comradeship in the yard. Some were grouped in small knots under and around the large oak tree to which Sherman's horse had been tied. Major Hitchcock had "quite a chat" with a Confederate major. The Southerner impressed him as a "quiet, gentlemanly, unassuming man." He "had evidently seen considerable service, though he had very little to say about it." Men in gray and men in blue unreservedly expressed the hope that the wretched business would soon be over and they could return to their families.

That hope brightened merrily when the three generals stepped out of the cottage. They told them an agreement had been reached and would be signed as soon as additional copies could be readied. Southern officers and Northern officers impulsively grasped each other's hands as though personally to seal the compact.

As soon as the copies of the agreement were ready, Sherman and Johnston re-entered the cottage. The sheets were placed on the table and signed, first by Sherman and then by Johnston.

Each took a copy. After shaking hands in the gathering darkness, they walked to their horses.

Major Hitchcock and his new friend were still engaged in conversation. Their strong hands met in a firm, cordial grasp. "Good-bye, Major," they said in unison. "Hope we shall meet again." The Southerner added: "In the right way."

Early the next morning Major Hitchcock left Raleigh by train for Morehead City and Washington. In his carefully guarded dispatch case he carried Sherman's copy of the agreement and two letters of explanation and clarification. One was addressed to General Halleck, the other to both Halleck and Grant. The latter was to be delivered to Halleck if he should be in Washington to receive it, otherwise to Grant.

In his letter to Halleck Sherman referred to his early fears that Lincoln's assassination would lead to serious trouble from his troops. But their indignation had "softened down" and "can easily be guided." As for a warning from Halleck—similar to the one from Stanton—that a member of the gang which had killed the President was on his way to Raleigh to kill him, Sherman treated the threat lightly. The would-be assassin, he wrote, "had better be in a hurry." Otherwise, "he will be too late."

No one, he said, had shown greater concern over the Lincoln assassination than General Johnston. Johnston realized that it "was calculated to stain his cause with a dark hue." The Confederate general had told him, he wrote, that the crime had extremely serious possibilities for the South. For the people there "had begun to realize that Mr. Lincoln was the best friend they had." [29]

Sherman asked Halleck to prevail upon President Johnson, insofar as he could, to make no changes in the terms agreed upon. For "I have considered every thing." He was convinced, he said, that "the Confederate armies once dispersed, we can adjust all else fairly well." [30]

The second Sherman letter also asked the recipient—as it happened, Grant—to try to get the Sherman-Johnston agreement approved by the President. If that could be done, it "will produce peace from the Potomac to the Rio Grande." Breckinridge had assured him, Sherman wrote, that Johnston would be able to carry out "to their full extent" all the provisions of the agreement. He had stated specifically that Johnston would be able to surrender other Confederate armies along with his own. If Grant (or Halleck, if he should receive the letter) "will get the President to simply indorse the copy, and commission me to carry out the terms," he promised to "follow them to the conclusion."

Sherman anticipated a possible objection from the President: the proposed peace terms might appear to be letting the Confederates off too easily. But, he contended, that was not true:

> You will observe that it is an absolute submission of the enemy to the lawful authority of the United States, and disperses his armies absolutely; and the point to which I attach most importance is, that the dispersion and disbarment of these armies is done in such a manner as to prevent their breaking up into guerilla bands. On the other hand, we can retain just as much of an army as we please. I agreed to the mode and manner of the surrender of arms set forth, as it gives the States the means of repressing guerillas, which we could not expect them to do if we stripped them of all arms.

Although both of the Confederate generals at the conference had conceded that slavery was no longer an issue, he wrote, he had not insisted upon inserting a specific antislavery declaration in the surrender terms: that could be made clear later to the individual states. The leading people of the South, he was sure, "sincerely want peace." He did not think they would resort to war again "during this century." There was no doubt in his mind that "they will in the future be perfectly subordinate to the laws of the United States."

His confidence that the President would approve at least that part of the agreement recognizing Confederate officials and governments was strengthened the day after Hitchcock's departure. His emissary was still off the North Carolina capes when he received a copy of the New York *Herald* of April 12. Prominently headlined was an article stating that General Godfrey Weitzel, in command of Federal troops in Richmond, had invited the Virginia Legislature, consisting of prominent Confederates, to assemble in that city. Presumably, Lincoln had approved. The newspaper writer indicated that the same recognition of Confederate legislators and other Confederate officials would be extended to other states. He gave the impression, moreover, that this show of generosity had met with widespread approval.

On April 14, however—the day Lincoln was assassinated and two days after the New York *Herald* published the Weitzel story —Horace Greeley's New York *Tribune* published a news story of an entirely different kind. General Weitzel, it said, had been removed from command at Richmond, and Secretary Stanton had declared himself "strongly adverse" to allowing the Virginia Legislature (or any other in the South) to meet. For some reason, however, Sherman did not see this story. Had he done so, he would not have written so confidently to General Johnston on April 21:

> By the action of General Weitzel in relation to the Virginia Legislature, I feel certain we will have no trouble on the score of recognizing the existing State Governments. It may be, however, the lawyers will want us to define more minutely what is meant by the guaranty of rights of persons and property. It may be construed into a compact for us to undo the past as to the rights of slaves and leases of plantations on the Mississippi. . . . I wish you would talk to the best men you have on these points, and, if possible, let us, in the final convention, make these points so clear as to leave no room for angry controversy. I believe, if you would simply and publicly proclaim what we all feel and know, that slavery is dead, that you would inaugurate an era of peace and prosperity that would soon efface the ravages of the past four years of war.

Two days later, Sherman, in a much different frame of mind, was writing out another message. Other papers had arrived from New York giving the important news he had missed. General Edward O. C. Ord, the new Federal commander at Richmond, reflecting the official mind at Washington, had withdrawn permission for the Virginia Legislature to meet. Sherman feared, he told Johnston, that Lincoln's assassination had so excited the public that politicians would be able to "thwart our purpose of recognizing 'existing local governments.' " However, he was not completely discouraged: he still felt "there must be good sense enough left on this continent to give order and shape to the now disjointed elements of government."

XVIII

PEACE

AFTER LEAVING the Bennett cottage General Johnston sent his copy of the compact to President Davis, then rode to Greensboro to rejoin his troops, arriving early the next morning. Soon after his arrival Colonel Archer Anderson, Adjutant General of the Army, handed him two messages from Davis. One directed him to obtain from J. N. Hendren, Treasury agent, thirty-nine thousand dollars in silver which Hendren was holding subject to his (Johnston's) orders, and use it for military expenses. The second message instructed him instead to send the money to Davis at Charlotte.

Johnston, who had conscientiously followed orders from his civilian and military superiors throughout the war, decided that this was a time he should disobey. He did not send the money to Davis. To his mind the army was the only agency of the Confederacy that still existed in fact. The government had come to an end. Even if it had still been functioning, it is problematical whether he would have felt morally justified in sending the money. His troops had not been paid in months. Their families were in want. Actually, he did not have thirty-nine thousand dollars to distribute, the Commissary-General having already withdrawn twelve hundred dollars. Johnston ordered that each man receive his proportionate share of the residue, regardless of rank.[31]

Jefferson Davis' stubborn optimism, which had caused him to bristle at Johnston's advice to seek armistice terms in the first place, asserted itself again. Again he took a stand for carrying on the war, in spite of Sherman's generous terms and against the advice of his cabinet, every member of which now urged him to sign. But pressures even sterner and more implacable than the strong urging of his advisers were working on him and shoving him relentlessly toward acceptance. One of them was the steady melting away of Johnston's army. During those days of indecision the troops who had fought bravely and uncomplainingly through many months fell victims to the boredom of idleness. Waiting in camp with nothing to do, they magnified their personal grievances and dislikes. They had more time to worry about their families. The army became a prolific rumor incubator, the most demoralizing rumor being that they would become prisoners of war after the surrender. The prospect of spending many months behind enemy barricades as a climax to their honorable war service made them sick at heart. They could see just one way of escaping, and they chose it *en masse.* Between April 19 and 24—less than a week—Johnston lost some four thousand men from his infantry and artillery. The cavalry lost almost as many. Added to the manpower loss was the loss of horses and mules, which the deserters took with them, leaving artillery and wagons stranded.

Davis now realized he had no choice. Yielding to his cabinet and to grim realities, he telegraphed Johnston, still in Greensboro, April 24:

> ...Your action is approved. You will so inform General Sherman; and, if the like authority be given by the Government of the United States to complete the arrangement, you will proceed on the basis adopted. Further instructions will be given after the details of the negotiation and the methods of executing

the terms of agreement when notified by you of the readiness on the part of the General commanding United States Forces to proceed with the arrangement.

Immediately after arriving in Washingon on the afternoon of April 21, Hitchcock delivered his dispatches to General Grant. Grant told him that the President would undoubtedly call a cabinet meeting to consider the agreement. Hitchcock therefore would probably have to spend forty-eight hours in the city. However, he was called back to Grant's office at 10 o'clock that same night where he was told he was to leave for Raleigh immediately. He learned, to his considerable surprise, that he was to have a distinguished traveling companion, none less than General Grant himself. Others in the party included Major General Montgomery C. Meigs, Army Quartermaster General, and three members of Grant's staff.

They reached Morehead City April 23 too late to take the afternoon train to Raleigh. Hitchcock sent Sherman a telegram telling of his arrival. He did not mention Grant's presence, however—"for prudential reasons," Sherman explained later. The party arrived in Raleigh about 6 o'clock the next morning, before Sherman was up and dressed. He received one of the greatest surprises of his life when, upon keeping a rendezvous with Hitchcock a little later, he recognized his old friend and military superior. His surprise would have been mingled with anger and resentment had he known the true significance of Grant's visit.

The bad news was not long delayed. Sherman's new orders were to give Johnston the agreed-upon forty-eight hours notice and, at the end of that time, resume the advance. At noon that day somebody at Johnston's headquarters handed him a single-sentence dispatch:

> You will take notice that the truce or suspension of hostilities agreed to between us will cease in forty-eight hours after this is received at your lines, under the first of the articles of agreement.

Sent at the same time was another and longer message, approved, like the shorter one, by Grant:

> I have replies from Washington to my communication of April 18. I am instructed to limit my operations to your immediate command, and not to attempt civil negotiations. I therefore demand the surrender of your army on the same general terms as were given to General Lee at Appomattox, April 9, instant, purely and simply.

Johnston telegraphed to Davis the contents of the messages. The next morning Davis, still in Charlotte, ordered him to disband his infantry after giving it instructions for reassembling later. He also ordered Johnston to have cavalry units escort him on his flight through the South to get out of the country.

Again Johnston flatly disobeyed an order from his commander-in-chief, more convinced than ever that it would be a crime to prolong the war. Instead, he sent another letter to Sherman:

IN THE FIELD APRIL 25, 1865

MAJOR GENERAL W. T. SHERMAN
  COMMANDING U. S. FORCES

GENERAL.

I have the honor to have received your dispatch of yesterday summoning this army to surrender on the terms accepted by Gen. Lee at Appomattox Court house.

I propose, instead of such surrender, terms based on those drawn up by you on the 18th for disbanding this army—and a further armistice & conference to arrange these terms.

The disbanding of Gen. Lee's army has afflicted this country with numerous bands having no means of subsistence but robbery, a knowledge of which would, I am sure, induce you to agree to other conditions.

Most respectfully
Your obt. servt.
J. E. JOHNSTON
GENERAL, C. S. A.

Peace

Distressed as he was, the sender of this message was in no more troubled frame of mind than the person to whom it was addressed. For by this time Sherman had learned what Grant's presence in Raleigh really meant. The realization came after he had had some talks with Grant and read some documents his friend had brought with him.

Neither Grant nor Hitchcock brought a message of any kind from Halleck or Stanton to Sherman. This was a surprising omission, considering that Sherman's dispatch regarding his negotiations with Johnston had been addressed to the Chief of Staff. However, Grant brought a letter which he himself had received from Stanton announcing the President's rejection of the agreement. Enclosed with it was a copy of a dispatch which Stanton, at Lincoln's direction, had sent Grant on March 3, a month and six days prior to Lee's surrender.[32] Grant also brought along a letter he had written to Sherman just before leaving Washington for Raleigh.

Stanton's message to Grant told in stilted but meaningful terms of the President's disapproval of the Sherman-Johnston pact: "The memorandum or basis agreed upon between General Sherman and General Johnston having been submitted to the President," it said, "they [sic] are disapproved. You will give notice of the disapproval to General Sherman and direct him to resume hostilities at the earliest moment."

The letter called attention to the enclosed copy of Stanton's telegram of March 3. That telegram strictly limited Grant in his negotiations with Lee and made it clear that the discussion of peace terms was outside a military commander's province. Lincoln's wishes of March 3, Stanton's letter said, were substantially the same as President Johnson's of April 21. Their wishes, it directed, "will be observed by General Sherman."

The real sting came in this final paragraph: "The President desires that you proceed immediately to the headquarters of General Sherman, and direct operations against the enemy."

281

That meant only one thing—Sherman was being relieved of his command.

The enclosed copy of the March 3 telegram from Stanton to Grant was of course a revelation to Sherman. It gave him, some seven weeks later than it should have, his first insight into the attitude of Washington officialdom regarding battlefield negotiations with the enemy:

> The President directs me to say to you that he wishes you to have no conference with General Lee, unless it be for the capitulation of Lee's army or on solely minor and purely military matters.
>
> He instructs me to say that you are not to decide, discuss or confer upon any political question; such questions the President holds in his own hands, and will submit them to no military conference or conventions.
>
> Meantime you are to press to the utmost your military advantages.

As for the letter Grant wrote in Washington, carried in his pocket to Raleigh and personally delivered to Sherman, it expressed complete agreement with Stanton and Johnson, but it was couched in much friendlier phrases. And it did much to ease the sense of insult and indignation incurred by Stanton's messages:

HEADQUARTERS ARMIES OF THE UNITED STATES,
WASHINGTON, D.C., APRIL 21, 1865

MAJOR-GENERAL WILLIAM T. SHERMAN, COMMANDING MILITARY DIVISION OF THE MISSISSIPPI:

GENERAL: The basis of agreement entered into between yourself and General J. E. Johnston, for the disbandment of the Southern army, and the extension of the authority of the General Government over all the territory belonging to it, sent for the approval of the President, is received.

I read it carefully before submitting it to the President and

Secretary of War, and felt satisfied that it could not possibly be approved. My reason for these views I will give you at another time, in a more extended letter.

Your agreement touches upon questions of such vital importance that, as soon as read, I addressed a note to the Secretary of War, notifying him of their receipt, and the importance of immediate action; and suggested, in view of their importance, that the entire cabinet be called together, that all might have an expression of their opinions upon the matter. The result was a disavowal by the President of the basis laid down; a disapproval of the negotiations altogether—except for the surrender of the army commanded by General Johnston, and directions to me to notify you of this decision. I cannot do so better than by sending you the inclosed copy of a dispatch (penned by the late President, though signed by the Secretary of War) in answer to me, on sending a letter received from General Lee, proposing to meet me for the purpose of submitting the question of peace to a convention of officers.

Please notify General Johnston immediately on receipt of this, of the termination of the truce, and resume hostilities against his army at the earliest moment you can, acting in good faith.

Very respectfully, your obedient servant,
U.S. GRANT, LIEUTENANT-GENERAL

Sherman was not a man to accept affronts docilely. He had considerable time on his hands while waiting for Johnston's reply to his demand for surrender. A great deal of it was spent working on letters to Grant, in whose eyes he especially wished to justify his actions, and to Stanton, for whom he now had contempt.

His letter to Grant pointed out that he had made his terms with Johnston "under the influence of the very liberal terms you extended to the army of General Lee." He had also been influenced, he said, by "the seeming policy of our Government, as evidenced by the call of the Virginia Legislature and Gov-

283

ernor back to Richmond." This call, he reminded Grant, had been issued "under yours and President Lincoln's very eyes."

He had, he wrote earnestly, "not the least desire" to interfere in any way with the Government's civil policy. However, "occasions do arise when a prompt seizure of results is forced upon military commanders not in immediate communication with the proper authority." Probably, the letter suggested, the Johnston-Sherman memorandum of agreement failed to make one point clear to the others, although it was perfectly clear to the participants: "our negotiations did not apply to any parties outside the officers and men of the Confederate armies." This oversight "could easily have been remedied."

Sherman, who liked to cite historical and military precedents, told Grant he knew of no precedent inconsistent with what he had done: no army "not actually at the mercy of an antagonist" had ever been surrendered without an agreement regarding the terms of surrender. The terms agreed upon "always define the miltary status of the surrendered." Grant himself had followed this principle of warfare at Appomattox: he had "stipulated that the officers and men of Lee's army should not be molested at their homes so long as they obeyed the laws at the place of their residence."

Nothing Sherman had done involved recognition of the "so-called" Confederate Government, he contended. Nor did any action he had taken make the Federal Government responsible for the Confederate Government's acts or debts. As for the individual states of the South, all laws and actions passed and performed while they were in rebellion against the United States were void "because done without the oath prescribed by our Constitution of the United States." That he called a "condition precedent."

As commander of an army, the letter went on, he had a right to use "any sort of machinery" to attain military objectives. He called it "the commonest thing" for military commanders to deal with the civil governments in existence at the time. He was sure, he said, that "we could and can use the present State governments lawfully, constitutionally, and as the very best possible means to produce the object desired." That "object desired" he defined as "entire and complete submission to the lawful authority of the United States."

No concessions he had made, Sherman wrote, could prevent punishment of Southerners guilty of crimes: that was the responsibility of the judiciary. He promised to do what he could to see to it that "rebels shall suffer all the personal punishment prescribed by law," as well as "the civil liabilities arising from their past acts."

President Johnson's chilly repudiation of his plan for the orderly demobilization of the Confederate armies, he predicted, would result in their dispersal instead. The United States would not have just six or seven states to deal with. Rather, "we will have to deal with numberless bands of desperadoes." They would be led by "such men as Mosby, Forrest, Red Jackson, and others, who know not and care not for danger and its consequences."

To Stanton he wrote:

> ...I admit my folly in embracing in a military convention any civil matters; but, unfortunately, such is the nature of our situation that they seem inextricably united, and I understood from you at Savannah that the financial state of the country demanded military success, and would warrant a little bending to policy.
>
> When I had my conference with General Johnston I had the public examples before me of General Grant's terms to Lee's army, and General Weitzel's invitation to the Virginia Legislature to assemble at Richmond.
>
> I still believe the General Government of the United States made a mistake; but that is none of my business—mine is a different task; and I had flattered myself that, by years of patient, unremitting, and successful labor, I deserved no reminder such as is contained in the last paragraph of your letter

to General Grant. You may assure the President that I heed his suggestion.

Grant's obligation to undertake command of military operations in the Raleigh area proved embarrassing to both men. General Howard was especially touched by Sherman's "deep chagrin." The episode hurt his chief, he said in his memoirs, not because Andrew Johnson had turned down the Sherman-Johnston peace terms—"for that was discretionary with the President"—but "because he had been so publicly and cruelly denounced by the War Department." It was no wonder, Howard felt, that Sherman, with three armies at his disposal, was angry about being treated in such summary and brutal fashion. Howard quoted his chief as saying: "I was outraged beyond measure, and was resolved to resent the insult, cost what it might." But no coldness developed between Grant and Sherman. Their unbroken friendship, Howard said, "allayed all asperities." The two men got along perfectly together. There was no friction, no working at cross-purposes, no unpleasant personalities. As a matter of fact, Sherman contended that "Grant did not relieve me." Nor did he "express a wish to assume command."

Sherman's men were in position to start moving the next day when, on the evening of April 25, a messenger handed Sherman Johnston's letter requesting a third meeting. Grant "not only approved, but urged me to accept." Sherman set the meeting for noon the next day, the hour when his troops were under orders to start moving.

Sherman's reply did not reach Johnston until after sunrise of the day the meeting was to be held. Jefferson Davis was advised of this development, and Johnston hurried off to the rendezvous.

Although the two men had lost none of their distaste for further fighting, they ran into a great deal of difficulty when they tried to agree on surrender terms. The contentious question of the status of surrendered Confederates seemed to defy compromise or meeting of minds. What rights and privileges of citizenship would they enjoy? What punishment might they receive? Grant's terms given Lee at Appomattox had indeed been generous. But people in many communities had been complaining bitterly to Johnston and to Jefferson Davis about outrages committed by Lee's paroled troopers. At Appomattox those men who had given such excellent account of themselves on innumerable battlefields had been suddenly released from the restraints of army life. They had lacked food or transportation or money with which to pay for either. They had even been left without guns with which to protect themselves. Their passage through Virginia and North Carolina had become a trail of thievery and other depredations. That would not happen to Johnston's men and the civilians with whom they would come into contact, if he could prevent it. So he contended that he should receive better terms, in that respect at least, than Lee had received, for the good of all concerned. Sherman could see his point and was sympathetic. But there was little or nothing he could do. President Johnson, Stanton and the others who had so summarily rejected his earlier peace terms would as summarily reject any concessions he might make now. And that would almost certainly bring on a resumption of fighting. It was to the best interest of all, Sherman believed, to hold Johnston to conditions which had already been agreed upon by his superiors.

The discussion went on and on, until it occurred to Sherman that General Schofield, who had shown considerable diplomatic and persuasive power, as well as exceptional military commandership, might be able to resolve the impasse. Sherman called him in.

That proved to be a wise move. Schofield came up with a solution. After Johnston's surrender Sherman expected to take most of his troops to Washington for demobilization, leaving him in command of the small force left to maintain order. He would have authority to handle the mechanics of the Confederate demobilization and promised to do what he could to avoid the conditions Johnston feared. Both Johnston and Sherman were satisfied. Schofield sat down at a table and wrote out the formal surrender terms which the other two men signed:

Terms of a Military Convention, entered into this 26th day of April, 1865, at Bennett's House, near Durham's Station, North Carolina, between General Joseph E. Johnston, commanding the Confederate Army, and Major-General W. T. Sherman, commanding the United States Army in North Carolina:

1. All acts of war on the part of the troops under General Johnston's command to cease from this date.

2. All arms and public property to be deposited at Greensboro, and delivered to an ordnance-officer of the United States Army.

3. Rolls of all the officers and men to be made in duplicate; one copy to be retained by the commander of the troops, and the other to be given to an officer to be designated by General Sherman. Each officer and man to give his individual obligation in writing not to take up arms against the Government of the United States, until properly released from this obligation.

4. The side-arms of officers, and their private horses and baggage, to be retained by them.

5. This being done, all the officers and men will be permitted to return to their homes, not to be disturbed by the United States authorities, so long as they observe their obligation and the laws in force where they reside.

With that major agreement achieved, Schofield reached for the pen again. A few minutes later he had put in writing the promises he had made orally to Johnston regarding the mechanics of demobilization:

Supplemental Terms

1. The field transportation to be loaned to the troops for their march to their homes, and for subsequent use in their in-

288

dustrial pursuits. Artillery-horses may be used in field transportation, if necessary.

2. Every brigade or separate body to retain a number of arms equal to *one-seventh* of its effective strength, which, when the troops reach the capitals of their States, will be disposed of as the general commanding the department may direct.

3. Private horses, and other private property of both officers and men, to be retained by them.

4. The commanding general of the Military Division of West Mississippi, Major-General Canby, will be requested to give transportation by water, from Mobile or New Orleans, to the troops from Arkansas and Texas.

5. The obligation of officers and soldiers to be signed by their immediate commanders.

6. Naval forces within the limits of General Johnston's command to be included in the terms of this convention.

Sherman arrived at the Governor's Mansion in the early evening. Officers, eager for news, were standing in small groups on the front patio. An army band was playing in the front yard, and bright lights were ablaze inside the building. Pulling his copy of the agreement from a pocket, Sherman handed it to Grant and asked him to sign it as evidence of his approval. Grant read it carefully, then took a pen and wrote "Approved: U. S. Grant, Lieutenant General" on the extreme left side of the sheet, opposite Johnston's and Sherman's signatures. He chatted awhile with Sherman, Howard, Schofield, Logan and others and then excused himself and went to bed. At 9 o'clock the next morning he was on his way back to Washington.

The news spread rapidly. The troops received it jubilantly. Band concerts burst forth all over town, and torchlight processions gave a carnival air. This went on for two days.

Sherman showed he could be as generous in victory as he was ruthless in war-making. "Now that the war is over, I am as willing to risk my person and reputation as heretofore, to heal the wounds made by the past war," he wrote Johnston April 27.[33] "And I think my feeling is shared by the whole army. . . . " To prove that these were not empty words, he ordered his top generals to do everything possible to make things easy for the civilian population. Foraging was forbidden. Whatever provisions the army required were to be paid for. Civilians needing horses, mules, wagons and carriages got them. Commissary food supplies were turned over to the needy. Sherman showed particular solicitude for farmers having trouble planting their crops and made a special effort to see that they had all the animals they needed.

In the gentle glow of victory, he was equally generous to the Confederate troops. They received sufficient rations to keep them satisfactorily fed for ten days, or until most of them could get back to their homes. He also conscientiously kept his promise to provide travel facilities for them. This double-barreled effort to prevent what Johnston so greatly feared largely achieved its purpose. Civilians living along the homeward trail experienced only a fraction of the thieving and other crimes that would otherwise have occurred.

Sherman's Special Field Orders, No. 66, sent his army, except for those units to be left behind under Schofield, on its final march, to Washington by way of Richmond. Two days later he left Raleigh for Savannah.

On May 2 Johnston issued his final orders, General Orders, No. 22—his farewell to "those matchless soldiers" who had served him and the Confederacy so well:

> Comrades: In terminating our official relations, I earnestly exhort you to observe faithfully the terms of pacification agreed upon; and to discharge the obligations of good and peaceful citizens, as well as you have performed the duties of thorough soldiers in the field. By such a course, you will best secure the comfort of your families and kindred, and restore tranquility to our country.

Peace

You will return to your homes with the admiration of our people, won by the courage and noble devotion you have displayed in the long war. I shall always remember with pride the loyal support and generous confidence you have given me.

I now part with you with deep regret—and bid you farewell with feelings of cordial friendship; and with earnest wishes that you may have hereafter all prosperity and happiness to be found in the world.

NOTES

1. Sherman's critics have accused him of building up his army at the expense of the army of General George Henry Thomas. Sherman answered a specific charge of this kind—from H. V. Boynton, a Washington newspaperman and author—by quoting from a letter he had received from Grant stating that he (Grant) had detached many of Thomas' best troops for service with Sherman because he did not think Thomas would be able to use them before spring. Grant's letter stated that Thomas' pursuit of General John B. Hood had been sluggish. Thomas, Grant wrote, was "possessed of excellent judgment" and had "great coolness and honesty" but was "not good in pursuit." Anxious to "give the enemy no rest," he had decided "to use his troops elsewhere." (Sherman's marginal notes on *Sherman's Historical Raid, The Memoirs in the Light of the Record, A Review Based Upon Compilations from the Files of the War Office,* by H. V. Boynton. Cincinnati: Wilstach, Baldwin & Co., 1875.)

2. Sherman greatly resented subsequent statements denying him credit for conceiving and planning the march to the sea and beyond. He was especially resentful of the claim by H. V. Boynton that Grant, not Sherman, conceived the march as part of the over-all 1864-65 campaign. When he saw a copy of the Boynton book, which also contained many other statements objectionable to him, he dictated to his aide-de-camp, Colonel John E. Tourtelotte, a vigorous denial. It declared that the entire scheme of operation was his own and that Grant was actually opposed to it until persuaded to approve it by himself. Sherman's statement was written on the margins of the book in Colonel Tourtelotte's handwriting. Another copy of the book containing Sherman's comments on the margins, in the handwriting of someone else, is in the Rare Book Room of the New York Public Library.

3. Sherman states in his memoirs that he did not learn about Kilpatrick's liaison with the fleet until after the assault upon Fort McAllister and planned the assault without knowing he could depend upon its help.

4. The Parrot gun was invented in 1861 by the American ordnance expert, Robert Parker Parrott, as an American adaptation of the gun in-

vented in 1857 by the Britisher, W. G. Armstrong. Both the Armstrongs and the Parrots were considered superior to earlier ordnance because of their greatly strengthened barrels, which reduced accidents and increased power. Perhaps through a clerical error, Parrott's gun is known as the Parrot gun.

5. President Davis, differing with Beauregard as to the wisdom of holding on to Savannah, instructed Lee to send two of his divisions to reinforce Hardee. But Lee replied that he could not do so without dangerously weakening his own position.

6. H. V. Boynton referred to this blunder at some length in *Sherman's Historical Raid, The Memoirs in the Light of the Record* and mentioned the widespread criticism it had aroused. Sherman dictated his answer to his aide-de-camp, Colonel John E. Tourtelotte. Colonel Tourtelotte wrote in longhand on the book's margin: "Nobody, except Mr. Stanton, ever expressed in writing, displeasure with me for allowing Hardee to escape."

7. Secretary of the Navy Gideon Welles wrote in his diary January 21 that the Secretary of War had reported on the trip at a cabinet meeting. Welles did not "get at the real object of his going, except that it was for his health." *(The Diary of Gideon Welles, Secretary of the Navy Under Lincoln and Johnson.* Boston and New York: Houghton Mifflin Company. Vol. II, p. 228.)

8. Sherman was misinformed on his geography. Raleigh is about 100 miles from the Roanoke at the nearest point.

9. Sherman may have forgotten Miss Poyas' first name when he wrote his memoirs. At any rate, this is the way he quoted the inscription.

10. Sherman flatly denied any responsibility whatsoever for the Columbia fire. At first he blamed the people who had welcomed his troops with the liquor that had inflamed them. Later he blamed Wade Hampton. The holocaust, he claimed, started from cotton bales which the Confederate cavalry leader had ordered fired just before evacuating the city. He said strong winds blew the flaming stuff over a wide area, and many buildings were ignited in that way.

"I saw the bridges burned and the depots burned whilst the Confederate troops were in Columbia, full 24 hours before we crossed the Congaree river," he claimed after the war. "And I saw smoke of burning cotton hours before we entered the city, and saw half-dozen separate piles burning as I rode down main street at the head of the 15th Corps." (Letter dated August 8, 1881. Parke-Bernet Catalogue, March 28, 1938, p. 128, No. 375 Manuscript Division, New York Public Library.)

Others, including Confederates, also mentioned cotton bales burning on the streets. Major John R. Chambless, C.S.A., for one, wrote three days later that "the air was illuminated with burning cotton" at 3 A.M. February 17.

Wade Hampton wrote in a letter to Senator Reverdy Johnson, read in the United States Senate April 21, 1866, "I deny emphatically that any cotton was fired in Columbia by my order; I deny that the citizens 'set fire to thousands of bales rolled out into the streets' (as Sherman had charged); I deny that any cotton was on fire when Federal troops entered the city."

Neither General Logan, General Wood nor Colonel Michael C. Garber, Howard's Chief Quartermaster General, made any mention of burning cotton in his official report—a striking omission, considering that Sherman gave the impression that burning cotton was blowing about everywhere when he arrived. Mayor Goodwyn testified that neither when he left the city to surrender to Colonel Stone nor when he returned was there any burning cotton on Main Street.

Sherman's case was weakened by one of his firmest friends and top generals. In 1867, when Howard was in Columbia as a commissioner of the Freedman's Bureau, Hampton asked him point-blank about the burning of that city. "It is useless to deny that our troops burned Columbia," Howard replied, "for I saw them in the act."

At hearings of the Mixed Claims Commission in 1873, Sherman admitted that he could have prevented the fire by keeping his men in formation, instead of allowing them to roam about the city at will. But, he went on, he had not been willing to do so, even to save Columbia. He backtracked somewhat on his earlier positive statement that Wade Hampton was to blame for the fire: "In my official report of this conflagration, I directly charged it to General Wade Hampton, and I confess I did so pointedly, to shake the faith of the people in him, for he was in my opinion a braggart, and professed to be the special champion of the people."

Sherman made much of the report of the Mixed Claims Commission— based upon testimony gathered by an American (not a Southerner), a British citizen and the Italian minister to Washington—which unanimously cleared both him and Wade Hampton, ruling that neither army, as such, was to blame.

11. Hampton was fully capable of carrying out his threat of retaliation on foragers. Against the thousand Confederate prisoners Sherman held at that time, he held some three thousand Federals. He added substantially to the number a short time later by a raid on Kilpatrick's camp.

12. Some authorities say the raid on Laurenburgh was made by the XVII Corps. Both the XV and XVII were in the vicinity.

13. Sherman, in his memoirs, says Hampton, thinking a major part of the Federal army was in the city, rushed to his horse and started to ride away across the bridge. But upon finding out that the Federals in the city consisted of only a small party of scouts—Sherman calls them foragers—he turned upon them, "bold and rash, as usual," killed some and took others prisoners, including Captain Duncan. He says Hampton then rode across the bridge and fired it.

14. Johnston, in his memoirs, says his inability to get his troops into position quickly prevented him from attacking while the Federals were in column and marching, thereby making a complete victory impossible, because of the great numerical superiority enjoyed by the enemy. He had only some 18,000 men, exclusive of cavalry. This was half as many as Sherman thought he had.

15. Neither Slocum nor Howard would concede that Carlin's men were routed. The former admitted that they made a forced retreat to prepared positions but said they "were handled with skill and fell back without panic or demoralization, taking places in the line established." Howard wrote: "There was some breaking here and there [in the Federal line], but Slocum's men were veterans, and quickly rallied."

16. There is a confusion of claims regarding the amount of credit due the Confederates for their successful coup. Wade Hampton (in *Battles and Leaders of the Civil War*, IV, pp. 700-05) says the Confederate force consisted of only about three hundred men. Others say there were more than two hundred effectives in Cumming's brigade alone and that they, added to those in Hampton's and Wheeler's cavalry and the 8th Texas Cavalry, made a total much in excess of three hundred. The magnitude of the Confederate achievement is reduced, too, by the relative weakness of Mower's force. Instead of being a powerful fighting unit, as widely believed, it consisted of only a single full-strength brigade and a brigade at less than full strength.

17. Sherman himself conceded that, in the light of later developments and subsequent revelations, it was probably a mistake. One of those subsequent revelations was that Johnston's force was much smaller and weaker than he thought. Another consideration was that he thought Mower had advanced too rashly and needed to be held back. (Sherman characterized him in his memoirs as "ever rash.") Still another—and this Howard called "probably the governing one at the time"—was that Sherman knew Johnston's retreat would have to be toward the north and would therefore leave an unimpeded road to Goldsboro.

18. Sherman had a somewhat different version. In his report on the Carolinas campaign he states that his army pursued the enemy two miles

beyond Mill Creek, at which point, he wrote, he halted the Federal advance.

19. Sherman's critics charge him with a serious error of judgment in putting an early arrival in Goldsboro ahead of the capture of Johnston's army. The latter, they say, would have virtually ended the war, while the former proved only an important step in that direction. His critics also accuse him of serious misjudgment and mismanagement of his troops prior to the battle. H. V. Boynton devoted an entire chapter of his book, *Sherman's Historical Raid*, to criticism of his actions at that time. The Yankee commander answered him in the notes he dictated for the book's margins: "This whole chapter is an absurdity. We were marching for Richmond, and did not wish to be diverted by minor events. The utmost care was taken from Fayetteville to Goldsboro, as detailed in the reports. Of course Johnston could attack, and did attack, but we were as well prepared for conflict on that [left] flank as was possible [sic] consistent with marching in a strange country. General Slocum had four divisions unencumbered with wagons—his head of column was driven back, but as soon as his Rear divisions came forward, checked the enemy & gave time for concentration."

20. Sherman actually had no grounds for criticism. In his letter to General Terry, written in Fayetteville, he had set April 10—sixteen days after the first train entered Goldsboro—as the date for completion of the repairs.

21. There have been those who scoffed at Lincoln's display of distress over the "effusion of blood." Johnston said in a letter to Colonel Thomas T. Gantt, "I believe that he never valued human life when it was in the way of his objects." He described a meeting between Grant and the President, in which he said Grant proposed to transport his army down the Potomac and up the James river and land it "as near Richmond as practicable." The expedition, Grant estimated, would save the lives of one hundred thousand men by avoiding that long overland advance. But it would also indicate that Lincoln's previous strategy was wrong. So "it was agreed that 100,000 men should be sacrificed to avoid the exposure of the President's military blunders." (Letter to Colonel T. Gantt, January 3, 1884, in the College of William and Mary Johnston Collection.)

22. It was later learned that Jefferson Davis was responsible for the cancellation of the safe conduct permit, not Johnston.

23. Sherman, in his memoirs, placed his own interpretation upon Vance's failure to return to Raleigh: "... but Governor Vance had fled, and could not be prevailed upon to return, because he feared an arrest and imprisonment."

24. At that time, Johnston wrote later, "8 or 10 per cent of my troops were without arms." (Letter to Colonel T. T. Gantt, January 3, 1884, in College of William and Mary Manuscript Collection.)

25. George Sanders was a Kentuckian involved in an abortive peace mission.

26. The South lost the war, Johnston believed, "from no want of courage, constancy and zeal" but "from their want of discretion in selecting a leader." (Letter from General Johnston to Colonel T. T. Gantt, in Johnston's Manuscript Collection, College of William and Mary Library.)

27. Sherman, who was given to questioning what others had reported as facts, wrote some time afterward that he had no recollection of the liquor bottle incident. After expressing doubt about another matter—the type of table in the room—he went on: "As to the black bottle I am even more incredulous. I doubt that Johnston or I"—he said nothing about Breckinridge—"drank anything, or if so, it must have been from the contents of a small flask, habitually carried by my orderly." (Unidentified letter quoted in "Legend Not Withstanding Sherman and Johnson [sic] Shared No Bottle at Bennett Place," by Fred G. Mahler, Raleigh, N.C., *News and Observer*, October 12, 1958.)

28. Sherman reacted with considerable heat to subsequent statements—by Johnston and others—that he accepted in principle the Johnston-Reagan-Breckinridge draft of the armistice terms. (In his memoirs Johnston says the Sherman draft of the memorandum "differed from mine only in being fuller.") The document he signed and agreed to transmit to the President, Sherman emphasized indignantly, was altogether his. "Neither Mr. Breckinridge nor General Johnston wrote one word of that paper," he says in his memoirs. "I wrote it myself and announced it as the best I could do, and they readily assented."

29. Johnston was later to express a different and far less favorable opinion of the late President.

30. In his report on the Carolinas campaign, Sherman wrote that the Sherman-Johnston memorandum "was designed to be, and so expressed on its face, as a mere 'basis' for reference to the President of the United States and constitutional Commander-in-Chief, to enable him, if he chose, at one blow to dissipate the military power of the Confederacy which had threatened the national safety for years." The memorandum, he went on, "admitted of modification, alteration, and change." And in his memoirs (page 354) he wrote: "I cared little whether they were approved, modified, or disapproved *in toto*; only I wanted instructions."

31. Davis ignored an urgent request from Johnston to make an additional payment to the soldiers out of "a large sum in specie" believed to be in Davis' possession.

32. If Stanton had sent him a copy of that dispatch at the time it was sent to Grant, Sherman complained, that "would have saved a world of trouble." It would have prevented "every barroom loafer in New York" from reading in his newspaper " 'official' matter that is withheld from a General whose command extends from Kentucky to North Carolina." He subsequently made a similar charge against Halleck when the Chief of Staff sent orders to Sherman's subordinates without informing him of his action. "When orders are thus sent," he wrote on the margin of Boynton's *Sherman's Historical Raid,* "a copy is always sent to the actual commander. This was not done."

33. An effort has been made by Sherman's friends and members of his family to dissipate the widespread belief that he was animated throughout the war by hatred of the South and its people. One who was particularly concerned was his daughter, Mrs. Minnie Sherman Fitch. She sent some of his letters to an old friend whom he had known in Louisiana in order that he and others in the South might know "how kind was my Father's feeling to those against whom he fought, even at the time of the War." That feeling, she wrote, did not come after the war, "but was in his heart all the time." (Letter from Minnie Sherman Fitch to Colonel David French Boyd, November 26, 1891, Walter H. Fleming Collection, Manuscript Division, New York Public Library.)

BIBLIOGRAPHY

BOOKS

ADAMS, GEORGE WORTHINGTON. *Doctors in Blue: The Medical History of the Union Army in the Civil War.* New York, 1952. Tells how the men of medicine used the crude equipment and scanty knowledge of their time to protect Sherman's troops and others against sickness and battle injuries.

AMERICAN BIBLE SOCIETY. Annual Reports, 1864 and 1865. New York, 1865, 1866. How this great religious organization, working with the United States Christian Commission, protected Sherman's men, as well as those of other armies, both Federal and Confederate, against the temptations of army life.

AMIS, MOSES N. *Historical Raleigh, With Sketches of Wake County and Its Most Important Towns.* Raleigh, 1913. The history of the last city Sherman reached on his way to victory.

ANDERSON, LUCY LONDON. *North Carolina Women of the Confederacy.* Raleigh, 1926. How the women of the Tar Heel State did their part while their husbands and sons were away at war.

BARRETT, JOHN G. *Sherman's March Through the Carolinas.* Chapel Hill, 1956. A detailed, thoroughly researched and thoughtfully written narrative of Sherman's campaign from Savannah to the end.

BATTLE, KEMP PLUMMER. *A History of the University of North Carolina.* In 2 volumes. An ardent North Carolinian tells how the war generally and Sherman's march particularly affected the State's principal institution of higher learning.

BOYNTON, H. V. *Sherman's Historical Raid, The Memoirs in the Light of the Record, A Review Based upon Compilations from the Files of the War Department.* Cincinnati, 1875. One of Sherman's bitterest critics attacks many of his actions and decisions.

BRADFORD, GAMALIEL. *Confederate Portraits.* Boston and New York, 1914. Appraisals of Beauregard, Johnston and other Southern leaders.

BUEL, CLARENCE CLOUGH. See Johnson, Robert Underwood.

BIBLIOGRAPHY

CHESNUT, MARY BOYKIN. *A Diary from Dixie,* edited by Isabella D. Martin and Myrta Lockett Avary. New York, 1905. This lively and intelligent observer includes vivid comment on Southerners' attitude toward Sherman's march.

The City of Raleigh, Historical Sketches from Its Foundations, A Review of the City in All Its Varied Aspects—Commercial, Industrial, Statistical, Religious, Social, Etc. Raleigh, 1887. More about the last city occupied by Sherman's army.

The Civil War As Told by James Street. New York, 1953. This unorthodox account of the conflict emphasizes many of the war's less well known aspects and finds much to criticize in Sherman and others.

Climatic Summary of the United States, Sections 98 and 99. Washington, 1933. Showing the kind of weather that prevailed during Sherman's march.

COMMAGER, HENRY STEELE, ed. *The Blue and the Gray. The Story of the Civil War As Told by Participants.* In 2 volumes. New York, 1950. Recollections of those with first-hand knowledge of the war's hardships and trials.

CONYNGHAM, DAVID POWER. *Sherman's March Through the South.* New York, 1865. The New York *Herald* correspondent with Sherman's army and Sherman's aide-de-camp gives a good newspaperman's story of the battles, the marches and life in camp.

The Correspondence of Jonathan Worth, collected and edited by Joseph Gregoire de Roulhac Hamilton. In 2 volumes. Raleigh, 1909. A letter-writing North Carolinian tells about civilian life in his State as Sherman's army advanced. Shows that many hardships and indignities were inflicted by lawless Confederates as well as by the invaders.

COX, JACOB D. *The March to the Sea—Franklin and Nashville.* New York, 1882. The commander of the XXIII Corps gives a matter-of-fact account of the final campaigns of the war. Treats Sherman more sympathetically than do many others.

DAVIS, JEFFERSON. *The Rise and Fall of the Confederate Government.* In 2 volumes. New York, 1881. The Confederacy's Chief Executive tells his side of the story, defends his actions and decisions and blames his critics.

The Diary of Gideon Welles, Secretary of the Navy Under Lincoln and Johnson. In 3 volumes. Boston and New York, 1911. A cabinet member's reminiscences, with appraisals of generals and other war leaders.

EATON, CLEMENT. *A History of the Southern Confederacy.* New York, 1954. An excellent single-volume history of the short-lived nation.

FREEMAN, DOUGLAS SOUTHALL. *R. E. Lee, A Biography.* In 6 volumes. New York, 1946. By far the most comprehensive of the many Lee biographies.

———. *Lee's Lieutenants, A Study in Command.* In 3 volumes. New York, 1942-44. The illustrious historian's appraisals of Confederate military leaders.

BIBLIOGRAPHY

GAY, MARY A. H. *Life in Dixie During the War, 1861-1862-1863-1864-1865.* Atlanta, 1897. Reminiscences of a Southern woman who saw and endured much suffering during the war, especially after it moved to her section of the country.

GIBBES, JAMES GUIGUARD. *Who Burnt Columbia?* Newberry, S.C., 1902. A vigorous presentation of the contention that the destruction of the South Carolina capital was an act of wanton hatred.

HOOD, JOHN B. *Advance and Retreat. Personal Experiences in the United States and Confederate Armies.* New Orleans, 1880. Military biography of the commander of the Army of Tennessee, presenting his defense against responsibility for one of the war's most disastrous defeats.

HORN, STANLEY FITZGERALD. *The Army of Tennessee, A Military History.* Norman, Okla., 1955. The story of the brave but often ill-led army that narrowly missed a great victory at Shiloh, met with disaster at Nashville and finally surrendered, with the rest of Johnston's army, near Durham.

HOWE, MARK ANTONY DE WOLFE, ed. *Home Letters of General Sherman.* New York, 1909. The informal, frank comments on the Georgia-Carolinas campaign and others by a military leader with an unusual flair for writing.

JOHNSON, ROBERT UNDERWOOD, and CLARENCE CLOUGH BUEL, eds. *Battles and Leaders of the Civil War.* In 4 volumes. New York, 1884, 1888. Veterans of both armies and other authorities tell about those phases of the war with which they were most familiar. Contains a wealth of portraits.

JOHNSTON, JOSEPH EGGLESTON. *Narrative of Military Operations Directed During the War Between the States.* New York, 1874. Sherman's chief antagonist during the last months of the war describes the battles in which he participated and emphasizes the difficulties under which he fought.

JONES, J. B. *A Rebel War Clerk's Diary at the Confederate States Capital.* In 2 volumes. New York, 1866. Life in Richmond during the war as seen by a civilian employee of the Confederate War Department.

KENNAWAY, JOHN H. *On Sherman's Tracks, or The South After the War.* London, 1867. A visiting Englishman's report on the devastation, ruin and poverty left by Sherman's troops, and also the brave optimism of many ruined Southerners.

LECONTE, JOSEPH. *'Ware Sherman, A Journal of Three Months' Personal Experience in the Last Days of the Confederacy.* Berkeley, 1937. A Confederate civilian official's reactions to war-ravaged Georgia and fire-swept Columbia.

LEWIS, LLOYD. *Sherman, Fighting Prophet.* New York, 1932. One of the most comprehensive of the Sherman biographies.

LOSSING, BENSON JOHN. *Pictorial History of the Civil War in the United States of America.* Hartford, 1887. Cameramen's narrative of Sherman's campaigns and others.

BIBLIOGRAPHY

Marching With Sherman, Passages from the Letters and Campaign Diaries of Henry Hitchcock, Major and Assistant Adjutant General of Volunteers, November, 1864-May, 1865. New Haven, 1927. One of Sherman's closest associates describes important and trivial incidents of the march and gives his impressions of his chief and other comrades in arms.

MIERS, EARL SCHENCK. *The General Who Marched to Hell; William Tecumseh Sherman and His March to Fame and Infamy.* New York, 1951. Sherman's Civil War biography.

NICHOLS, GEORGE WARD. *The Story of the Great March, From the Diary of a Staff Officer.* New York, 1865. Informal sketches of life in Sherman's army—how the men amused themselves in camp as well as how they fought in battle.

OATES, JOHN A. *The Story of Fayetteville and the Upper Cape Fear.* Charlotte, 1950. Tells about the capture of Fayetteville and Sherman's men's conduct toward the section's civilian population.

ROBINSON, BLACKWELL P., ed. *The North Carolina Guide.* Chapel Hill, 1955. Describing Fayetteville, Raleigh, Durham, Bennett House and other historically significant places in the Old North State and the parts they played in Sherman's triumphal march.

SALLEY, KATHERINE BATTS, ed. *Life at Saint Mary's.* Chapel Hill, 1942. Wartime pleasures and privations of the students at one of the South's most fashionable girls' schools.

SANDBURG, CARL. *Abraham Lincoln, The War Years.* In 4 volumes. New York, 1939. Lincoln's dealings with Sherman and his other generals in a biography that leaves very little untold about the war President.

SHERMAN, WILLIAM TECUMSEH. *General Sherman's Official Accounts of His Great March Through Georgia and the Carolinas.* New York, 1865. The victor's version of the campaign.

————. *Memoirs of General William T. Sherman, Written by Himself.* In 2 volumes. New York, 1875. Recollections, impressions and reactions a decade after the war's end.

SIMMS, WILLIAM GILMORE. *Sack and Destruction of the City of Columbia, S. C.* 1865. An ardent and aroused Southern author describes the greatest single catastrophe of the war.

SNOWDEN, YATES. *Marching With Sherman.* Columbia, 1929. A Southerner's comment on the war and some of its leading participants.

UPSON, THEODORE F. *With Sherman to the Sea, The Civil War Letters, Diaries and Reminiscences of Theodore F. Upson,* edited by Oscar Osborn Winter. Baton Rouge, 1943. An Indiana teen-ager's adventures as a soldier under Grant and Sherman. Tells a great deal about what the men in the ranks did and thought about in battle, in camp and on the march.

BIBLIOGRAPHY

WALLACE, DAVID DUNCAN. *South Carolina, A Short History, 1520-1948.* Chapel Hill, 1951. How the war affected the people of the first state to secede.

The War of the Rebellion; A Compilation of the Official Records of the Union and Confederate Armies. In 128 volumes. Washington, 1901. Letters and other correspondence of the war's most prominent participants, badly arranged and poorly indexed but complete.

WELLMAN, MANLY WADE. *Giant in Gray, A Biography of Wade Hampton of South Carolina.* New York, 1949. The brilliant career in war and peace of perhaps the war's greatest cavalryman.

WRIGHT, MARCUS F., ed. *Battles and Commanders of the Civil War.* Washington, 1902. Descriptions of the great clashes and the parts played by the leading participants.

ARTICLES IN PERIODICALS

ALLEN, W. G., JONES, JOSEPH A., and BENNETT, SAM. "About Fight at Fayetteville, N.C.," *Confederate Veteran,* XIX (September, 1911), 433-4.

ANDERSON, MRS. JOHN H. "Confederate Arsenal at Fayetteville, N. C." *Confederate Veteran,* XXXVI (June, 1928), 222-3, 238.

ARTHUR, BILLY. "They Loved Vance," *The State,* XXV (June 1, 1957), 9.

BARNWELL, ROBERT W. "Bentonville—The Last Battle of Johnston and Sherman," *Proceedings of the South Carolina Historical Association,* XIII (1943), 42-54.

BASYE, E. T. "Burning of Columbia," *Confederate Veteran,* XVII (September, 1911), 465.

BENNETT, SAM. See Allen, W. G.

BOYD, DAVID F. "W. T. Sherman, His Early Life in the South and His Relations with Southern Men," *Confederate Veteran,* XVIII (September, 1910), 409-16.

BYERS, S. H. M. "Some Personal Recollections of General Sherman," *McClure's Magazine,* III (August, 1894), 212-24.

COFFIN, JAMES PARK. "Chapel Hill at the Close of the Civil War—Letter from James P. Coffin to R. H. Battle," *North Carolina University Magazine,* XVIII (June, 1901), 270-5.

COX, J. D. "Sherman-Johnston Convention," *Scribners,* XXVIII (October, 1900), 489-505.

DANIELS, JONATHAN. "Tar Heel Capital," *Holiday,* XIX (February, 1956), 40-41, 128, 130-131.

DAVES, GRAHAM. "The Battle of Averasboro," *Southern Historical Society Papers,* VII (March, 1879), 125-8.

DODSON, W. C. "Burning of the Broad River Bridge," *Confederate Veteran,* XVII (September, 1909), 462-5.

BIBLIOGRAPHY

DuBose, John W. "Fayetteville (N.C.) Road Fight," *Confederate Veteran*, XX (February, 1912), 84-6.

Eaton, Clement, ed. "Diary of an Officer in Sherman's Army Marching Through the Carolinas," *Journal of Southern History*, IX (May, 1943), 238-54.

Hamilton, Posey. "The Effort to Capture Kilpatrick," *Confederate Veteran*, XXIX (September, 1921), 329.

————. "Incidents of the Fighting at Aiken, S.C.," *Confederate Veteran*, XXXII (February, 1924), 58.

Hill, James D. "The Burning of Columbia Reconsidered," *South Atlantic Quarterly*, XXV (July, 1926), 269-82.

Johnston, Joseph Eggleston. "My Negotiations with General Sherman," *North American Review*, CXLIII (August, 1886), 182-97.

Jones, Joseph A. See Allen, W. G.

"The Last Telegrams of the Confederacy," *Southern Historical Society Papers*, VII (1879), 127.

Lord, William Wilberforce, Jr. "In the Path of Sherman," *Harper's Magazine*, CXX (February, 1910), 438-46.

Luvaas, Jay. "Johnston's Last Stand—Bentonville," *North Carolina Historical Review*, XXXIII (June, 1956), 332-58.

McClurg, Alexander C. "The Last Chance of the Confederacy," *Atlantic Monthly*, L (September, 1882), 389-400.

Milling, Chapman J. "Ilium in Flames," *Confederate Veteran*, XXXVI (April-May-June, 1928). 135-8, 179-82, 212-6.

Morgan, D. B. "Incidents of the Fighting at Aiken, S.C.," *Confederate Veteran*, XXXII (August, 1924), 300-1.

Mullen, James M. "Last Days of Johnston's Army," *Southern Historical Society Papers*, XVIII (January, 1890), 97-109.

Olds, Frederick A. "Story of the Surrender of Raleigh to Federal Army," *Orphan's Friend and Masonic Journal*, L (November 27, 1925), 1, 8; L (December 4, 1925), 7-8; L (December 11, 1925), 7-8.

Overley, Milford. "The Burning of Columbia, S. C.," *Confederate Veteran*, XI (December, 1903), 550.

Pickett, W. D. "Why Sherman's Name Is Detested," *Confederate Veteran*, XIV (September, 1906), 397-8.

"Recollections of General Sherman," *Harper's New Monthly Magazine*, XXX (April, 1865), 640-6.

Rhodes, James Ford. "Who Burned Columbia?" *American Historical Review*, VII (April, 1902), 485-93.

BIBLIOGRAPHY

SANDERS, ROBERT W. "The Battle of Bentonville," *Confederate Veteran*, XXXIV (August, 1926), 299-300.

SANDERSON, WILLIAM H. "Union Veteran Upon War-Time Deeds," *Confederate Veteran*, XIX (September, 1911), 434-5.

SMITH, JESSIE S. "On the Battlefield of Averasboro, N.C.," *Confederate Veteran*, XXXIV (February, 1926), 48-9.

SPENCER, CORNELIA PHILLIPS. "Old Times in Chapel Hill, No. IX, Governor Swain," *North Carolina University Magazine*, VII (May, 1888), 214-21.

STROUPE, HENRY S. "The Beginnings of Religious Journalism in North Carolina," *North Carolina Historical Review*, XXX (January, 1953), 1.

"Unpublished Letters of General Sherman," *North American Review*, CLII (March, 1891), 372-4.

WELLMAN, MANLY WADE. "The Last 'Might Have Been,'" *The State*, XXVI (August 9, 1958), 99-100, 130.

"Where the War Between the States Ended," *North Carolina Teacher*, I (November, 1924), 81-2.

YATES, RICHARD E. "Governor Vance and the End of the War in North Carolina," *North Carolina Historical Review*, XVIII (October, 1941), 315-38.

MANUSCRIPTS

FITCH, MINNIE SHERMAN. Letter to Colonel David French Boyd, dated November 26, 1891, denying Sherman's hatred for the South. In Manuscript Division, New York Public Library.

GIBSON, JOHN M. Article tentatively titled " 'Surrender House'—North Carolina's Second Appomattox," to be published by New York *Herald Tribune*.

HARSHBARGER, H. B., Acting Director, United States Department of Commerce Weather Bureau, Asheville, N. C. Letter to author dated January 8, 1958, describing weather conditions at Hilton Head, S. C., on February 17, 1865.

JOHNSTON, JOSEPH EGGLESTON. Letter to General Sherman dated April 25, 1865, replying to demand for surrender on terms accepted by General Lee at Appomattox. In Manuscript Division, New York Public Library.

————. Letter dated January 3, 1884, to Col. Thomas T. Gantt, declaring Civil War probably would not have occurred if the South had properly prepared for it by increasing its output of military supplies and placing a large army on the northern frontier. In College of William and Mary Manuscript Collection.

————. Letter to Col. Gantt, dated February 2, 1884, blaming loss of the war upon Southern leadership, especially Jefferson Davis. In College of William and Mary Manuscript Collection.

307

BIBLIOGRAPHY

Johnston, Joseph Eggleston. Letter to Col. Gantt, dated June 23, 1888, criticizing Southern Members of Congress for their attitude toward the approaching crisis. In College of William and Mary Manuscript Collection.

——. Letter to Col. Gantt, also dated June 23, 1888, referring to "blunders" contributing to Confederate defeat. In College of William and Mary Manuscript Collection.

——. Letter to Col. Gantt, dated June 26, 1888, discussing in considerable detail the causes of the South's defeat. In College of William and Mary Manuscript Collection.

Merritt, B. F., Mayor of Macon, Ga. Letter to author, dated January 5, 1959, discussing mayorality of his predecessor, Stephan Collins, at time of Sherman's campaign.

"North Carolina Confederate Sites." Manuscript prepared and supplied by North Carolina Department of Archives and History, April 18, 1958.

"Register of Meteorological Observations Under the Direction of the Smithsonian Institution, Adopted by the Commissioner of Agriculture for His Annual Report, for the Month of February, 1865," showing wind velocity at Hilton Head, S.C. Photostatic copy furnished by U. S. Deparment of Commerce Weather Bureau, Asheville, N. C.

Sherman, William T. Letter to General Kilpatrick, dated April 14, 1865, telling of plan to prevent Johnston's escape into Georgia by blocking his retreat by joint action of Sheridan's and Kilpatrick's cavalry. In Manuscript Division, New York Public Library.

——. Letter dated December 29, 1864, to General Kilpatrick at Savannah, praising him for protecting main Federal army from attack by Confederate cavalry. In Manuscript Division, New York Public Library, 326 T. Marigan, 1935.

——. Letter dated August 8, 1883, stating he saw fires in Columbia twenty-four hours before Federal troops entered the city. Parke-Bernet Catalogue, March 28, 1938, p. 128, No. 375. In Manuscript Division, New York Public Library.

——. Letters, 1859-1861, W. L. Fleming Collection, Manuscript Division, New York Public Library.

Vance, Zebulon Baird. Letter to Sherman surrendering Raleigh and asking for protection of public buildings and private property. In Manuscript Division, New York Public Library.

——. Papers, 1827-1903. In North Carolina Department of Archives and History.

——. Correspondence, 1852-1874. In North Carolina Department of Archives and History.

——. Letter Book, 1863-1865. In North Carolina Department of Archives and History.

BIBLIOGRAPHY

Various manuscripts in the Hugh MacRae Letters, the Alonzo G. Beardsley Papers, the Charles S. Brown Papers, the Augustus William Law Papers, Official Telegrams of Robert Edward Lee, William Tecumseh Sherman Papers, the Augustus White Long Papers and other collections in the Manuscript Division of Duke University Library.

Various manuscripts in the LaFayette Laws Papers, the John Bragg Papers, the William T. Sherman Letters, the Robert Phillip Howell Memoirs and other collections in the Southern Historical Collection, University of North Carolina.

NEWSPAPERS

Augusta *Chronicle and Sentinel*
Augusta *Constitutionalist*
Charleston *Mercury*
Charlotte *Observer*
Chicago *Tribune*
Durham *Morning Herald*
Fayetteville (N.C.) *Observer*
Laurinburg (N.C.) *Exchange*
Macon *Telegraph*
Montgomery *Advertiser*
New York *Herald*
New York Times
New York *Tribune*
North Carolina *Presbyterian*
Raleigh *News and Observer*
Raleigh *Times*

INDEX

INDEX

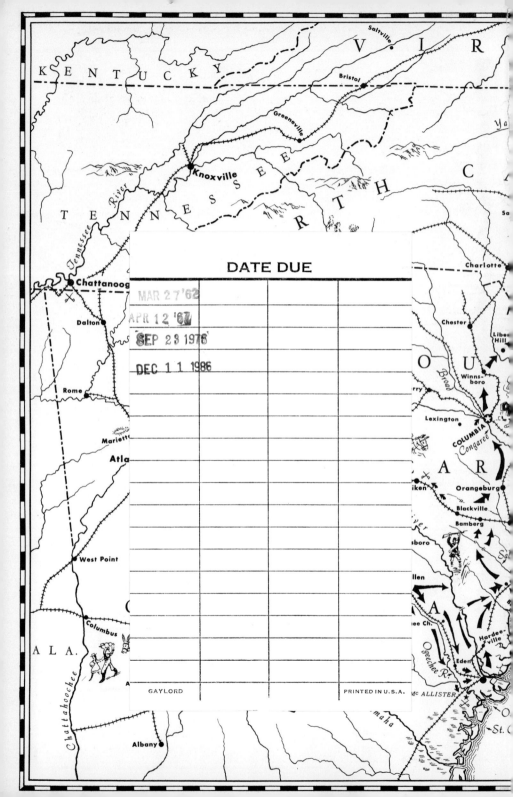

DATE DUE